ENTANGLED TERRITORIALITIES

Negotiating Indigenous Lands in Australia and Canada

Edited by Françoise Dussart and Sylvie Poirier

Under unequal relations of power and often traumatic conditions – colonization, sedentarization, dispossession, and arduous processes of land rights recognition – Indigenous involvement with and knowledge about the land have been reshaped through time and space, and have now become entangled with mainstream societies. Grounded in vivid ethnographic examples, *Entangled Territorialities* analyses how contemporary Indigenous people in Canada and Australia "live" the land, and how their changing knowledge of the land remains at the heart of their indigeneity.

Most of the lands to which Indigenous peoples are connected have been physically transformed, resulting in destruction of their ecological balance. But long after the agents of resource extraction have abandoned these lands, Indigenous people continue to claim ancestral ties and responsibilities towards their territories, however transfigured and degraded. Each chapter in this volume discusses specific circumstances in which Indigenous peoples have become intertwined with non-Aboriginal institutions and projects, such as the construction of hydroelectric dams and open-pit mines. Together the editors and contributors offer an integrated, in-depth comparative study that advances the larger debates about the vexed relationships between settlers and Indigenous peoples over the meaning, knowledge, and management of traditionally owned lands.

FRANÇOISE DUSSART is a professor in the Department of Anthropology at the University of Connecticut.

SYLVIE POIRIER is a professor in the Department of Anthropology at Université Laval.

Entangled Territorialities

Negotiating Indigenous Lands in Australia and Canada

EDITED BY FRANÇOISE DUSSART
AND SYLVIE POIRIER

UNIVERSITY OF TORONTO PRESS
Toronto Buffalo London

ISBN 978-1-4875-0169-3 (cloth)   ISBN 978-1-4875-2159-2 (paper)

Library and Archives Canada Cataloguing in Publication

Entangled territorialities : negotiating indigenous lands in Australia and Canada / edited by Françoise Dussart and Sylvie Poirier.

Includes bibliographical references and index.
ISBN 978-1-4875-0169-3 (cloth).—ISBN 978-1-4875-2159-2 (paper)

1. Aboriginal Australians – Land tenure. 2. Aboriginal Australians – Social conditions. 3. Aboriginal Australians – Economic conditions. 4. Land tenure – Government policy – Australia. 5. Native peoples – Land tenure – Canada. 6. Native peoples – Canada – Social conditions. 7. Native peoples – Canada – Economic conditions. 8. Land tenure – Government policy – Canada.
I. Poirier, Sylvie, 1953–, author, editor II. Dussart, Françoise, author, editor

GN666.E58 2017   305.89915   C2016-907937-6

This book has been published with the help of a grant from the Federation for the Humanities and Social Sciences, through the Awards to Scholarly Publications Program, using funds provided by the Social Sciences and Humanities Research Council of Canada.

University of Toronto Press acknowledges the financial assistance to its publishing program of the Canada Council for the Arts and the Ontario Arts Council, an agency of the Government of Ontario.

Canada Council   Conseil des Arts
for the Arts   du Canada

ONTARIO ARTS COUNCIL
CONSEIL DES ARTS DE L'ONTARIO
an Ontario government agency
un organisme du gouvernement de l'Ontario

Funded by the   Financé par le
Government   gouvernement
of Canada   du Canada

Canadä

Contents

Foreword

JOHN BORROWS

To be alive is to be entangled in relationships not entirely of our own making. We are born to parents whom we did not choose. Our families pre-existed our arrival. We receive languages, cultures, and world views before getting much choice in the matter. Our formative years are threaded with social, emotional, and economic relationships that we did not conceive. They are woven into our very being, largely without our permission. We are structured by race, class, and gender without much ability to resist, at least at first. These identities are generally knitted into our very being without our active and autonomous choice. We often live with the consequences of these decisions throughout our lives. Sometimes these decisions affect generations of people, through vast epochs of time. And it is not only individuals who deal with this reality. Nations, peoples, and species face the same circumstances. Free, prior, and informed consent is weakly deployed when receiving life's first endowments.

And the choices pressed upon us are complex. Though some might claim otherwise, no one lives with perfect integrity. Nobody resides in a truly unitary/indivisible/undivided/untroubled/holistic world. We absorb contradictory, cross-cutting, and parallel ideas throughout our lives. Conflicting impressions received at birth often last through adulthood. These threads can follow us to the grave, even when identified and actively resisted. Received patterns exert a tremendous pull on how we perceive and react to the world.

Some of us hold onto our bequests with fierce loyalty. Others unquestioningly accede to what we do not perceive. Some people try to make sense of our inherited mess by rejecting the very idea of heredity. They believe tradition can be discarded like an old cloak. In fact, many of the world's most powerful political stories tell us we are born free – without communal bonds. Liberalism is one of these tales. Like every good yarn it has attractive qualities. Many versions tell us we craft our own destiny. But liberalism isn't alone in this regard. Strands of thought that decontextualize sociality are found in many groups' lore. My own people, the Anishinaabe of the North American Great Lakes, sometimes spin "outside-of-time," essentialist tales. I have seen similar themes in other Indigenous groups.

Human societies appear to have a penchant for creating state-of-nature fictions. These stories can de-emphasize or deny a past era's complex entanglements. These stories are often deployed to distinguish a group's contemporary circumstances from a perceived simpler, purer past. Tradition is even recited to bolster these origin stories (and it can be recounted without irony or self-reflexivity). These narratives are used to explain how we live in "post-something" worlds: post-Edenic, post-evolutionary, post-contact, post–social contract, post-colonial, post-industrial, etc. These stories seem invented to resist relationality's always present reality. Thus, original positions are created. A priori worlds are fashioned. Essentialism has great appeal because it allows for the telling of a less tangled story. It is an attempt to embroider the truth with a few simple stitches. This book is an antidote to these proclivities.

To be alive is to be entangled – with a past and in the present. No group or individual can function without being subject to prior conditioning; our received contexts structure our very beings. In making this point I am not being deterministic. Greater and lesser degrees of choice are available to both individuals and societies. Human agency can always be exercised to alter our thoughts and change our environments. However, in making these choices we never act with complete independence. We cannot fully step outside of our past conditioning or present circumstances and totally recreate ourselves in the process. We do not make anything whole out of entirely new cloth. We must use the materials at hand in fashioning our alternatives.

At the same time it must also be recognized that our entanglements can be either liberating or oppressive. In common parlance, entanglement sounds like a bad thing – as if we are caught, bound, constrained, tied up, and in need of liberation. Yet, in the real world, entanglement with other human beings can enhance our lives. Thus, I do not want to suggest that entanglement is always and entirely problematic. Most of what we enjoy in life flows from other people's labour, received through our entanglement with people long dead or living people whom we will never meet. Such entanglement can be a good thing. Our enmeshment in unfolding routines and patterns often facilitates greater connections. It builds our stock of shared ideas and resources. Our received conditions can augment our growth and broaden our horizons through mutual aid and participatory structures.

Moreover, our entwined languages, cultures, and world views can also generate innovation and creativity. Conflicting, contrasting, parallel, and mutually reinforcing life-ways can present alternatives for taking new actions. Their combinations and permutations can sometimes provide unexpectedly positive opportunities. Habits, customs, routines, and conventions can be turned upside down, for good as well as for ill. We can challenge tradition while recognizing that (even in its rejection) tradition is a source of different ways of living.

The essays in this book discuss entanglement in an Indigenous context. They demonstrate how Indigenous peoples resiliently struggle to strengthen their agency by resisting, deepening, or transforming their entanglements. Each of these essays paints a complex picture of how power is deployed, subverted, or reshaped in response to state policies and practices. Each essay situates these struggles in concrete territorial contexts. Each author also grounds their analysis in specific community settings. This approach illuminates entanglement's many facets. As such, each essay effectively illustrates how Indigenous peoples reconstruct their distinctive identities, notwithstanding ongoing colonial encounters.

Thus, these essays are works of significant academic merit. They contribute to our understanding of how Indigenous peoples maintain their responsibilities and transmit their unique world views despite many constraints. As such, this book will be useful to many audiences, particularly within the academy and within Indigenous communities. A dominant message is that Indigenous peoples can largely remake their worlds in their own ontological images; this is possible even as they struggle through unbalanced alliances and live with uneven distributions of power.

These are important insights, even if they are not entirely new insights.

Basil Johnston, an elder from my reserve who passed away while this foreword was being prepared, communicated this message using another language and genre. We are from Neyaashiinigmiing on the southern shores of Georgian Bay, Ontario, and, in his 1976 book

Ojibway Heritage, Basil discusses entanglement from an Anishinaabe perspective by using a traditional story (4–5). The story involves our own net-maker, Asabikeshiinh (*asab* = net, *ke* = maker, *shiinh* = little): the spider. I will tell this story in my own words.

Asabakeshiinh was busy. His subtle strands of light cloaked every rock, plant, and hollow. Silver nets shrouded the forests, prairies, and shorelines. The world was tied together. Sinuous ropes twisted through time, with a nearly invisible force. There was no escaping his grasp.

In the midst of this tangle, deep in the forest, Snake was caught fast. The more he struggled, the tighter his bonds grew. He first thought he could escape on his own. Hours passed without any success. He quietly wound his way into a larger coil of knots. As hours turned into days, Snake began calling out for help. But no one answered. He grew desperate. The silent trees stood mute; the air gathered around him without aid. His struggle continued, but he only succeeded in twisting himself into an ever-tightening snare.

Nanabush was walking through the forest when he felt the pull. Tiny filaments of light spun round him. He stopped, stock still. All his senses came alive. Nanabush watched the subtle shift in the breeze. He tasted the fear welling up from the darkest tangle of woods. He tilted his head towards the source of this change. Then he heard a faint cry. Nanabush began following it to its source.

Snake heard the footfalls. His tongue gathered information about the approaching stranger. When Nanabush emerged from the glade, Snake was waiting. He immediately called out to his visitor, "Boozhoo. Aaniin ezhi-ayaayan. Aaniin ezhinikaazoyan? Giin ina Nanabush?" I know you; you're that trickster.

Nanabush stood at the clearing's edge, carefully surveying the scene. A dense mesh of webs looped around Snake. With his every twitch Nanabush saw waves of resistance ripple through the net. Nanabush could not help but feel pity.

Snake felt this change and noticed a shift in his visitor's form. Sensing opportunity, Snake called out, "Wiidookawashin! Help me Nanabush. I can't get free. Every time I move I get further entangled. I've been here for days. I'm starving. I don't think I can hold on much longer."

Nanabush was suspicious. He knew about Snake's reputation but he also saw his awful predicament. Snake was feared throughout the forest. His stealth and subtlety brought death and pain. At the same time Nanabush could not stifle his compassion. Nookomis, his grandmother, taught him to help those in need. While Nanabush had a disposition to play mean tricks, he also had a big heart. Snake's skin was lacerated; his fight against the web had cut him deeply. Open wounds lay across his back. Raw flesh attracted flies. Small insects were feeding on Snake's blood. Nanabush couldn't resist his pleas. Nanabush replied, "Will you promise not to eat me if I let you go?"

"Of course," said Snake. "I'll not even touch you; you and I are not of the same kind. I don't really want anything to do with you or this wretched place. Once I'm free I'll get as far away from here as I can."

With this promise Nanabush made his way carefully towards the web. Transforming himself into Man, Nanabush picked up a sharp green rock on the forest floor below him. Raising his arms to the work, he cautiously began slicing at the fine strands around Snake.

It took some time, but Snake was eventually freed.

For a moment.

Upon release, Snake immediately coiled around Nanabush's body. Snake writhed and thrashed. He twisted Nanabush firmly in his grip.

Nanabush fought back. He wound his arms and legs around Snake's neck. His hands flailed at Snake's wounds, trying to open them further. But Nanabush couldn't quite reach. Snake was strong; he resisted. Snake managed to hold Nanabush at bay. At the same time he couldn't tighten himself sufficiently to stop Nanabush from breathing.

Snake and Nanabush wrestled for hours. They securely wound themselves together, with no one gaining the upper hand. They thrashed through the clearing. Their conflict reverberated through the forest.

Fox, hearing the commotion, ran towards the scene. Emerging from the woods, he saw Man and Snake entangled with one another. He said, "Ahow! What's happening here? I don't like what I'm seeing."

Snake turned to Fox, hissing in derision. "It's none of your business. Go back where you came from. This is not your concern."

"But I think it is," Fox replied. "I can't stand idle and watch this damage to our home. And I will not be responsible for the harm you are causing one another. Tell me what's going on here, or I'll call a council. The other animals might not be as kind to you as I, when they see you."

Nanabush, sensing Fox's concern, took the initiative. "Help me, Fox. Snake tricked me. He was tangled in these woods. He was wrapped in Spider's webs. I offered to free him if he would flee from here. He promised he would leave, but then he turned on me, as soon as I let him go."

Fox knew Man could not always be trusted, but he also knew Snake was a sly one too. Fox asked Snake, "Is this true? Did you turn on Man when he rescued you?"

Snake said, "He lies. He's hiding things. And look at me. Do you think I'd be foolish enough to get tangled in that spider's web? And even if did, look at me: I'm strong. I could easily escape a spider's frail tendrils."

"I don't believe you," Fox said. "You don't look as bright or as strong as you say."

Snake was infuriated. "You don't believe me? You would challenge my power? I'll show you who's smart around here. I can prove my strength."

With those words, Snake flung Nanabush away and scrambled back to the nets. Twirling a strand around himself, he mocked Fox and scorned his doubt. "See my strength? These bands are no match for me. You'll see."

But as Snake took each thread to himself, he soon became entangled. Each attempt to extricate himself further embedded him in the snare.

Nanabush, now free, saw his fortune. Realizing that Fox's cunning had delivered him, Nanabush fell to his knees. He cried out, "Fox, I'll be forever grateful for what you have done for me today. I'm in your debt. Can I do something for you? If ever you need anything I will always honour that request."

Fox, turning again to face Man, said, "That's not how we do things around here. We don't think in terms of debt. We don't make contracts. We help others when needed. I'm glad you're free, and I see Snake's treachery here, but please don't make that request of me. I only did what any other good-hearted being would do. I was just doing my duty."

Fox and Nanabush went on for some time in this vein, each insisting that the other accept his position.

Eventually, however, Nanabush prevailed. Fox relented. Fox agreed that Man could do one thing for him. "Whenever you hunt, if you would leave a small piece for me, my family would be deeply grateful."

Nanabush agreed. "No problem. I promise. I will always honour you. I will always leave something for you whenever I hunt. We are connected, you and me. I won't forget that."

With that promise, the two parted, going their own ways, leaving Snake on his own to contend with the nets.

Years passed and Nananbush remembered his promise. Whenever he hunted, small parts of the animal would be left for his friend Fox. In the process, Fox's life became ever more tightly knitted to Man. Nanabush fed this relationship whenever he could. He was always grateful for his rescue.

One night, Nanabush was in his home, when his son came rushing in. "Ambe! Something's rummaging around your sled. I think they're stealing your moose. Come quick."

With that, Nanabush ran outside, weapon in hand.

He notched his bow and he crept towards his sled. All was quiet. Then he saw a slight movement. Something shifted in the shadows of the carcass, beside the sled.

Nanabush pulled back on the bowstring. He took aim and let his arrow go.

At that moment Nanabush caught Fox's eye, just as he emerged from the gloom.

The arrow was true; it struck its mark; it lodged deep in Fox's heart.

Fox's life spilled onto the snow. Dark crimson webs of blood spread at Nanabush's feet.

There is a truth, debwewin: To be alive is to be entangled in relationships not entirely of our own making.

The book you hold in your hands develops these themes in intricate and finely woven ways.

Weweni …

ENTANGLED TERRITORIALITIES

Negotiating Indigenous Lands in
Australia and Canada

1 Knowing and Managing the Land: The Conundrum of Coexistence and Entanglement

FRANÇOISE DUSSART AND SYLVIE POIRIER

The very ways societies change have their own authenticity, so that global modernity is often reproduced as local diversity.

(Sahlins 1993: 2)

Introduction

More than thirty years ago, Marshall Sahlins provided us with a model that he called "structures of conjuncture" to trace out the trans-formability of social systems, of systems of meaning and structures of power, and the relationships between local practices and social change (Sahlins 1981). For anthropologists working with contemporary Indigenous peoples in Australia and Canada, Sahlins's approach has proven quite salient to studying the modernizing and indigenizing processes taking place especially with regard to "managing" Indigenous customary territories (see also Sahlins 1993). Grounding their work in vivid ethnographic examples, the authors of this volume analyse how Indigenous peoples, in both countries, "live" the land, and how their changing knowledge of the land remains at the heart of their contemporary "indigeneity." Under unequal relations of power and mostly stressful encounters – colonization, sedentarization, dispossession, and arduous processes of land rights recognition – Indigenous involvements with and knowledge about the land have been reshaped through time and space and have now become entangled with mainstream societies as well as among Indigenous groups. As Frances Morphy aptly notes here in her chapter, "The nature of the articulation between Indigenous and Euro-Australian societies has not as yet often been conceptualized in terms of entanglement, although the notion of the intercultural (Merlan 1998; Hinkson and Smith 2005a, 2005b), with its emphasis on relationality and the co-production of contemporary Indigenous sociality, certainly implies an entanglement of the Indigenous in the non-Indigenous" (see this volume, p. 71). So before going on any further, let us address what we mean by entanglement, and how we see this volume contributing to larger debates about the vexed relationships between settlers and Indigenous peoples over the meaning, knowledge, use, and management of their customary lands.

The Relevance of Entanglement in Indigenous Studies

Understanding how entanglements are lived in various parts of the world can illuminate how Indigenous knowledge and practice in land management are reshaped by encounters with modernity, by neoliberalism, by reified oppositions between Indigenous and non-Indigenous, and by the proximity of other practices and engagements with customary lands; hence the concepts of entangled territorialities and entangled places. Together, the contributors show how each local variation of engagement with and knowledge of the land must be understood on its own socio-historical terms. They also draw attention to the contexts of entanglement of Indigenous and non-Indigenous societies, ontologies, and values within the land but also with the land, the places, and the non-human constituents.

The American Merriam Webster dictionary defines entanglement as "the condition of being deeply involved," and explains how such involvement can be complicated and even compromising.[1] While this definition focuses on the depth and complexity of involvement, it does not focus on the correlation aspect of the process of entanglement, as we have come to understand it. As illustrated in each of the chapters in this volume, studying the complexity of processes of entanglement illuminates how close or distant interactions between and among Indigenous and non-Indigenous groups, institutions, and organizations over the use and the management of the land retain an everlasting type of connectedness. They become part of a process of correlations, as it is known in quantum physics, that Albert Einstein has called "spooky action at a distance." Quantum physicists outline that when systems of particles become entangled with one another, one part of a system will come to systematically affect the state of another, regardless of how far apart they are. In other words, neither can any longer be described independently, no matter how far apart they are, and such correlations among the systems are unpredictable.[2] However, and while the systems are correlated, they also remain distinct. In fact such kinds of entanglement may not only be unpredictable, unexpected, unseen, or emergent, but also harmful, decomposing, and reshaped, while remaining inextricably connected. As two different cultural groups coming into contact through colonization, they become irreversibly connected, even if in direct or indirect proximity they continue to be correlated and affect each other. While quantum physics does offer some basic elements to engage with the concept of entanglement, we are aware that the phenomena of entanglement between social and cultural worlds, and thus between different meanings, praxes, and relationships with lands and places, may involve a higher level of complexity or, at least, a different kind of complexity.

Nicholas Thomas presented one of the seminal anthropological analyses of the notion of "entanglement" in his book titled *Entangled Objects* (1991). Thomas writes, "The notion of entanglement aims to capture the dialectic of international inequalities and local appropriations; it energizes a perspective situated beyond the argument between proponents of the view that the world system is essentially determinate of local social systems and those asserting the relative autonomy of individual groups and cultures" (1991: 207). As far as Indigenous people are concerned, as Sylvie Poirier argues in this volume, "the concept of entanglement allows us to inquire into the dialectical and the dialogical dimensions of the encounters and the coexistence between Indigenous and non-Indigenous worlds, ontologies, and actors" (p. 215) and their practices. Regarding relationships to customary lands, the concept of entanglement helps us better understand the complex local Indigenous "responses to State policies and ideologies and to dominant modernity and 'global coloniality' (Escobar 2008)" on their own terms, "which are not necessarily those expected by the State and the majority society" (Poirier in this volume), responses with the aim of securing for themselves a relative autonomy and, as Sahlins would say, being more like themselves (1993: 17).

Whatever is entangled, in a given place and time (context), cannot easily be undone. And no matter, if changes are made to the distinctive dimension of one entity, they will impact in some fashion the other directly or indirectly. Each thread-entity-agent-world involved in the entanglement keeps its identity, relative autonomy, and potentiality, while the spatial and temporal interactions with the other components do bring transformations to each one of them; it is an ongoing and somehow embodied process. The concept of entanglement suggests also no coherence and ordering, no given direction and fixed categories, no boundaries, and leaves room for principles of uncertainty and unpredictability. The challenge for anthropologists is to figure out what *does* become entangled.

Françoise Dussart (2010) offers a fine ethnographic example of entanglement between the Warlpiri people from Central Australia suffering from diabetes and the biomedical regime of care. In her article, she articulates the ontological obstacles between Warlpiri forms of subjectivity and sociality and those expected from the biomedical establishment that assesses their "health." The routine of a medical regimen for chronic illness limits considerably a Warlpiri person's capacity for moving (over the land and neighbouring communities) and caring for kin. Painfully, patients and relatives have to rethink kinship and the very foundations of the Warlpiri person. As Dussart explains, Warlpiri people need to remain mobile to attend to their obligations to their kin scattered around, to partake in religious and other secular events, and to maintain and nourish their social and cosmological networks of relationships in order to remain, according to them, healthy social beings (Dussart 2010: 80). But the local realities of Warlpiri people and their notions of "health" have also become entangled with, as well as alienated from, biomedical diagnoses, treatments, and finger pointing to their non-compliance, in turn prompting the biomedical establishment to engage with its failure to reduce health disparities between Indigenous and non-Indigenous Australians. This does not mean, of course, that notions of health have merged; in fact, they have remained dynamically distinct.

A similar sort of entanglement has been wonderfully articulated in a video about Yolŋu people from northeast Arnhem Land describing their feelings about Christmas celebrations. For the camera, the director – a senior Yolŋu man, Paul Gurrumuruwuy – explains what an entanglement of cultural traditions comes to mean in the context of neo-colonial life, "Aboriginal and non-Aboriginal cultures. Two Together. But not mixed up.[3] They're connected through feeling. You and me" (Gurrumuruwuy et al. 2012). In other words, wherever people who celebrate Christmas are for Gurrumuruwuy, they can all feel and celebrate Christmas, and while those feelings are correlated, connected, the people are rooted in their own local and historical distinctiveness. Non-Indigenous

Christian congregations have made changes to their way of celebrating in order to dialogue with indigenized forms of Christianity, changing in turn how Indigenous people engage with and indigenize non-Indigenous beliefs and practices (see also Schwarz and Dussart 2010). Similarly, Petronella Vaarzon-Morel, in this volume, offers us a potent example of entanglement in Central Australia between the Warlpiri people's and the Pitjantjatjara people's cosmological order (the Dreaming) and Christian cosmology and values in order to resignify and renegotiate their relationships with feral camels – associated with colonial expansion, Indigenous mobility, and Christmas celebration – that are roaming free in large numbers and destroying the fragile ecosystem of the people's customary landscapes.

As Poirier writes in her chapter, "entanglement stresses the politics of coexistence and difference and provides a window into social change" (p. 216). With this concept, we seek also to underline the ongoing tensions, conflicts, readjustments, compromises, negotiations, but also alliances going on between Indigenous and non-Indigenous actors within the territories, and thus between their respective ontologies, practices, and life projects (Blaser 2004).[4] Encounters and coexistence between Indigenous and non-Indigenous worlds and actors, within the land, and as their worlds become more and more entangled, are always a matter of politics, in the widest sense of the term, but also of ontological differences and obstacles (Clammer, Poirier, and Schwimmer 2004; Blaser 2013; Poirier 2010).

Partial Connections and the Encountering of Ontologies

The complexity of the entanglement lies also at the level of the manifold social relationships, meanings, and values each group of actors involved attaches to the relationships and to whatever is exchanged or acted upon. The notion of "partial connections" elaborated by Marilyn Strathern (1991) is relevant here, and the examples discussed in this volume testify to such "partial connections" and conflicts of interpretation between Indigenous and non-Indigenous ways of knowing, managing, and relating to the land and the non-humans. A case in point is Elodie Fache's analysis of the so-called "two way approach" – a program of land and resource co-management and conservation in the tropical region of Arnhem Land (Northern Territory, Australia) – that seeks to merge Indigenous and Western scientific knowledge systems. Fache demonstrates how these two systems of knowledge become only partially connected and brokered, considering, among other things, the unequal relations of power and their differing ontologies.[5] Colin Scott's chapter offers another example of partially connected worlds, this time between Cree and sport hunters in northern Quebec. Both groups come in contact with each other on the lands, but the nature of their respective relationships with the hunted animals and the places is grounded in differing ontologies. Partial connections between Indigenous and non-Indigenous worlds and actors stem also from another factor, well illustrated in this volume, and that is the enduring kin-based nature of Indigenous relationships to and sense of responsibility towards the land of their ancestors, which differ from non-Indigenous individuated relationships to the land.

To better understand what is at play in the interactions between Indigenous and non-Indigenous worlds, ontologies have thus to be taken into account. The recent interest in anthropology in ontologies allows us to better understand and seriously consider not so much the diversity of world views – that is, varying representations of the same world – but the multiplicity of worlds. Furthermore, and as Arturo Escobar has noted, "in cases where different ontologies are involved, the theoretical and political treatment of difference becomes even more important" (2008: 25), and the entanglement and the processes of social changes are even more complex.

We understand ontologies as ways of being and acting in the world of cultural and social subjects and agents, which are shaped by the subject's knowledge of what the world is and how it is constituted. Ontologies are not only metaphysical and concerned with theories of being and reality, but have real practical, political, aesthetic, and phenomenological implications. As John Clammer, Sylvie Poirier, and Eric Schwimmer have argued, "ontologies are consequently political in the widest sense (body politics, cultural politics) and are the key to the phenomenological forms that order actual everyday life" (2004: 6). Considering that "ontologies are basic to the construction of culture, then it is reasonable to assume that differing conceptions of being-in-the-world necessarily enter into conflicts between systems (societies or cultures) based on different ontological premises" (2004: 4).

The dominant naturalist ontology of the Western-modern world "supposes a world from which spirit and subjectivity were long ago evacuated" (Sahlins 1995: 163). In the traditional and contemporary worlds of Indigenous Australians and Canadians, spirits of various kinds and non-human beings and agencies have, for their part, an enduring presence within the land and contribute actively to the unfolding of local historicity (see also Poirier 2013). "Relational ontologies," as they have come to be termed, and as discussed by Colin Scott, Brian Thom, Clinton Westman, and Petronella Vaarzon-Morel in this volume, consider thus the volition and agency of non-human others to be facts of life, and that sociality and historicity are indisputably inclusive of non-human others. For contemporary Indigenous Australians, knowing, managing, and relating to the land means being receptive to the voices, moods, and presence of ancestral beings and spirits of deceased relatives, as presented, for example, by Morphy and Sachiko Kubota in this volume. In a similar vein for Indigenous hunters in Canada, for whom animals are "partners" in life (Feit 2000), the agencies and volition of animals and the spirits of deceased relatives are forever present in the land (see also Poirier, Scott, and Thom in this volume).

There is another particularity to such "relational ontologies" that needs to be stressed. Unlike a naturalist ontology, relational ontologies place relatedness/relationality as a paramount embodied value, perception, and experience, such that relations take on a reality of their own. In such ontologies, relations and relationality are not only constitutive of the forms of sociality and subjectivity but also constitutive of being (human and non-human) (see also Poirier 2013). That is to say that, on the one hand, ontological considerations add to the complexity of the entanglement between Indigenous and non-Indigenous worlds and their respective practices on and experiences of the land. On the other hand, the ontological perspective offers us conceptual tools to reconfigure our understanding of such cultural encounters and spaces of interculturality in today's context.

What we propose thus in this volume is to better understand the complex involvements between Indigenous peoples and mainstream Australian and Canadian societies over land, and shed light on how they are experienced in all their difference and singularity. On the one hand, we see the concept of entanglement reflecting a wide range of complex types of Indigenous dynamic engagements with different forms of governmentalities, and, on the other, the processes of entanglement point to the fact that settler societies are also changed by how Indigenous societies engage with what we call state policies of partial recognition and management. We suggest that, in countries such as Canada and Australia, one of the defining aspects of Indigenous entanglement with the settlers is that Indigenous peoples are caught in a double bind, depending on the State and non-Indigenous people, who in turn also depend on the traditionally owned territories. As Jean Dennison has pointed out: "The term 'entanglement' also serves to negate the easy divide of colonized and colonizer, illustrating the ways few can escape the logic of settler colonialism" (2012: 8), which permeates both time and space.

Our volume provides "tangled stories" (Stoler 2002: 2) of different narrative perspectives of change, and of mutability (Thomas 1991), in relation with customary Indigenous territories. It is important to note at this juncture that such tangled stories and partial connections continue to be transformed through entangled times and places. Our contributors provide examples of culturally situated practices regarding land management, of how systems of knowledge and meanings change and in turn affect the deployment of social practices and structures of power in neo-colonial situations. In examining some of the specific tangled stories of "Indigenous" and "non-Indigenous" people in the commonwealth states of Australia and Canada, we join other anthropologists who have analysed contemporary cultural projects tethered to processes of accommodation, collaboration, and appropriation. Among these, Fred Myers in his seminal work on Australian Central Desert Aboriginal people speaks of "intercultural articulation" (1989) and "intercultural space" when analysing the global circulation of Aboriginal knowledge and Aboriginal art (2002: 6). Myers analyses how meanings are continually renegotiated depending upon various practices and positions of power. Francesca Merlan in her study of Aboriginal groups in the Australian town of Katherine in the Northern Territory (1998) analyses also how different "forms of Indigenous–non-Indigenous relationality" may be direct but also indirect (2013: 637). More recently, Howard and Frances Morphy have urged anthropologists to re-examine the Australian situation, to go beyond an understanding of the different forms of relationality between Indigenous and non-Indigenous as social processes and "analyze what differences are brought to the relationship" (2013: 639). They propose to move away from seeing such interactions as just intercultural, to better understand how Indigenous people embedded within specific historical processes resignify what the authors call their "relative autonomy." Such processes of mutability are also echoed by anthropologists working with Indigenous people in Canada, as articulated by Feit, Scott, Poirier, Thom, and Westman in this volume. The collective work edited by Scott, *Aboriginal Autonomy and Development in Northern Quebec and Labrador* (2001), offers potent ethnographic examples of the "dynamics of resistance" and the manifold strategies deployed by First Nations in redefining territory within an "intersystemic negotiation of meanings" (2001: 8).

Readers may ask at this stage why we are privileging the concept of entanglement over "relative autonomy," "forms of relationality," or "dynamics of resistance." It makes it possible to grasp the complexity of situations such as "relative autonomy," "hybridity," the "intercultural," or "resistance," without privileging any of them.[6] Moreover, unlike these later notions, the concept of entanglement invites the non-humans into the equation – as agents in the becoming and the unfolding of whatever is entangled and with their own practices and "relative autonomy." The concept of entanglement is opposed to ideas such as separate objects or discrete operators, and, as illustrated in each of the chapters in this volume, it is best suited to analyse "what is going on," since it draws attention to imaginative possibilities and unexpected consequences of colonization, neo-colonization, and commodification. Entanglement is a flexible concept that helps us envisage the complexity of the politics of representation and recognition, making us aware of Indigenous and non-Indigenous projections about "modernity" and "tradition," especially when examining entangled territorialities. The concept of entanglement forces us to engage with the multiplicity and the variability of connections, with the inevitability of the correlations, the uncertainty of their outcomes, and the unintended consequences. In short, entanglement is more than the sum of its parts, and our task as anthropologists is to understand what exactly is encompassed by such connections.

Why Australia and Canada?

This volume has its origin in a panel we organized at the 10th Conference on Hunting and Gathering Societies (CHAGS) held in Liverpool in June 2013. The original title of our panel read as follows: "Relationships to the Land: Ontological Resistance and Entanglement in the 21st Century." Our intent was to bring together scholars working with Indigenous people in Canada and Australia in order to exchange ideas on how, under rather similar colonial histories and faced with the imperatives of "development" on their lands, (former) hunters and gatherers have managed to dynamically reproduce relationships with their customary lands. Such transformative and entangled reproduction "assumes the dual appearance of assimilation and differentiation" (Sahlins 1993: 19). In organizing our panel, we were particularly interested in exploring the complexity of ongoing encounters about and on customary territories between non-Indigenous and Indigenous groups, among Indigenous groups, and between humans and non-humans. The papers provided convincing ethnographic examples of the transformative power of entangled relationships that enable distinct but interdependant realities specifically grounded in local colonial and neo-colonial histories.

In the course of the past two centuries, traditional hunters and gatherers in Australia and Canada have been dispossessed of their lands, forced to settle, "invited" to engage in the market economy, and more recently involved in long and arduous processes of partial recognition of their land rights and titles. However, and in spite of these constraints and new deals, contemporary Indigenous peoples in Australia and Canada have been involved in some forms of maintenance of their intimate relationships with territories, some of which have been repossessed while others have been irretrievably lost. Through such a prism, we can come closer to understanding the different local strategies deployed to renegotiate relations to land and illuminating how Indigenous ongoing forms of engagement with the land remain distinctive and forever entangled with the settler society at large. It is important to point out that Indigenous lands in both countries share a number of characteristics. They are above all the products of the entanglements of pre-colonial patterns of spiritual, political, and economic uses, of colonial and neo-colonial histories of dispossession and repossession, of environmental changes (mining, pastoralism, deforestation, urbanization, to name just a few), of legal systems, and ultimately of capitalism.

From the first colonial encounters to the present, Indigenous-State relations in both countries show similarities and differences. In both countries, the states justified and declared their sovereignty over these newly "discovered" lands through the doctrine of "Terra Nullius" and the "settlement" thesis (see Asch 2002). While we acknowledge that the doctrine of Terra Nullius was not as explicit in Canada as it was in Australia, nevertheless, considering the Royal Proclamation (1763) and the treaty-making process,[7] Indigenous-State relations amounted to similar outcomes: land dispossession and the denial of Indigenous sovereignty. In Australia, the *Mabo* decision and the ensuing Native Title Act signed in 1993 acknowledged the fiction of the Terra Nullius doctrine and provided a platform for a legal concept of customary rights. In Canada as in Australia, conflicts of interpretation over the meaning and the value of land, but also over the meaning of the agreements negotiated between these groups, have durably tainted the nature of the coexistence between Indigenous peoples and settlers.

Since the middle of the nineteenth century, respective Canadian and Australian colonial histories and governmental policies towards Indigenous peoples have followed rather similar paths. Their policies of management have moved from policies of protection and land dispossession (with the Indian Act in Canada, and the establishment of reserves, missions, and/or governmental settlements in both countries), to policies of assimilation (with residential schools), to policies of self-determination, and, since the 1990s, and under the strategies of neoliberal governance, to what we call the policies of contradictions or partial recognition. In the last decades, Indigenous peoples in Australia and Canada have been engaged in major political and legal challenges over the recognition of their rights and titles to land. They have been involved with the negotiations of various forms of alliances, "modern" treaties, at least in Canada, as well as more viable partnerships over the use and management of traditional lands. Our volume examines specific cases of such forms of engagement; thus, our contributors direct the lens towards "what is going on out there." In other words, each chapter examines what is happening on and with the land, where Aboriginal people and Torres Strait Islanders in Australia and First Nations in Canada reimagine their entangledness as well as their distinctiveness. In bringing theoretical and ethnographic insights into how Indigenous relationships to, on, and with the land become rearticulated under different forms of neo-colonial governmentality, each chapter highlights how Indigenous and non-Indigenous Australians and Canadians produce history and possible entangled futures. Each narrative of entanglement presented here evokes a singular life project and local strategies of coexistence. In spite of increasing constraints, inequity, and "amoral forms of global capital" (Appadurai 2013: 295), these narratives call to mind the enduring, transforming, but also creative and imaginative relationships of Indigenous people to their territories and places. From the Indigenous perspectives, these entangled life projects are fuelled by politics of hope and ethics of possibility (Appadurai 2013) as well as by a deep and everlasting ethics of responsibility towards customary lands and places.

All the authors of this volume, as ethnographers and anthropologists, share a long-term engagement with Indigenous groups in Australia and Canada. Each one of them, in varying degrees, has made political and methodological claims and strives to understand the multiple realities and ways of being in the world deployed by Indigenous peoples historically embattled with settler states. Furthermore, the authors take the position that contemporary Indigenous conceptions of the land and how these conceptualizations play out in practice are not divorced from the direct and indirect entanglements of socio-political life and the structures of bureaucratic institutions. In other words, understanding these processes of entanglement, we argue, helps us engage with the messiness, the ambiguities, and the limits of the politics of recognition and reconciliation as well as with the dangers of reifying cultural domains as if they were not correlated and always in flux. Furthermore, and as anthropologists studying what Stuart Hall has called "politics without guarantees" (1997: 4), we need to reassess how we examine not only the tangled stories of what and how it means to be Indigenous today, but also our own entangled roles as anthropologist (see Morphy, Nicolas Peterson, Poirier, and Westman in this volume).

What it means to live and to know the land remains among the most vexing socio-political and economic issues to the processes of entanglement. Indigenous lands have long been spaces of encounters, where conflicts and negotiations have been played out, and where different regimes of values, sets of practices, and interests come to coexist. Indigenous territorialities are increasingly constrained and entangled within the agendas of settler states and global capital, and of their industries such as mining, forestry, hydroelectricity, and tourism, to name just a few. If the hegemonic role of settler states in managing the land has been emphasized by many anthropological works, many Aboriginal, Torres Strait Islanders, and First Nations peoples continue to distinctively and ingeniously engage with the land and the circulation of their knowledge of their territories.

With these overall considerations in mind, our volume addresses the following issues: Under unequal relations of power and different kinds of mostly stressful encounters, constraints, and entanglements (colonization, sedentarization, dispossession, arduous processes of land right recognition), how are Indigenous relationships to and with the land rearticulated in today's context? How do the interactions between Indigenous and non-Indigenous peoples within the land become entangled? How do Indigenous peoples maintain their manifold responsibilities towards their territories and the non-human constituents of their world? How do they transmit local knowledge of the land to younger generations? How, as anthropologists, are we to convey the expression and the redefinition of their relational ontologies in their encounters with dominant ontologies of the settler society? Entangled with each other, Indigenous and settler societies rearticulate the meaning of distinctiveness through strategic alliances, unbalanced mediations, and uneven processes of appropriation. The key issue here has become how distinctiveness – a by-product of entanglement – is manoeuvred by both Indigenous and non-Indigenous peoples through time and place.

Contributors in this volume reflect upon some of the current and manifold challenges experienced by Indigenous people in Australia and Canada, in regard to land management. In his Foreword, John Borrows teases out the meaning of entanglement and relationality from an Anishinaabe perspective. In his Afterword, Michael Asch engages with the themes of this volume from the perspective of an anthropologist long seeking to reinvent the State's alliances and treaties with Indigenous peoples and neighbours. Taken together, the Foreword, the chapters, and the Afterword speak of trans-local entanglements and strategic relationality, of coexistence, of knowledge and relationships lost and transformed, of re-articulation, of resilience, and of resistance.

In his chapter, Harvey Feit presents a fine ethnography of dialogues occurring in the early 1970s between hunters on the one hand and government and Hydro-Quebec representatives on the other over the construction of the James Bay hydroelectric project on Cree lands. For Indigenous peoples, in Canada and Australia, the 1970s marked the beginning of the era of negotiating "modern" land rights with the states and the industries, and of engaging thus into new forms of alliances, entanglements, and dialogues, as well as their unpredictable and at times vexing outcomes. Feit stresses the "subtle and contradictory connections" between Cree and non-Cree worlds. In examining diverging Cree and non-Cree meanings over "development," "education," "knowledge," or "economies" on the land, he highlights precisely what became entangled. In order to engage in a fair dialogue with the Whitemen and in the hope that their knowledge, experiences, and memories of the land would be taken at face value, Cree hunters made use of a dominant metaphor in Western thought, that of the "garden": "The country and the land is my garden." Feit highlights in his chapter how Indigenous people are prepared to go to great lengths to dialogue with powerful others, so that their entangled land continues to be "looked after" to some extent on their own terms – a strategy touched upon by all contributors in this volume. While the James Bay Cree people have since then signed two "modern treaties" (James Bay and Northern Quebec Agreement, 1975; La Paix des Braves, 2002), the diverging meanings, conflicts of interpretation, and ontological obstacles endure. Feit's chapter points to the unpredictability of negotiations and social changes. As Colin Scott puts it in his chapter, "From Feit's analysis, one learns that Eeyouch [Crees] insist upon respectful and consensual relationships, not because they are ignorant of the real presence of self-ish, competitive, and violent forms of human interaction, but out of a conviction that, inherent in the equally real nature of relationship, such forms are ultimately self-defeating" (p. 51).

While the dialogues analysed by Feit occurred some forty years ago, they already foresaw the forms of entanglement that were to take place over Cree lands in the following decades. Scott finely explores some of these dialogues in his chapter. Like Feit, Scott also observes in his own work among the Cree people that the entanglement as a status quo is necessary for the "survival" of Indigenous people. Scott shows how they enter into what he calls "strategic relationality" with sports hunt-ers, to realign what they hold central to the management of their land and what lives on the land by using forestry and hydroelectric roads and befriending non-Indigenous recreational hunters. The deploy-ment of strategies to form such friendships with non-Indigenous hunt-ers as well as politicians makes it possible to maintain harmonious relationships with the land. Scott here reflects on how hunting and reciprocal relationships between hunters and animals endure, as well as on how, following Cree logic and ethic of responsibility, old friends and newcomers become incorporated to reproduce the harmony of the world (see also Poirier and Westman in this volume). He shows how the Cree people indigenize the use of the hydroelectricity infrastruc-ture to hold steady jobs, hunt on their distant territories, and engage with a physically transformed landscape they now share and use with non-Indigenous hunters' groups. Relying on their friendship with one group of non-Indigenous hunters, they are able to fence off other new-comers, a seemingly perfect entanglement.

Frances Morphy's contribution echoes Scott's chapter and discusses how Yolŋu people from Arnhem Land (Australia) have engaged with the Indigenous Protected Areas (IPA) policy of land management on two fronts: as a way to ensure their religious, political, and economic involvement as customary caretakers of the land, and as a way to con-trol the kind of articulations Yolŋu people try to create with mainstream society. Through "politics of persuasion" (p. 81) and "'cross-border' negotiations" (p. 82), and under neoliberal politics of contradictions, Yolŋu people recalibrate how they care for their land and sea on their own terms. Morphy examines Yolŋu motivations for engagement with the IPA and how they frame the IPA as part of a long trajectory of a particular kind of engagement with settler Australian society and as a vehicle for intergenerational cultural transmission.

With their respective notions of relative autonomy and strategic relationality, Morphy and Scott point to specific processes of entanglement illustrating how the degree of Indigenous control is correlated to how settler societies and individuals engage and are engaged by Indigenous hunters, rangers, and communities. Furthermore, both authors articulate how Indigenous identity becomes grounded in what happens to customary territories and what lives on these lands.

The use of Indigenous and settler knowledge and technologies to manage their customary land is also at the heart of Elodie Fache's analysis of the rangers at Ngukurr in the Northern Territory (Australia). While Morphy focuses on the strategies deployed by the Yolŋu people to retain control over the management of land and sea, Fache argues that, for the area where she worked, mediation and brokerage transform not only all constituencies involved but also the nature and the future of such entangled territorialities.

The hunting trips described by Scott and Westman and the roles of rangers discussed in Morphy's and Fache's chapters illustrate, albeit quite differently, how local knowledge of the land is transmitted among the generations as well as how relationships between humans and nonhumans are reproduced. These are fraught with conflicts over the use of the land, its ownership, and the uncertain future that lies ahead.

In his chapter, Clinton Westman, through his work with Cree First Nations of northern Alberta, documents "the lived vitality of Aboriginal politics, identity, ontology, and livelihood in what has been, and likely will again be, a very busy part of the boreal forest" (p. 117). Like all the Indigenous groups discussed in this volume, the Cree First Nations of northern Alberta "maintain their engagement with the land principally on two interrelated levels: by negotiating with the state and with corporations for jurisdiction and benefits, and through their hunting practices" (p. 121). While the Cree people of northern Alberta have seen their lands invaded by various industries like forestry, gas, and oil sands, "hunting and fishing continue to supply key nutritional resources and remain an important part of family economic strategies" (p. 127). Moose remain "a focal species ... the subject of much specialized knowledge and discussion, and the target or subject of rituals, spiritual utterances, and much pragmatic labour and speech" (p. 127).

Westman's narrative of a family hunting trip exemplifies how modern technologies such as mobile homes and satellite phones and values and practices embodied within an animistic and relational ontology become entangled.

In his chapter, Brian Thom explores how Coast Salish people living in southwest British Columbia and Vancouver Island reshape the distinctive indigenousness of their relationships with the spirit powers of the lands and waters of their territories under assault. Thom's chapter is a poignant exploration of how, despite disrespectful private landowners, suburbanization, and industrial forestry, mortuary landscapes and other sacred places over many decades are guarded so that their ancestors' agency can continue to mediate relationships in contemporary Coast Salish lives. In doing so, the Coast Salish people labour to connect the real possibility of that power to a non-native audience – to resituate the consequences of something that can happen to all of us, not just an "us" and "them" situation but one that incorporates and includes settlers in ancestral lands. This is also what entanglement is all about.

Sachiko Kubota explores as well the ways in which the Yolŋu people from Galiwin'ku in Arnhem Land (Australia) labour intergenerationally to resignify their relationships with ancestral spirit powers and agencies, their deeds to lands, myths, and legacies. Kubota, like Thom, points to how systems of knowledge and know-how are transmitted, safeguarded, lost, and changed. Both authors illuminate what it means today for Indigenous people to maintain their knowledge of the land and the ancestral world as well as to reproduce their responsibilities to their customary lands and the world at large. Kubota's analysis of conversations, struggles, and conflicts erupting over the selection of burial sites exemplifies how the Yolŋu people recontextualize their ties to the land, their clan's identity, and their cosmological beliefs, as well as the agency of supernatural beings such as sorcerers.

While most Indigenous people are concerned with the movement of people, animals, and spirit powers on the land and at sea, governmental environmental policies are concerned with the control of weeds, invasive species, and feral animals. In her chapter, Petronella Vaarzon-Morel provides us with an example of what happens when Indigenous people from Central Australia have to cope with new species introduced on their land, prompting an ontological shift. Vaarzon-Morel shows how local knowledge of the land and what is on the land is reinterpreted, and how it feeds into current crises about identity and relations with the wider Australian society and with other Aboriginal groups. The land – as living and interacting places, interactive spaces of living memory, dwelling places of the ancestors and deceased relatives, home to non-human entities – remains *the* important social, religious, and legal dimension for the (re)making of personhood and citizenship. Vaarzon-Morel engages with ongoing processes of re-significations by examining how several groups of Aboriginal people from Central Australia have to deal with dromedary camels gone wild and how these animals' existence on their customary lands impacts their contemporary life-worlds. Her analysis shows how worlds become entangled in their distinctiveness. Such ontological entanglements – and here we are not suggesting that these are processes of hybridity as underlined by Poirier's chapter – over land and what is negotiated, reinterpreted, and transmitted on the land have economic and political dimensions in the everyday lives not just of Indigenous peoples but of other citizens and, of course, of different nation-states.

In her chapter, Sylvie Poirier analyses the conditions under which the Atikamekw Nehirowisiw people maintain their relationships with the land and deal with different levels of state involvement as well as with industries directly affecting their customary territories, such as forestry and tourism. Such involvement is *hard work*, a point made by all the authors in their respective chapters. Under stressful conditions, it is indeed exhausting to look after the land and transmit the knowledge of the land. Poirier describes how Indigenous people willingly engage in entangled gift economies with the society at large in order to continue to care for their land under difficult circumstances. The absence of a clear framework of rights institutionalized by the State (unlike the situation described by Scott in his chapter) renders coexistence difficult, since the Atikamekw Nehirowisiw people have to rearticulate their resistance around failed negotiations, which in turn impacts how as individuals and families they come to understand their place as Canadian citizens. Poirier points to how neocolonial acts of "resistance" by the Atikamekw Nehirowisiw people may need to be understood as part of a structure of domination – within which the settler state treats Indigenous people differently from one area to the next – determining in turn the outcome of Indigenous and individually driven initiatives. This is another dimension of how relational ontology and entanglement become constructed.

In our last chapter, Nicolas Peterson explores the ethical, political, and ontological dimensions of the use of maps produced in the

Australian context of Aboriginal land claim procedures by subsequent generations of Aboriginal people. Peterson shows how maps of sacred sites and key itineraries of ancestral beings – created by close collaborations between Aboriginal claimants and anthropologists and originally used to demonstrate knowledge and ownership of customary territories during land claims – have now become a vexed tool for the Aboriginal groups concerned. As Peterson remarks, these Indigenous claims have become claims to "culture" which are tied to political, economic, and ontological entanglements in settler states (see also Poirier 2004). Disenfranchised people must promote values to be recognized, even if they are only partly recognized. So how and what kinds of Indigenous knowledge can or should be transmitted? Lost? Retrieved? As Peterson suggests, how should we as anthropologists and, by default, the State get involved? As anthropologists we are inevitably tied to the production and deployment of Indigenous identities, and we have to come to terms with such entanglement in the politics of recognition of Indigenous peoples in settler states such as Australia and Canada.

We conclude with an open and difficult issue, which relates to the inalienable character of customary lands and places, or, in other words, their sheer materiality. Most of the customary and entangled lands, places, and landscapes portrayed in this volume have been, over the last decades, physically transformed, some more drastically than others. They have been turned into hydroelectric dams or large open mining pits, and their ecological balance has been destroyed, to name just some of the most visible transformations. When the resources are depleted, the actors of extractive economies usually abandon the places to their fate, while Indigenous people continue to claim ancestral ties and responsibilities towards their metamorphosed territories. For Indigenous Australians and Canadians, territories and places are not means to an end, and, whether people, non-humans, and things come to intersect and become entangled on and in the land, their sense of belonging and responsibility remains deep and everlasting. Regardless of the degree of physical degradation and transfiguration, in their sheer materiality customary lands and places retain their sovereignty, their autonomy, and their inalienable dimension. The cultural logic of capitalism cannot explain such unexpected consequences, which in turn prompt us to see how entanglement speaks theoretically, politically, and practically to the work of coexistence.

ACKNOWLEDGMENTS

We want to thank the organizers of CHAGS 10 for inviting us to submit our session titled "Relationships to the Land: Ontological Resistance and Entanglement in the 21st Century." Our contributors' enthusiasm and hard work have been remarkable. Thank you! We are grateful to the three anonymous reviewers for their insightful comments, as well as to Doug Hildebrand for his constant encouragement and support. Finally, we both want to express our profound gratitude to the Indigenous people, in Canada and Australia, whom we have worked with for more than three decades and who have guided us into their world. All infelicities remain our own.

NOTES

1 See http://www.merriam-webster.com/dictionary/entanglement.
2 We particularly want to thank here Professor Nora Berrah (University of Connecticut) for explaining the notion of entanglement in quantum physics and recommending key readings.
3 In Aboriginal English, "not mixed up" means that things retain some of their own cultural priorities.
4 "Life projects," writes Blaser, "are embedded in local histories; they encompass visions of the world and the future that are distinct from those embodied by projects promoted by state and market ... Life projects are premised on densely and uniquely woven 'threads' of landscape, memories, expectations and desires" (2004: 26). The "woven 'threads'" alluded to here may stand as a metaphor of entanglement.
5 See Nadasdy (2003) for a critical approach to land and resource co-management programs in Canada.
6 We want to acknowledge our conversations with Frances Morphy for articulating this dimension of the concept of entanglement.
7 See Miller (2009) and Asch (2014) for sound analysis of the treaty-making history and process in Canada. For a comparative analysis between Canada and Australia as regards treaties vs Terra Nullius, see Pratt (2004).

REFERENCES

Appadurai, Arjun. 2013. *The Future as Cultural Fact: Essays on the Global Condition.* London: Verso.

Asch, Michael. 2002. "From Terra Nullius to Affirmation: Reconciling Aboriginal Rights with the Canadian Constitution." *Canadian Journal of Law and Society* 17 (2): 23–39. http://dx.doi.org/10.1017/S0829320100007237.

Asch, Michael. 2014. *On Being Here to Stay: Treaties and Aboriginal Rights in Canada*. Toronto: University of Toronto Press.

Blaser, Mario. 2004. "Life Projects: Indigenous Peoples' Agency and Development." In *In the Way of Development: Indigenous Peoples, Life Projects and Globalization*, ed. Mario Blaser, Harvey A. Feit, and Glenn McRae, 26–44. London and New York: Zed Books and Ottawa: Canadian International Development Research Centre.

Blaser, Mario. 2013. "Ontological Conflicts and the Stories of Peoples in Spite of Europe: Toward a Conversation on Political Ontology." *Current Anthropology* 54 (5): 547–68. http://dx.doi.org/10.1086/672270.

Clammer, John, Sylvie Poirier, and Eric Schwimmer, eds. 2004. *Figured Worlds: Ontological Obstacles in Intercultural Relations*. Toronto: University of Toronto Press.

Dennison, Jean. 2012. *Colonial Entanglement: Constituting a Twenty-First Century Osage Nation*. Chapel Hill: University of North Carolina Press. http://dx.doi.org/10.5149/9780807837443_dennison.

Dussart, Françoise. 2010. "'It Is Hard to Be Sick Now': Diabetes and the Reconstruction of Indigenous Sociality." *Anthropologica* 52 (1): 77–87.

Escobar, Arturo. 2008. *Territories of Difference: Place, Movements, Life, Redes*. Durham, NC: Duke University Press. http://dx.doi.org/10.1215/9780822389439.

Feit, Harvey. 2000. "Les animaux comme partenaires de chasse: Réciprocité chez les Cris de la Baie James" [Animals as Hunting Partners: Reciprocity among the Cree of James Bay]. *Terrain* 34 (34): 123–42. http://dx.doi.org/10.4000/terrain.1005.

Gurrumuruwuy, Paul, Fiona Yangathu, Jennifer Deger, and David Mackenzie, eds. 2012. Manapanmirr, in Christmas Spirit. 60 min. Electronic document. http://miyarrkamedia.com/projects/manapanmirr-in-christmas-spirit/, accessed 16 December 2014.

Hall, Stuart. 1997. Race, the Floating Signifier. Media Education Foundation. Transcript. Pp. 1–17. Electronic document. http://www.mediaed.org/transcripts/Stuart-Hall-Race-the-Floating-Signifier-Transcript.pdf, accessed 12 December 2014.

Hinkson, Melinda, and Benjamin R. Smith. 2005a. "Introduction: Conceptual Moves towards an Intercultural Analysis." *Oceania* 75 (3): 157–66. http://dx.doi.org/10.1002/j.1834-4461.2005.tb02877.x.

Hinkson, Melinda, and Benjamin R. Smith, eds. 2005b. "Figuring the Intercultural in Aboriginal Australia." *Oceania* 75 (3): 209–21.

Merlan, Francesca. 1998. *Caging the Rainbow: Places, Politics, and Aborigines in a North Australian Town*. Honolulu: University of Hawai'i Press.

Merlan, Francesca. 2013. "Theorizing Relationality: A Response to the Morphys." *American Anthropologist* 115 (4): 637–8. http://dx.doi.org/10.1111/aman.12045.

Miller, Jim R. 2009. *Compact, Contract, Covenant: Aboriginal Treaty-Making in Canada*. Toronto: University of Toronto Press.

Morphy, Howard, and Frances Morphy. 2013. "Anthropological Theory and Government Policy in Australia's Northern Territory: The Hegemony of the 'Mainstream.'" *American Anthropologist* 115 (2): 174–87. http://dx.doi.org/10.1111/aman.12002.

Myers, Fred. 1989. "Truth, Beauty, and Pintupi Painting." *Visual Anthropology* 2 (2): 163–95. http://dx.doi.org/10.1080/08949468.1989.9966508.

Myers, Fred. 2002. *Painting Culture: The Making of an Aboriginal High Art*. Durham, NC: Duke University Press. http://dx.doi.org/10.1215/9780822384168.

Nadasdy, Paul. 2003. *Hunters and Bureaucrats: Power, Knowledge, and Aboriginal-State Relations in the Southwest Yukon*. Vancouver: University of British Columbia Press.

Poirier, Sylvie. 2004. "La (dé)politisation de la culture? Réflexions sur un concept pluriel" [(De)politicization of Culture? Reflections on a Plural Concept]. *Anthropologie et Sociétés* 28 (1): 7–21. http://dx.doi.org/10.7202/008568ar.

Poirier, Sylvie, ed. 2010. "Cultural and Political Imagination in Indigenous Communities in Canada and Australia." *Anthropologica* 52 (1).

Poirier, Sylvie. 2013. "The Dynamic Reproduction of Hunters-Gatherers' Values and Ontologies." In *A Companion to the Anthropology of Religion*, ed. Janice Boddy and Michael Lambek, 50–68. Malden: Wiley-Blackwell. http://dx.doi.org/10.1002/9781118605936.ch2.

Pratt, Angela. 2004. "Treaties vs. Terra Nullius: 'Reconciliation', Treaty-Making and Indigenous Sovereignty in Australia and Canada." *Indigenous Law Journal at the University of Toronto Faculty of Law* 3: 43–60.

Sahlins, Marshall. 1981. *Islands of History*. Chicago: University of Chicago Press.

Sahlins, Marshall. 1993. "Goodbye to Tristes Tropes: Ethnography in the Context of Modern World History." *Journal of Modern History* 65 (1): 1–25. http://dx.doi.org/10.1086/244606.

Sahlins, Marshall. 1995. *How "Natives" Think: About Captain Cook, for Example.* Chicago: University of Chicago Press. http://dx.doi.org/10.7208/chicago/9780226733715.001.0001.

Schwarz, Carolyn, and Françoise Dussart. 2010. "Christianity in Aboriginal Australia Revisited." *Australian Journal of Anthropology* 21 (1): 1–13. http://dx.doi.org/10.1111/j.1757-6547.2010.00064.x.

Scott, Colin, ed. 2001. *Aboriginal Autonomy and Development in Northern Quebec and Labrador.* Vancouver: University of British Columbia Press.

Stoler, Ann. 2002. *Carnal Knowledge and Imperial Power: Race and the Intimate in Colonial Rule.* Berkeley: University of California Press.

Strathern, Marilyn. 1991. *Partial Connections.* Lanham: Rowman and Littlefield Publishers.

Thomas, Nicholas. 1991. *Entangled Objects: Exchange, Material Culture and Colonialism in the Pacific.* Cambridge, MA: Harvard University Press.

2 Dialogues on Surviving: Eeyou Hunters' Ways of Engagement with Land, Governments, and Youth

HARVEY A. FEIT

Introduction

This chapter is about dialogues that Eeyou hunters initiated in 1972 and 1975 when the James Bay hydroelectric project started to be built on their lands. These dialogues were part of Eeyou efforts to become effective participants in decisions about the project. Eeyouch (plural) sought recognition of their governance and stewardship of their lands from Quebec and Canada.[1] Some hunters also spoke to Eeyou youths about the survival of Eeyou families and ways of life when they are at risk. Under threats to their lands and lives from the project, they talked about starvation and Eeyou hunters' ways of surviving. Accounts like these have been told in new forms in the decades since.

Some of the Eeyou hunters' dialogues on the project were reported in public media and newspapers, as well as in books and documentary films.[2] Among the topics taken up by public media and non-Indigenous supporters were Eeyou affirmations of their active stewardship of land and animals, their calling the hydroelectric project a social and environmental crisis for Eeyouch as well as for other Quebecers and Canadians, and their statements that survival of the Eeyou way of life was at risk. Eeyouch shared these dialogues with journalists, in courtrooms, with environmental movement supporters and the public, and in their communities.

But some aspects of what Eeyouch were saying were not so readily reported or understood by media or the wider public. When Eeyou hunters talked about differences between Eeyou and non-Indigenous ways of life, they also recalled their mutual histories of engagements in the fur trade and the ontological commensurabilities with non-Indigenous people. Dialogues on hunters' experiences and reflections on hunger, starvation, hardship, death, and survival did not get widely circulated. These are dialogues on Eeyou hunters' ways of surviving.

The Context of Eeyou Dialogues, 1972

The great majority of Eeyouch in 1972 lived in families for whom hunting was the main component of their domestic social economy. Their responses to the project were primarily rooted in their histories of hunters' governance of their family hunting lands, their multi-generational relations within their communities, and the histories of their relations with non-Indigenous people. Relationships with fur traders went back three hundred years, and government agents had been present for three decades, but the hydroelectric project created new threats and destruction.

In the summer of 1972, a year after the hydroelectric project was announced and a few months after the decision was made to begin the construction of dams on the Chisasibi River, Robert Kanatewat, the Chisasibi chief and a regional leader, summarized for journalist Boyce Richardson and for non-Eeyou why Chisasibi families at Fort George opposed the hydroelectric project:[3]

> They are already building the roads. There goes your nature right away. Our people want to go back to the land whenever they feel like it. They will never go down south to the labor market. They will always be here in this last remote area that has never been trod by any white man, and when this is gone, there is nothing left. It is just like destroying these people completely. (Richardson 1972: 173)[4]

Philip Awashish, who was at the time a senior councillor at Mistissini, an inland village, and who also was a key leader in organizing Eeyou responses, has recently written and spoken about this period. I invited him to read and advise me on an earlier and rather different version of this chapter. He said that more of "the political context of the time for Eeyou" needed to be included, and he shared some of his knowledge of the period. I have drawn on his commentaries here and below.

Philip Awashish stressed that, at the time, "the government exercised a politics of exclusion and denial. Exclusion and denial of relations. We were excluded from planning, a denial of our mere presence" (Philip Awashish, personal communication, 7 June 2015; from my keyword notes).

There was a denial of Eeyou rights, "including rights to hunt, fish, and trap, and to govern ourselves" (personal communication, 7 December 2015).

> When the project was announced we were immediately opposed. We agreed to oppose because of our anger and rage. There was that anger and rage. It was their actions that determined how we perceived them. We had no information on it, and were not consulted.
>
> It was hard to rationalize it for Crees, no one lived with electricity. There were only generators for the Hudson's Bay Company and Indian Affairs staff, Eeyou people at home had no electricity ... it was not an issue. People did not need it, and did not understand it. The thought of using land and rivers to produce electricity was hard to understand. This was being done to meet needs elsewhere, our demand for electricity came after.
>
> Eeyou people joined together. Environmentalists joined us, but we each had our own agenda. We were trying to stop the project. Eeyouch took an interlocutory injunction, then a permanent one. (Personal communication, 7 June 2015)[5]

In other discussions and in publications, Philip Awashish described some of the ways Eeyou people spoke of the issues at the time (Awashish 2012, 2014). The English translations of Eeyou terms that he mentions also appear throughout the texts, cited below in translation:

> In the meetings that came as the result of the announcements of the hydro project, that is the Cree meetings, not the meetings with the hydro or government, people talked about what they call *Eeyou Eedou-wun*, it means literally, *Eenou* way of doing things. It encompasses everything respecting the *Eenou* way of life. And that was what they talked about ... the Cree pursuit of *Eeyou pimaat-tahseewin*, holistic well-being. And the paths chosen to maintain *Eeyou pimaat-tahseewin* determined *Eeyou Eedou-wun*, that is the Cree way of life. It is the pursuit of survival and the Cree way of life.
>
> So people talk about *Eeyou Eedou-wun*. How this project, and not only the project but how the government, conduct their relations with people constituted a big threat to *Eeyou Eedou-wun*. (Awashish 2012, transcribed using Eeyou spellings and italicizations found in Awashish 2014)

The statements cited below are not texts of Eeyou meetings, but dialogues among approximately twenty Chisasibi hunters in 1972, 1974, and

1975, and later Eeyou statements that are related to them. These statements are supplements to oral histories, memories, and other records of the community meetings and leadership discussions of these years, records which Philip Awashish and other Eeyouch share in their work.

Chisasibi lands were the areas where project construction was most advanced and would be most extensive, and there was a consensus among Eeyouch from other communities that the Chisasibi people should take the lead in making decisions about Eeyou responses. This chapter does not follow all of the Eeyou responses to the hydroelectric project or the subsequent negotiations and treaty, nor does it assess the results of their initiatives during the years, since these analyses are available elsewhere.[6]

Dialogues about and for Whitemen on Differences, Suffering, and Relationships, 1972

Job and Mary Bearskin's statements in the summer of 1972 were among the earliest by Eeyou hunters that were widely circulated to non-Eeyou. Job Bearskin talked to Boyce Richardson at the suggestion of Gilbert Herodier, a younger member of the community who was helping Richardson make a public film for the Chisasibi people (Richardson 1974). Richardson wrote about what Job said with his wife Mary's encouragement:[7]

> "I know, I'm the one who's telling the truth" he said. "I'm over fifty years old and I've been hunting over this territory since I was a young boy." He spoke of the relatives buried on some of the most beautiful spots along the river. "The person who gave the word to go ahead with this project," said Job, "the Indians think he has no consideration for all the graves of our ancestors. I have to say this about him: he has no consideration for the Indian at all. I would tell him exactly this if he were sitting right in front of me."
> "*Gee-wa*," said Mary, "*gee-wa*" – right, right …
> Now Job said that he heard that the man who launched this project believed this was just a wasteland, that there was nothing here. How could he believe such a thing when so many people are surviving here? That man should come north and see for himself. "He is made the same way we are," said Job. "He would still survive if he lived with Indians. He has the same soul we have. Everybody was given the same. But he is not using his soul properly, he's using it only for his own gain. He is trying to

destroy lots of men. The Creator did not intend that this land should be destroyed." (Richardson 2007: 146–7)

The meeting proposed by Job and others with Quebec Premier Robert Bourassa took place in Quebec City in the fall of 1972. The meeting began with Eeyou and Inuit opening statements, but it was cut short by the premier just as elder Eeyouch were beginning to speak in detail (Diamond 2011).[8] Immediately after that failed and disrespectful meeting, the Eeyou leaders accelerated the legal case they had begun in the spring.

In the late fall of 1972, several Eeyouch gave statements as preparation for the court case. The speakers and dialogues were likely organized in Fort George by Eeyou leaders and interpreters working with their non-Eeyou lawyers, whose notes these may be.[9]

The first sets of questions to respondents were about their involvements with and feelings about the land, subsistence hunting and diets, family life on the land, and evidence about the immediate effects of developers' works. Later questions addressed issues of Eeyou survival that had been raised by government and corporate spokespersons who claimed that Eeyouch were losing their ties to lands and their distinctive ways of life. These questions addressed the effects of Eeyou interactions with the school systems, industrially produced technologies, Christian religions, money and markets, store-bought foods, government assistance programs, more settled villages, and increasing involvements in wage employment (see Poirier in this volume).[10]

In response to the first set of questions, William Ratt said in part:

Yes, I have always trapped west of LG-4 [a dam site], and am forty years old. That is why I can't speak English, because I was always in the bush. I have trapped and hunted for thirty years ...

The country and land is my garden. When it is destroyed, everyone will be in an awkward position including the Whiteman. This is why the people oppose the Project, because what the Indian survived on is being destroyed and the future is being destroyed. The Whiteman brings up his children through his garden of education and technology, it is just the same for the Indian. He wants to bring his children up by his country garden. The diet is different between the Indian and the Whiteman. The Indian does not feel right when he eats Whiteman's food ...

I don't want the land destroyed where my father brought me up and I was brought up this way. I want to bring up my children like my father brought me up. I will be sad when the land is destroyed because it provided for me.

The pollution of the river by gas and oil will affect the drinking water, of our children and their children's children. No one was brought up to drink gas.

The fish are being destroyed by this pollution. This affects the Indian food.

In the future, the Indian land will decrease, getting smaller all the time. This will cause the Indian to lose his land. The same will happen as happened in the States. It is on Indian land that they are working.

Indians will not know what to do; there will be nothing but confusion. Where will he hunt? (1972a)[11]

When William Ratt was asked what he would do if he could no longer hunt, he said:

No way that he could survive, he has grown up from hunting and trapping. He cannot learn from white people ...

About the young people ... It is his hope that they will carry on his way of life. This is true for both cultures. The Whiteman teaches his children his way. Indian is the same. He cannot criticize either culture. (1972b)

William Ratt expresses his anguish about his family's future survival, and worries as well about the future for Whitemen.

None of the statements made by the eight speakers can be called typical, but William Ratt's are not dramatically different from the others. Some of the circumstances and concerns expressed by others give a sense of differences and commonalities. Fifty-year-old Philip Cox, parts of whose hunting lands were to be flooded, said: "All my trapline is destroyed except for a few spots. What is left for me to survive on? Very little, very very little" (1972a). He also said: "He could not survive, everything would be destroyed, he would have nothing left. He could not support his family" (1972b). Joseph Pepabino said, "If the Project is finished, I don't know how the Indian will survive. I just don't know how, maybe this is why I speak against the James Bay Project. Indians can't plant vegetables for food," implicitly referring to Chisasibi's northern lands and poor soils (1972a).

David Sandy, forty-five years old, said, "How can there possibly be harmony with the Indian and Whiteman when the Whiteman has done this damage already? I will be very very sad if I am not able to hunt and fish. I wouldn't be able to live too long if I continue to eat store foods too long" (1972a).

Harry Bearskin, who worked in the village but who said he hunted on his days off and on weekends with Philip Cox, said: "There will be no benefits for the Indian after the project is completed. The Indian will be left to starve to death. The Creator put us Indians on this land to live off of it and I see that this will be destroyed. A person who did not create the land should not be allowed to destroy the land" (1972a).

These statements express how bio-physical and social wellness depended on self-provisioning and livelihoods from lands people knew well and that were healthy. And how sustaining confidence in the Eeyou way of life was essential if they were to continue living on the land and youth were to choose to follow these ways of living.

Governments and corporations never did take these dangers of individual and collective survival, well-being, and health seriously. Nor did they acknowledge that Eeyou ways of life would be endangered for future generations. Social changes were inevitable, they said, and they were certain that Eeyouch would not really be personally or collectively endangered (see the government negotiators' statements in Chisasibi in the spring of 1974 quoted in Feit 2010).

In the course of responding to the second set of questions about the government characterizations that their way of life was already transformed and dependent on Whitemen, speakers offered their views of the recent course of their lives and their complex relationships to Whiteman institutions.

For example, Joseph Pepabino said: "The outboard motor was the first [motor] to be adopted. It is easier and faster to go for a hundred miles up the river, but it was the return of the beaver which brought in the outboard motor ... But it still leaves us Indians" (1972a). He thus notes that access to technologies depends on the land and the abundance of animals, in this case the recovery of beaver populations, whose pelts provided the needed cash. Technologies in this view do not necessarily cut ties to land; they can create new ties. And, he notes, this technology improved access to the land.

Notes on the speakers' discussions of the effects of Christianity on their ways of life were concise. Philip Cox said:

The Church came before my time. It was accepted by our old people. We have been Anglicanized, this is no change, they did not force their religion on us, but we accepted it. It was accepted by our old people. It has been

handed down like our traditions. But nobody thinks about the Church
when he is hunting or fishing, this is funny, but it is there. You do not drop
your rifle while in the bush and decide to go to church. (1972a)

William Ratt also stressed acceptance of Christianity by the old
people and its becoming "like our own tradition" (1972a). But Harry
Bearskin stressed fights within the church, which had a non-Eeyou
minister at that time, and said: "The church doesn't help you to survive
in the bush" (1972a).

Speakers also spoke about the effects of Whiteman education on
Eeyou youth, and the need of youth to be educated in Eeyou ways.
Job Bearskin said:

Since education started for our children, our children are not the same.
Our children and grandchildren do not think of the future like we old people think of the future. The education system has mixed up and confused
our children and they are lost between two worlds, the Indian world and
the Whiteman's world. The Project and the coming of the Whiteman has
ruined our culture and our culture is being lost. The white school teaches
you not to think like an Indian but only like a Whiteman. Children are no
longer Indian minded today ...

The people are not the same since the Whiteman came, everyone is
becoming strangers. The Whiteman is trying to throw their culture, if they
have any, on us. They are trying to make us become like the Whiteman.
Our children are affected and their future is uncertain. (1972a)

William Ratt stressed that Eeyou education is threatened (1972a).
David Sandy also put priority on Eeyou education while valuing both:
"I have one child, sometimes I let her go to school, but I am the father
of that child. I know what is best for her. So I have led the trapper and
hunter's life, I want her to be able to live like this also. I want to bring
her up my way. I have taken her out of school many times" (1972a).

Thomas Pachanos, Philip Cox, and Joseph Pepabino stressed
the importance of schools being local so that Eeyou and Whiteman
education could both be pursued (all 1972a). "Education is good for
the children when the children are attending school on the settlement
but the problem starts when the child is sent to the schools down
south" (1972a).

Harry Bearskin reversed the logic of the government and corporation arguments that schools were the means to secure future survival

through jobs. He was himself employed and had worked at several jobs, although he says that he had never been to school: "The White-man's education system has caused ... the disappearance of the Indian culture. Hunting skills of the young people are gone. If the student doesn't get the job, how is he able to survive?" (1972a). He doubted the reliability of jobs, or that employment can offer the same survival security as knowing how to live on the land.

The speakers repeatedly stressed the differences between Eeyou ways of doing things and those of Whitemen. They spoke of two cultures, two worlds, and two ways of thinking, two ways of living, two ways of educating, two diets, and two ways of surviving.

Along with differences, and anger over the destruction of the land and the effects of school education on youth, there were acknowledgments of Whitemen's capacity to learn and to change. Job Bearskin said to the premier of Quebec, in absentia, that all humans are the same, both calling on the premier to remember that, and affirming Job's view of an underlying ontological and spiritual relationship (see Scott in this volume). William Ratt said he expected that "both will suffer" from the project, that both peoples want to continue their ways of life, and that he "cannot criticize either culture" for that. Others noted that Eeyouch accepted new technologies and Christianity, and made them their own. And they did so without losing relations to land, hunting, or Eeyou ways (see Morphy in this volume). Whitemen and Eeyouch have shared Christianity, and education in both ways of life is needed by Eeyou youth. Calling attention to these subtle and contradictory entangling relationships is an impetus to these diverse dialogues (see Dussart and Poirier in this volume).

The Context of Eeyou Dialogues, 1975

About one-third of the people who gave these statements in 1972 got the chance to testify and were among the forty-six Eeyouch and Inuit who were witnesses. Those Eeyouch and Inuit who did testify found that presenting what they had to say in court was not easy. The frustrations and anger of dialogues under constant lawyers' interruptions, repeated misunderstandings, and a lack of respect in questioning are clear in the transcripts. Nevertheless, significant portions of what Eeyouch intended to say was communicated, and much was said between the lines (Richardson 2007).

In late 1973 Judge Albert Malouf ruled in favour of a temporary interlocutory injunction against the project, pending a full hearing on Eeyouch's legal rights. He ruled more strongly on Eeyou legal rights than he needed to do. However, it was more than a legal victory.

He accepted much of what Eeyouch and Inuit witnesses sought to communicate. He concluded that their continuing hunting, trapping, and fishing throughout the territory were "still of great importance to them and constitute a way of life for a very great number of them," that they "have a unique concept of the land ... and any interference therewith compromises their very existence as a people. They wish to continue their way of life" (Malouf 1973).

The ruling was circulated in the Eeyou villages, parts were read in meetings, and it was understood as a great victory. The Quebec Court of Appeal suspended Malouf's ruling one week later, until it could decide on an appeal against the ruling by Quebec and the corporations, allowing construction to continue during the appeal.

The premier of Quebec made a public offer to the Eeyouch after the Malouf ruling late in 1973. Philip Awashish highlights the importance of this change, commenting;

> You do not mention their refusals. We were willing to talk, but they refused ... When Bourassa made his offer a week to ten days after Malouf's ruling it was based on a list we prepared. Bourassa's office had called and they asked what it would take to stop the court case. We were still set on stopping the project, and on recognition of rights – called "Indian Rights" then ...
>
> The Cree chiefs, Billy Diamond, and I spent days and long nights discussing the Bourassa offer. We discussed what to do with the project, oppose it or seek a modified project? But rights were first. There was harassment of hunters, schools were under the federal government, children were being taken away, we only had nursing stations ... There were a lot of social ills in Cree communities ...
>
> We decided to get recognition of rights and a modified project. That is why the agreement has all those sections. At the moment when we reviewed the Bourassa offer we decided to seek a treaty, and of course a modified project, and an out of court settlement. We rejected the offer but we sought to negotiate. (Personal communication, 7 June 2015)

The negotiations resulted in an agreement-in-principle in November 1974 which received approval in communities as a basis for continuing negotiations. Negotiations continued in 1974 and 1975, and a final agreement was signed on 11 November 1975 (on related processes, see Westman in this volume). The texts that follow come from the period of continuing negotiations, when the Eeyou negotiators and people were engaged in significant dialogues but the outcomes were unknown.

Dialogues for Youth on Starvation, Determination, Relationships, and Surviving, 1975

In the summer of 1975 two young Eeyou researchers, James Bobbish and Buckley Petawabano, spoke with elders about their lives.[12] The hunters' dialogues with the young researchers were probably intended to address Eeyou youths more generally, and some of the 1975 speakers referred to youth not knowing the things the speaker would be talking about (see Samson Neacappo and Clifford Bearskin in Bobbish and Petawabano 2014 [1976]).[13]

The speakers told detailed and sometimes moving personal and family histories. Ernest Herodier said:

> Years ago I used to feel sorry for my people and myself. How we used to survive; of course it was very difficult in those years. There wasn't that very many mammals to kill, or rather it wasn't easy for us to catch or kill them.
>
> One time there was this man, who was very weak all over his body, all because of hunger. That man didn't eat one or two days and he would say that he didn't even feel a bit hungry. Even if he didn't eat for a day or so, he would only drink. Sometimes when he was really trying hard to hunt he could hardly walk back to his camp because he was very weak. There were some families that were living near to that guy's camp, an old man knew about this poor man but he only ignored him.
>
> Then this poor man approached some other camp and he went right in and he put down his pack sack. They only gave him a little food, because they didn't want to give a lot of food to him right away. They were afraid something wrong might happen to him. As the days went by that poor man got stronger and stronger every day.
>
> Then from that time on everyday he killed different kinds of animals. In exchange he helped other people who were too old to hunt for themselves and other people that were starving. This man that I'm talking about – my father had lived and survived the same way as this man had years ago.
> (Ernest Herodier, in Bobbish and Petawabano 2014 [1976])

Noah Sealhunter told a story of his great-grandfather saving another family from starvation. Emma Wesabo said her parents starved to death, along with other families, when there were no fish, rabbits, and partridges. It happened when she was a young child living with an uncle (Bobbish and Petawabano 2014 [1976]). Abraham Martinhunter told of his own father, who had died of starvation when he was three (Martinhunter, 1974).

Descriptions of periods of personally experienced life-threatening hunger were told by Emma Wesabo, Samson Neacappo, James Rupert, Sr, James Rupert, Ronnie Sam, and Edward Kitty (Bobbish and Petawabano 2014 [1976]). Edward Kitty explained:

> I've seen how hard it was in the years back. All the men and women didn't eat all day. Still the men would go hunting even if they don't have food with them to keep them going. At that time there were no rabbits or partridges. Yes, I went hungry a lot of times but I still tried with all my strength to hunt for my family. Then it came to pass when a white man came to the post to build a store and he had everything we need in his store. That's when we all didn't have that much difficulty when he had the store. There were many mammals like mink, fox, partridge, marten and rabbits at that time, including what the white man had in the store. In the summer I used to work for that Company. (Bobbish and Petawabano 2014 [1976])

Ronnie Sam also discussed surviving:

> I'm going to tell about how I survived in the past. One time I was living near a river and I was very hungry. So I walked back to the post. When I got there I named everything that I needed. But the store manager told me I had some bills. But I couldn't even pay for my bills. I was just given a little of food.
>
> So I started my way back to my camp. When I was there I didn't have anything left to eat. I went out to hunt and I didn't take any food with me for me to go on. I didn't walk that far when I saw fox's tracks. One of its hind legs was gone, by the way I looked at its tracks. I followed its tracks until I saw him hiding behind the trees. The colour of its fur was black. That was the year the fox's black pelt was very expensive. That's what I thought anyway ...
>
> When I was close enough to shoot him the tree was in my way ... When I saw him again, it wasn't close enough for me to shoot him ...

I couldn't go any further so I went back to my camp ... I told them about what I have been doing while I was out. My brother told me that he had to go and get some food and their other things [from their camp]. Then he told his son to go with him ... Sure enough his son came back to my camp with the supplies and I saw a fox tied to the sled too. I saw that it was the same fox I saw while I was out hunting. His father asked him how he had killed the fox. His son said that he saw its tracks, so he just set the trap up anywhere in the snow, just in case if the fox had turned back. And he said that it just walked into his trap.

In a couple of days I did kill a few mammals. So I went to the post with my brother's son; we wanted to sell our pelts ...

So we went to the store to sell our pelts and the manager started measuring my pelts first. He said that the fox pelts were not going to be expensive. I told him what do you mean? Look I said, when I came here before you didn't want to give me anything just because I had a few bills. So he started apologizing to me for what he had done to me. I told him I was going to take my pelts to another trading post, which was not far from where we were. He said to me "Why are you taking your pelts to another post?" I said they gave me a good bargain when I sold my pelts at their post. So he didn't say anything; what can he say. The next morning we started loading our luggage on a sled and the manager was there watching us leave the post.

After we sold our pelts we went back to our camp and my wife was waiting for me. And my brother's wife was there too. What me and my brother's son bought from our pelts, we were running out of food in no time. We could hardly catch any fish from our fishing nets. In the springtime we didn't have enough food for all of us. (Bobbish and Petawabano 2014 [1976]).

Ronnie Sam then went on to tell another story that he heard from his father about the coming of Frenchmen long ago. They claimed they discovered "our land" first. But an old Indian man said to people that the Indians used to make fish nets out of the "stems" of trees (roots?), which implied the Indians were there first, before the Frenchmen brought twine for net making.

Another time Frenchmen stayed a year, and when they were leaving an old man "was lonesome for those Frenchmen. Then one of those Frenchmen gave him an [old-fashioned] gun," and taught him how to use it. After they left he was "anxious to use the gun," and when he saw a caribou, "he killed it right away. He was very thankful to the

Frenchman who had given him the gun" (Bobbish and Petawabano 2014 [1976]).

Several stories attribute starvation or near starvation to the absence of animals, as in stories by Emma Wesabo and Edward Kitty. Ronnie Sam's story of the easy capture of the black fox shows another relationship with animals, that animals can be generous to hunters. His brother's son set a trap for a black fox that he knew was around and that was missing a leg, probably because it had been caught and injured in a trap before. He set the trap "anywhere," and the same fox just "walked into his trap." Many of the 1972 statements indicate how hunting families have been surviving on animals' generosity over generations, although not without very hard times, and sometimes starvation.

Ernest Herodier's account starts out recalling the uncertainties of catching animals. But he corrects himself, saying: "There wasn't that very many mammals to kill, or rather it wasn't easy for us to catch or kill them." This implies that animals or others may have made animals hard to capture, and that there were reasons why they could not be caught – reasons probably caused, wilfully or not, by human negligence or malevolence. In this case he implies that the old man who knew of but ignored his father's starving condition was the cause of his father not being able to catch animals.

Others cared for and nursed his father when he literally "went right in" to their home in his weakened condition, ignoring Eeyou ways visitors should announce their approach to an abode. And having survived with their careful nursing, he in exchange helped others as he hunted every day. Eeyou malevolence and caring both occur.

Edward Kitty tells listeners that fur traders' stores and goods made a significant difference to reducing hunger and sometimes starvation. And Ronnie Sam's second story tells how, in an earlier period, the relationships with French traders or explorers brought the gift of a gun that made life easier. Even though the exchange took place in the midst of relationships that involved fundamental disagreements over claims to the land, the Eeyou man felt an attachment to the Frenchman, which was reciprocated. The relationship expressed mutual recognition and caring, the Eeyou elder offering friendship in response to mutual loneliness or inquisitiveness, and being in turn thankful to receive an old gun as a gift.[14]

Ronnie's story of abuse by a trader misusing indebtedness, goods, money, and power shows malevolence and dangers of trading, putting the lives of Ronnie's extended family at risk. Ronnie did not go to the other trader at first because he was meeting his debt obligations to the first. When that was not reciprocated, he was fortunate to have an alternative. And Ronnie made the trader aware of his disapproval for not reciprocating responsibly. But the help from the second trader was still limited, because trade purchases could not be the basis of sustained subsistence and of survival by themselves. Eeyouch were still fundamentally dependent on the land, animals, and their own everyday hunting and trapping to live.

Speakers repeatedly told hunger stories about how surviving is grounded in the land, and how surviving can be both aided and threatened by relationships to animals, Eeyouch, and Whitemen (see Thom in this volume). They also give a clear sense of the sometimes exceptional efforts and wilful determination required of hunters who must keep hunting when they and their families are starving and in grave danger, even when their health and strength are diminishing. Not to seek to renew efforts to encounter and re-establish relationships with animals or nearby caring humans would settle the fate of oneself and one's family.

These stories of starving are told partly for the benefit of youth in a time of increasing destruction and uncertainty. They highlight hunters' everyday wilful pursuit of family survival, in conditions of hardship and danger. The speakers give few details on the hunting techniques and strategies that are also often vital to surviving, for some strategies enhance chances of surviving and others can put people at greater risk and sometimes contribute to their deaths. Instead, many stories focus on relationships. Speakers talk about families seeking out relationships, or cutting other relationships short, or avoiding, criticizing, or calling for renewed relationships. Thus speakers indicate the diversity of relationships that can endanger survival, as well as the multiplicity of relationships that may be crucial for surviving and that need to be attended to and valued in everyday life, even when they need to be changed (see Borrows in this volume).

Dialogues on Changes, Histories, and Survivances, 1991–2014

We do not have records of direct Eeyouch responses to these Chisasibi dialogues, but they are part of a long history of narratives and discussions of starving, surviving, and resisting Whitemen among Eeyou and related peoples. Mary Black-Rogers has analysed fur trader records from northern Ontario between 1750 and 1850 that include many mentions of the root term "starv-". Traders' writings from that century refer to numerous hunters' accounts of starvation and hunger, along with reports of traders' hunger, and other dialogues on strategies of hunting, trapping, trading, and starving (Black-Rogers 1986).

Anishinaabe scholar and activist Gerald Vizenor has written extensively on the importance of surviving in Indigenous narratives and histories, and he has revived an earlier term, "survivances," for the ensemble of practices, including what is passed on across generations. He explores how disappearances are central themes of colonial and contemporary claims for Indigenous peoples' removal and assimilation, and how surviving is a set of themes in Indigenous narratives about how people are continuing to live as Indigenous peoples, and for the active processes of surviving, for Indigenous resistance, and for the passing on of survivances (1999 [1994], 2008).

In the decades since 1972, recorded Eeyou dialogues have periodically referred to earlier narratives of surviving. These dialogues are told in a time when starvation is not a regular threat. But they are still sometimes spoken about in court cases, in addressing youth, and also as part of new stories of Eeyou nation building. Between 1974 and 1991 nineteen storytellers at Whapmagoostui, the community immediately to the north of Chisasibi, recorded stories that included many narratives and reflections on starvation and other themes that are related to the narratives recorded here (Marshall and Masty 2013).

In 1991 Jimmy Happyjack, a hunter who would have been about the same age as some of the Chisasibi speakers above, was cited by Paul Dixon, a younger hunter from the southernmost Eeyou community, in "Quoting the Old and Young Hunters, Trappers and Fishermen of Waswanipi":

> Our ancestors learned from starvation, they were determined not to let it happen again. They taught us to respect the animals, the young and their habitats, we learned a lot from the animals. We were taught, at an early stage, conservation and preservation methods, rotating our lands, [changing our hunting] from one species of animal to another, eating blueberries and fish in summer [when many mammals are nurturing young]. Taking into careful consideration the balance between men and nature. Like our ancestors, we were determined to maintain the survival of the animals, so our children would survive also. (Dixon 1991: 2–3)

In a 1999 affidavit for a court case against unregulated forestry on inland Eenou hunting lands, fifty-nine-year-old Yvonne Cheezo Neeposh from Nemaska, north of Waswanipi, spoke of a childhood experience:

> At the age of ten, when life was harsh and we were close to starvation and when my father was very ill, I remember that I helped him hold his weapon in order to kill some game. After having our meal, we were well and regained our strength from the land. This event is very important for me since the land saved us from starvation. I am thus very attached to the hunting territory and I have great respect for our land. (Yvonne Cheezo Neeposh 1999: 1)

For still younger Eeyou generations, accounts of hardship and survivance told by grandparents are important in new contexts.

Michael Neeposh from Waswanipi submitted an essay as part of a Millennium youth project. Many of the contributions to that project mentioned grandparents and learning from them. Then nineteen years old, Michael Neeposh titled his essay "Changes in Life in the Bush and Land," and in it he discussed his relationship to his grandfather:

> Over the last twenty-five years, Cree society has changed a great deal – or at least many parts of it have. Particularly the Life in the bush and the Land are two areas in which changes have been extremely fast ...
>
> My grandfather lived and survived from the land all his life ... A lot of what I know about the life in the bush and land comes from him. I feel pity for him because he is still living off the land but pollution is stopping him. He feels pity for the younger people because he says they will never know the good hard bush life because of the changes in the land ...
>
> Today, in modern Cree life, life in the bush is seasonal. The times that people live in the bush are spring and fall. This does not mean that all Cree people don't live in the bush throughout the year any more. I am saying that Cree culture has been modernized. It has been balanced with both modern and the Cree way of life ...
>
> All of these changes that occurred during the last 25–30 years have been very surprising, hurting, negative and positive. (Michael Neeposh 2000)

Michael Neeposh concluded his essay:

> Together throughout the 25–30 years of change the foreign people had tried to take Cree culture, land, language, beliefs away. They have tried

to take lands and rivers away, in return for money. Money cannot be exchanged for land that a society needs to survive from. Always remember the Cree culture is weak and materially impoverished. It is very fragile. The Cree people can blame Governments, Churches, Companies, but the blame also lies in the people themselves. We did not protect our own culture, land and rivers, when we did it, it was a little too late. Also, let the Cree people remember that the past cannot be changed, but the changes in the past can guide the future, so that their children's children will be able to share the Cree way of life among themselves and others. (Michael Neeposh 2000)

In the last decade, Eeyou leaders and organizations have undertaken a series of initiatives to enhance Eeyou youth's awareness of the histories of Eeyou Nation building that have been continuous since the fight against the James Bay project. A number of these initiatives include publications, streamed internet videos, community gatherings, educational programs, electronic cafés, museum exhibits, and touring plays. These are aimed at giving Eeyou youth of today an awareness of the struggles since 1971, some of the results of which many take for granted. The Eeyou leaders of today see these histories as a way to assist current generations to meet the challenges and responsibilities they are encountering (see Peterson in this volume).

As these new narratives are developing, there are occasional references to earlier dialogues on surviving. In 2014, Ashley Iserhoff, the then deputy head of the Eeyou Nation political and governance organizations, gave a presentation at a community youth day in Waswanipi on an "Overview of the 75 Agreements" the Eeyou had signed since 1975. In his impromptu introduction he said:

In 1970s, I was born in 1974, and around that time the Cree nation was already working at making sure that our rights were always protected. And we wanted to make sure, that the way we live life today still continues ...

You might be wondering ... "What am I doing here? Why did they ask us to come out of school?" It's important for you, as young people, to know where we came from as people. If you know your history – just like grandma and grandpa, when there were days they almost didn't survive because there was no food at the camp. That's where they came from.

They showed us something in our life here today, that if they gave up back then we would not be sitting here in this room. The schools that you have ...

You might be wondering "Is it important for me to be here?" Yes, it is. For you to know where we came from as a nation ... and continue on with the work that we did. (Iserhoff 2014: 3)

These recent Eeyou dialogues highlight familial and community gifts of life and ways of living. They recall hunters' dialogues, which show how it is necessary to act with resoluteness every day in order to continue surviving. Everyday relations are means of surviving, and reasons for life and living.

Dialogues, Relationships, and Surviving

In the hunters' dialogues, when they are confronting life-threatening starvation, refusals of proper trade and reciprocity, disruptive development of lands, or life-threatening denials of their presence and governance, they repeatedly seek relations and dialogues with those potentially caring or responsive animals, family members, neighbours, traders, judges, and government officials who may help to enhance opportunities for surviving.

Dealing with persons or officials like the fur trader who refused to properly offer provisions or pay for pelts, the judge, or the premier who Job Bearskin said showed no concern while "trying to destroy lots of men," hunters seek dialogues and take other initiatives that might change those people and their mutual circumstances. These relational initiatives are part of using all the means they have to survive. When hunters went to another trader, into the courtroom, and into negotiations, in order to survive and to instruct and seek to change others, these officials did change. The trader came to offer an apology, the judge understood hunters' dialogues and changed the legal and political situation, the premier sought an agreement and entered negotiations.

These trader, judicial, and government changes appear to have occurred out of self-interest, and out of some new insights into the mutuality of relationships. These changes were brought about by Eeyou initiatives in trading, courts, and negotiations. It is also clear that these Cree initiatives have had wider and longer-term effects, although it is difficult to know the distinct impacts of these specific events as government policies, negotiations, judicial rulings, and Indigenous governance have been elaborated in subsequent years in Canada. The effects of the changes for Crees have also been much debated and contested by Crees themselves as well as others (see, for example, Awashish 2002; Feit 2009).

These initiatives were part of the Eeyou hunters' means of surviving the currently urgent situations. These initiatives were also part of hunters' ways of everyday surviving, and Eeyou ways of living, and they are part of their dialogues and histories.

In these accounts, surviving is never certain. Surviving is sought in a multiplicity of ways, there are not always opportunities for potentially effective initiatives, and one cannot know in advance the effects of one's initiatives or if they will be timely. Yet, resolute everyday situated actions are vital, as are initiatives that seek to engage both potentially caring and currently destructive people, amidst entangling relations.

Eeyou dialogues on surviving over decades and across generations are deeply moving and thought-provoking, and they continue to be recalled and recreated in diverse ways today.

ACKNOWLEDGMENTS

This research is funded by the Social Sciences and Humanities Research Council of Canada (SSHRC) and the Canada Council. I want to acknowledge and thank James Bobbish and Buckley Petawabano, who, as young researchers in 1975, working on a grant I had received, engaged in dialogues with Eeyou hunters and families, some of which are quoted here. I also want to thank Philip Awashish and Samuel C. Gull, who over many years have aided my understanding of Eeyou knowledge, practices, and visions. In recent years Philip Awashish, Sam C. Gull, Jasmin Habib, and I have had new and expanded exchanges with the assistance of an SSHRCC research grant, of which this chapter is one outcome.

NOTES

1 "Eeyou" and "Eeyouch," plural, are used along with "Cree(s)" as terms of self-reference for James Bay Cree people in general and for people from northern coastal Cree communities in particular. "Eenou" and "Eenouch" are used as terms for inland and southern James Bay Cree people. The linguist Kevin Brousseau notes that the term "îyiniw" can refer to a human, a Native American of any nation, or a person of Iynu, Iyyu, or Innu descent (2007). In quoted texts, the original usage and spelling are retained.
2 For example, see those of the activist journalist and film-maker Boyce Richardson (1972, 1974, 1975, 1991, 2007 [1976]).
3 Fort George is an Eeyou village on an island in the mouth of the Chisasibi River where the majority of Chisasibi Eeyouch lived seasonally in the early

1970s. The term "Chisasibi" translates as "Great River" or "Big River" in English or "La Grande Rivière" in French. The Eeyou term also refers to the people, the Chisasibi Eeyouch or "Big River People," and the Cree Nation of Chisasibi. The present village, a few miles upstream of the island on the shore of the river, to which they relocated their main community between 1978 and 1980, is called Chisasibi.

4 The term "white man," or "Whitemen," gender inclusive, was in common use in Eeyou English, and in regional non-Indigenous English. In Eeyou usage it was generally an English cognate of the Eeyou-language *wemistikushu* or *wemistikusiw* (various spellings). It often indicated non-Indigenous people, but the term could be used with varying inclusiveness, with the context clarifying the meaning. So it might be used for fur traders, for all the non-Eeyou in a village, for Euro-Canadians in general, for English-speaking Canadians, or for people of European descent (see Brousseau 2007).

5 The term "Cree" was the common term for Eeyouch at that time in English, and it remains in use. The term "Indian" was also commonly used by Eeyouch and non-Indigenous people then. It could refer to Eeyouch, Indigenous, Aboriginal, or First Nations People.

6 On the main events of this period and since see: Recherches amérindiennes au Québec 1971; Awashish 1972, 1988, 2002, 2005, 2014; Diamond 1972, 1977, 1990, 2011; Richardson 1972, 1975, 1991, 2007; Feit [1985], 1986, 1989, 2009; Salisbury 1986; Vincent and Bowers 1988; Scott 2001, 2005; Gnarowski 2002; Gagnon and Rocher 2002; Blaser et al. 2004; Petit et al. 2010.

7 On the process see Richardson 2007: 124, 134; 2003: 211–12; and on Job's life see Pashagumiskum 1989–90.

8 Eeyouch were joined in opposition to the project, in the court case, and in the agreement, by the Inuit of northern Quebec, one of the peoples who were formerly called "Eskimo." Their more northerly lands and lives were also affected by the hydroelectric development.

9 Internal evidence in these English notes suggests that they were made as part of the court preparations with the lawyers involved, although their purpose and timing are a matter of surmise. The notes record responses to a continually evolving set of questions, which are sometimes written with the responses. These notes are concise and not verbatim, but they include what appear to be original phrasings. There are eight notes from male Chisasibi hunters of varying ages (1972a), three of whom also made statements on another occasion in a somewhat different format (1972b), which may have been before or after the 1972a statements. Each note includes the respondent's name, and one set is labelled "Dialogue with [name]." Efforts to identify others involved in the discussions have not succeeded to date.

10 These statements by government and corporate spokespersons and by some social scientists were discussed with media and were referred to in one of the 1972 "Dialogue" records. A summary statement of these views appears in the unpublished report of the Joint Federal-Provincial Task Force (1971). And they were repeated in questioning by lawyers for the hydroelectric state corporation and the government in the court case (Richardson 2007).

11 On the widespread Eeyou use of the garden metaphor, see Feit 2001. In this and other passages I have made minor typographical corrections and altered sentence and paragraph breaks in these working manuscripts.

12 James Bobbish was from Fort George, Buckley Petawabano was from Mistissini, and his wife Bella (Moses) Petawabano was from Eastmain to the south of Fort George. James Bobbish recorded and transcribed conversations with eleven men and one woman from Fort George, and a similar number of people were recorded from Eastmain by Buckley Petawabano. James Bobbish's and Buckley Petawabano's conversations were more extended than those in 1972, one running to seventeen typed pages (Bobbish and Petawabano 2014 [1976]). I cite from the Chisasibi conversations, as well as from notes of a discussion with Abraham Martinhunter from the year before, provided by Martin Weinstein, who conducted research in Fort George for the Eeyouch. I visited Fort George and Eastmain several times during these years, mainly as an advisor to Eeyou negotiators, and my conversations with hunters were mainly about issues in negotiation.

13 The 1975 texts were recorded on cassettes and then translated into English by James Bobbish, for the Chisasibi conversations, and by Buckley Petawabano, for those from Eastmain. The original recordings were lost in transit. Copies of all the translated texts from 1972 and 1975 have been deposited at the archives of Aanischaaukamikw-Cree Cultural Institute.

14 This story of relations with the Frenchman may have been meant by the speaker to extend to Frenchmen more generally. In the 1970s, when French-speaking staff were becoming more common among the newly arrived Quebec government representatives, some were former fur traders.

REFERENCES

Awashish, Philip. 1972. "Report of Philip Awashish Communications Worker James Bay Development Project, Huron Village, June 23 1972," 11. Photocopied typescript, retyped 2013.

Awashish, Philip. 1988 "The Stakes for the Crees of Quebec." In *Baie James et Nord québécois: dix ans après [James Bay and Northern Quebec: Ten Years Later]*, ed. Sylvie Vincent and Garry Bowers, 42–9. Montreal: Recherches Amérindiennes au Québec.

Awashish, Philip. 2002. "Some Reflections on Eeyou Governance and the James Bay and Northern Quebec Agreement." In *Reflections on the James Bay and Northern Québec Agreement*, ed. Alain-G. Gagnon and Guy Rocher, 153–63. Montreal: Québec Amérique

Awashish, Philip. 2005. "From Board to Nation Governance." In *Reconfiguring Aboriginal-State Relations*, ed. Michael Murphy, 165–83. Montreal and Kingston: McGill-Queen's University Press.

Awashish, Philip. 2012. Discussion with Harvey Feit, 11 April 2012. Transcript. Pp. 13.

Awashish, Philip. 2014 "Eeyou Governance in Eeyou Istchee." In 2014 Report of the Cree-Naskapi Commission. Ottawa: Cree-Naskapi Commission. Electronic document. http://www.creenaskapicommission.net/, accessed 10 December 2015.

Black-Rogers, Mary. 1986. "Varieties of 'Starving': Semantics and Survival in the Subarctic Fur Trade, 1750–1850." *Ethnohistory* 33 (4): 353–83. http://dx.doi.org/10.2307/482039.

Blaser, Mario, Harvey A. Feit, and Glenn McRae, eds. 2004. *In the Way of Development: Indigenous Peoples, Life Projects and Globalization*. London and New York: Zed Books and Ottawa: Canadian International Development Research Centre.

Bobbish, James, and Buckley Petawabano. 2014 (1976). "Conversations and Stories by Crees of Fort George (now Chisasibi) and Eastmain – Summer, Fall, Winter 1975–76." Unpublished typescript. Pp. 144.

Brousseau, Kevin. 2007. *The Practical Iynu Dictionary*. N.p.: Nikan Publishing.

Diamond, Billy. 1972. "Report from: Chief Billy Diamond, Communications Worker on the James Bay Development Project, February 15, 1972 to April 3, 1972." Huron Village: Indians of Quebec Association.

Diamond, Billy. 1977. "Highlights of the Negotiations Leading to the James Bay and Northern Quebec Agreement. Val d'Or." Grand Council of the Crees.

Diamond, Billy. 1990. "Villages of the Damned: The James Bay Agreement Leaves a Trail of Broken Promises." *Arctic Circle* 1 (November/December): 24–34.

Diamond, Billy. 2011. "Billy … In his own words – My Dad told me 'Use the white man's law to get our rights recognized.' *Air Creebec Destinations*, special issue: Special Tribute – Grand Chief Dr. Billy Diamond 1949–2010," 16–17.

Dixon, Paul. Ca. 1991. "Quoting the Old and Young Hunters, Trappers and Fishermen of Waswanipi." Unpublished photocopied typescript. Pp. 3.

Feit, Harvey A. 1985. "Legitimation and Autonomy in James Bay Cree Responses to Hydroelectric Development." In *Indigenous Peoples and the Nation State: Fourth World Politics in Canada, Australia, and Norway*, ed. Noel Dyck, 27–66. St John's: Memorial University, Institute for Social and Economic Research.

Feit, Harvey A. 1989. "James Bay Cree Self-Governance and Land Management." In *We Are Here: Politics of Aboriginal Land Tenure*, ed. Edwin N. Wilmsen, 68–98. Berkeley: University of California Press.

Feit, Harvey A. 2001. "Hunting, Nature and Metaphor: Political and Discursive Strategies in James Bay Cree Resistance and Autonomy." In *Indigenous Traditions and Ecology*, ed. John A. Grim, 411–52. Cambridge, MA: Center for the Study of World Religions, Harvard Divinity School, and Harvard University Press.

Feit, Harvey A. 2009. "Governmental Rationalities and Indigenous Co-Governance: James Bay Cree Co-Existence, from Mercantilist Partnerships to Neoliberal Mechanisms." In *Unsettled Legitimacy: Political Community, Power, and Authority in a Global Era*, ed. Steven Bernstein and William D. Coleman, 97–128. Vancouver: University of British Columbia Press.

Feit, Harvey A. 2010. "Le peuple cri de la Baie James parle aux gouvernements: développement, gouvernance et co-gouvernance." In *Les Inuit et les Cris du Nord du Québec – Territoire, Gouvernance, Société et Culture* [The Inuit and the Cree of Northern Quebec – Territory, Governance, Society and Culture], ed. Jacques-Guy Petit, Yv Bonnier Viger, Pita Aatami, and Ashley Iserhoff, 119–32. Rennes, QC: Presses Universitaires de Rennes and Presses de l'Université du Québec.

Feit, Harvey A. 2014 (1986). "Hunting and the Quest for Power: Relationships between James Bay Crees, the Land and Developers." In *Native Peoples: The Canadian Experience*, 4th ed., ed. C. Roderick Wilson and Christopher Fletcher, 115–45. Toronto: Oxford University Press.

Gagnon, Alain-G., and Guy Rocher, eds. 2002. *Reflections on the James Bay and Northern Québec Agreement*. Montreal: Québec Amérique.

Gnarowski, Michael, ed. 2002. *I Dream of Yesterday and Tomorrow*. Kemptville, ON: Golden Dog Press.

Iserhoff, Ashley. 2014 Grand Council of the Crees (GCC) — Cree Nation Government – Agreements – Round Table on Capacity Building at Waswanipi, Quebec, 18 February 2014. //livestream.com/accounts/5362528/events/2778745/videos/42735468/player?autoPlay=false&height=360&mute=false&width=640" width="640" height="360" frameborder="0" scrolling="no" allowfullscreen></iframe>, accessed 9 September 2014.

Joint Federal-Provincial Task Force. 1971. "A Preliminary Study of the Environmental Impacts of the James Bay Development Project." N.p.: JF-PTF.

Malouf, Albert. 1973. *Superior Court, No: 05–04841–72. Chief Robert Kanatewat et al, vs The James Bay Development Corporation et al, Judgement*, 178. Montreal: Superior Court. Typescript.

Marshall, Susan, and Emily Masty, eds. 2013. *Mind's Eye. Stories from Whapmagoostui*. Oujé-Bougoumou: Aanischaaukamikw Cree Cultural Institute.

Martinhunter, Abraham. 1974. "Abraham Martinhunter, 21 June 74," 11. Manuscript notes by Martin Weinstein.

Neeposh, Michael. 2000. "Changes in Life in the Bush and Land." In *Voices of Waswanipi Eeyou in 2000*, ed. The Contest Editorial Committee. [Waswanipi]: The Contest Editorial Committee.

Neeposh, Yvonne Cheezo. 1999. Affidavit. In *Mario Lord, et al. v. The Attorney General of Québec et al. and Domtar Inc., et al.* Affidavits. Volumes 1, 2, and 3. Pp. 6. Canada, Province of Quebec, District of Montreal, Superior Court. No. 500–05–043203–981.

Pashagumiskum, Nellie. 1989–90. "In Memory of Joab Bearskin." *Northland* 46 (2): 7.

Petit, Jacques-Guy, Yv Bonnier Viger, Pita Aatami, and Ashley Iserhoff, eds. 2010. *Les Inuit et les Cris du Nord du Québec – Territoire, Gouvernance, Société et Culture* [The Inuit and the Cree of Northern Quebec – Territory, Governance, Society and Culture]. Rennes, QC: Presses Universitaires de Rennes and Presses de l'Université du Québec.

Recherches amérindiennes au Québec. 1971. "La Baie James des Amérindiens" [James Bay of the Amerindians]. *Recherches amérindiennes au Québec* 1 (4–5).

Richardson, Boyce. 1972. *James Bay: The Plot to Drown the North Woods*. San Francisco and Toronto: Sierra Club in association with Clarke, Irwin and Company.

Richardson, Boyce. dir. 1974. "Job's Garden." 60 min. Tamarack Productions. Made for the Indians of Quebec Association, Huron Village, QC.

Richardson, Boyce. co-dir. 1975. "Our Land Is Our Life." 60 min. Ottawa: National Film Board of Canada.

Richardson, Boyce, dir. 1991. "Flooding Job's Garden." 60 min. Toronto: CBC TV series "As Long As the Rivers Flow."

Richardson, Boyce. 2003. *Memoirs of a Media Maverick*. Toronto: Between the Lines.

Richardson, Boyce. 2007 (1976). *Strangers Devour the Land*. White River Junction, VT: Chelsea Green Publishing.

Salisbury, Richard F. 1986. *A Homeland for the Cree*. Montreal and Kingston: McGill-Queen's University Press.

Scott, Colin H., ed. 2001. *Aboriginal Autonomy and Development in Northern Quebec and Labrador*. Vancouver: University of British Columbia Press.

Scott, Colin H. 2005. "Co-Management and the Politics of Aboriginal Consent to Resource Development." In *Reconfiguring Aboriginal-State Relations*, ed. Michael Murphy, 133–63. Montreal and Kingston: McGill-Queen's University Press.

Vincent, Sylvie, and Gary Bowers, eds. 1988 *James Bay and Northern Quebec: Ten Years After*. Montreal: Recherches amérindiennes au Québec.

Vizenor, Gerald. 1999 (1994). *Manifest Manners: Narratives on Postindian Survivance*. Lincoln: Bison Books.

Vizenor, Gerald. 2008. "Aesthetics of Survivance." In *Survivance: Narratives of Native Presence*, ed. Gerald Vizenor, 1–24. Lincoln: University of Nebraska Press.

3 The Endurance of Relational Ontology: Encounters between Eeyouch and Sport Hunters

COLIN SCOTT

Introduction

As I write this chapter, I have in mind a recent conversation with Eduardo Kohn, about the conundrum posed by the somewhat commonplace anthropological treatment of "ontology" as a proxy for radical cultural difference. Even if, as Kohn (2013:10) and others[1] have asserted, ontology deals in different worlds, not just different cultural views of the same world, the question remains what anthropology (indeed what anyone) can say about the world in general. The more power is accorded culture (understood as a conventionalized but arbitrary and relative construct) to generate or reveal distinctive worlds, the deeper is the refutation of the original philosophical sense of ontology as getting at the fundaments of being – a true (perchance universal?) story, not a culturally contingent one. For ontology to amount to something more than cultural relativism, it must surely, for humans at least, involve cultural grappling with realities, truths irreducible to culture alone. When it comes to relations among humans, and between humans and other forms of life, Eeyouch (eastern Cree people)[2] whom I have known profess certain truths understood to transcend their own social and human context, both analytically (Scott 2013a) and politically (Scott 2013b), in their relationships with the larger world. Harvey Feit (2004) has written about how such truths shape Eeyou "life projects" and political agendas vis-à-vis non-Eeyou human actors, including representatives of the state. From Feit's analysis, one learns that Eeyouch insist upon respectful and consensual relationships, not because they are ignorant of the real presence of selfish, competitive, and violent forms of human interaction, but out of a conviction that inherent in the equally real nature of relationship, such forms are ultimately self-defeating. Hence, sociological, ecological, and ethical truths, at once factual and normative, are conjoined in narratives alleging a transcendent relationality beyond human cultural differences.[3] Relationality is ontologically primary. Relationships of (dis)respect and reciprocity (whether positive or negative) are ubiquitous and profoundly consequential in the living world, whether or not a particular cultural framing is alert to such truth. This perspective has fundamental implications for how we engage – intellectually, politically, and processually – Marshall Sahlins's "structures of conjuncture" (see Dussart and Poirier in this volume).

In this chapter, I explore these themes in a prosaic setting of competition and cooperation between Eeyouch who hunt for their livelihoods and so-called "sport hunters" who are one factor in the many challenges to the security of those Eeyou livelihoods. I do so by way of reflection on nearly four decades of experience with a family at Wemindji, a community on the east coast of James Bay, with whom I have had the privilege of working, socializing, and hunting across this span of time.

Thirty-eight years ago, as a graduate student, I lived in an Eeyou hunting camp two hundred kilometres inland from the coast of James Bay, in the high subarctic of northern Quebec. Accessible only by bush plane and inspiring to me for its "isolation," the land on which it was situated was the centre of the world for my hosts. It was the hunting territory of their extended family, one of about three hundred that make up Eeyou Istchee, as the ten federated communities of the Cree Nation now call their territory. Each of two households in the camp was headed by a couple whose livelihoods and identity were those of hunters, *nituuhuu iiyiyiu*. The literal and simple translation of this phrase is "hunting person," but the term *iiyiyiu* enfolds complexities to which I will return; and the term *nituuhuu*, conceptually and etymologically, is not just about self-provisioning but about fostering the vitality of the land. That fostering depends on various forms of respect that reciprocate and reinforce a flow of animal gifts. Appreciation, thanks, and respect are synonyms in Wemindji speech; the common translation of the English "thank you," for example, is *chiniskuumitin*, literally "I respect you," and it is uttered to human and animal partners alike.

My age-mates in the camp in 1977, fresh out of residential school and apprenticing to their parents as hunters, were children of the more senior couple. That autumn, as we travelled by canoe to hunt and check traps and fishnets, we heard the faint rumbling of explosives, some fifty kilometres northward, where the first phase of the James Bay hydro-electric project was under construction. Cautious animals displayed unprecedented behaviours in response to the distant tremors; beavers would exit their lodges only later in the afternoon, closer to dusk than was normal. Much of the flow of the Sakami River, a main artery of this family's territory, was scheduled for diversion into the vast system of reservoirs. My hosts and their children, who became my friends, faced an uncertain future. The leadership of the federated Eeyou communities of the region, the Grand Council of the Crees, had two years previous negotiated the James Bay and Northern Quebec Agreement (JBNQA, 1975), a comprehensive land claim settlement that was the first treaty with an Indigenous nation in Canada since the 1920s; in the intervening half-century, federal and provincial governments had come mistakenly to believe that Canada was done forever with making treaties with Indians.

Feit (in this volume) describes the outward-looking, extra-territorial alliances that Eeyouch have cultivated since the inception of the James Bay hydroelectric project, as they have navigated a field of mutual entanglement among diverse societal actors with converging and diverging interests. My focus here is on local-scale practices of strategic relationality in which Eeyou hunters engage to maintain their responsibilities and interests vis-à-vis family territories, a deeply personal, kin-embedded, and sacred connection to the land with strong parallels in the practices of "caring for country" described for Indigenous Australia (Morphy, Fache, Kubota in this volume), and similar engagements in Indigenous Canada (Poirier, Thom, Westman in this volume).

Hunting Today – New Challenges

In recent years, I have been blessed with invitations to go moose hunting with Elmer Georgekish, one of my friends and age-mates from those early years, now retired from a career as a community police officer and enjoying the hunting life. At his camp on the eastern end of the family's territory, we have shared a cabin with one of his sisters (Gerda) who had also been with us all those years ago, and a younger brother (Wilfred) who is now the hunting territory leader. The old people have passed away. It is no longer necessary to fly in; I am able to make a twenty-hour drive from my house in Montreal to this camp. Five years ago, following Elmer's telephoned instructions, I met him there and was surprised to find the camp within a stone's throw of massive hydro towers, from which transmission cables the thickness of a forearm hung, crackling in the autumn humidity.

I learned that recreational moose hunters, employees of Hydro-Quebec, had been guests on the territory the week previous, during part of the sport hunting season, welcomed by Elmer and his siblings for particular reasons that I'll come to. But now my friends had the territory to themselves once more. By day we used a hydro service road, contouring the transmission corridor that carries electricity two thousand kilometres to southern Quebec and onward to New England markets in the northeastern United States, to get to strategic points of access branching into promising hunting areas, from which we walked and paddled miles in search of moose and bear. Overnight, if we had not ventured so far as to have to pitch a tent, we returned to the warmth of the cabin and the conviviality of family. There, I heard Elmer croon *nituuhuu iiyiyiu* to his brother's grandson, a toddler, gently imparting the hope and prospect of his future as a hunter. For Elmer, like many if not most of his community, is keenly aware that the wellsprings of cultural knowledge are the lived and embodied experiences of relations with the land; he would no doubt agree with Nicolas Peterson (in this volume) that, in the absence of that experience, no amount of documenting "Eeyou culture," or communicating it through school programs, cultural centres, and digital media, can possibly substitute.

My annual trips for moose hunting with Elmer include a biology doctoral student, Jeremy, with whom I have collaborated on the use of GPS-equipped handheld devices for community-based biodiversity monitoring. Elmer is a councillor with the Cree Nation of Wemindji, and like many of his fellow community members and leaders, adopts a generous and inclusive attitude towards non-Eeyouch equipped in one way or another to assist the community with the many issues it faces in conservation and development, and in reinforcing land-based livelihoods and lifeways. My own relationship with the community illustrates as well as any other the primacy of reciprocity in the ontology and ontological politics of Eeyou society. An important context of my developing relationship with Wemindji, and the many relationships that have emerged between community members and members of an interdisciplinary research team that I have directed at Wemindji, is our shared project to establish a comprehensive conservation plan for the community, including an extensive network of terrestrial and marine protected areas (Mulrennan, Mark, and Scott 2012; Mulrennan, Scott, and Scott forthcoming; Scott, Brown, and Labrecque forthcoming).

Eeyouch, like numerous other Indigenous peoples in northern Canada and northern Australia (Morphy in this volume), see in protected areas the potential for an added measure of local autonomy in Eeyou use and stewardship of the land, buffered from external development demands. Elmer and his family, along with many others at Wemindji and other Eeyou communities, have proposed portions of their family territory for "biodiversity reserve" status within Quebec's protected area system, a bid to safeguard spaces of relative autonomy discussed elsewhere (Mulrennan, Scott, and Scott forthcoming). Whatever the outcome of this initiative, the reality is that the majority of Eeyou families' territories, under various regimes of "protection," "conservation," and "development," are (and for the foreseeable future will be) legally accessible to recreational hunters and fishers, among other newcomers, with whom these territories must now be shared. Like their neighbours the Atikamekw (Poirier in this volume, pp. 212–33), Eeyouch are ontologically disposed to strike up relations of sharing with Québécois, even if the latter sometimes prove disappointing partners in reciprocity, and like Yolŋu (Morphy in this volume, pp. 70–90), Eeyouch "continue to welcome visitors to their country, because they see the necessity for articulation, but they look for opportunities where articulation can be on [their own] terms." (p. 81). One "conundrum of coexistence" (Dussart and Poirier in this volume) is that recreational hunters and fishers seek limited resources that are also important to Eeyouch, so there is a need for control and selectivity in forms of "welcome" and degrees of "sharing."

An Eeyou logic of relationships is extended to old friends and to newcomers alike, in caring for a world whose face is changing, and the ethics of those relationships are simultaneously referenced to other-than-human actors in the world. It is a world maintained, in places, amidst the "ruins" of capitalism (Tsing 2015), but a giving world, nonetheless, worthy of respect and care. I would not have been happy to think, those many years ago before the Sakami had been diverted and transmission lines and corridors had been pushed through, that I might one day visit my friends in a camp with access defined by Hydro-Quebec lines and service roads. Hunters pay a price for this infrastructure, both aesthetic and practical. It is harder now to paddle canoes up a river greatly reduced by damming and diversion. The residual flow is too shallow in many places, requiring us to wade and drag our canoes where before there was freeboard. Shallow water makes return trips, loaded with several hundred kilos of moose meat, even more difficult. Rapids that could once be run, poled, or lined require many more pull-overs and portages today.

There have been advantages, at the same time. The existence of a road network to service hydroelectricity infrastructure means that in a few hours people can travel from the village, three hundred kilometres away – a trip that in their grandparents' generation required weeks of paddling and portaging, or expensive charter aircraft in their parents' generation. Even abandoned service roads now afford points of access by all-terrain-vehicle or snowmobile, depending on the season, taking hunters well beyond stretches passable by pick-up truck. This increased ease of access has expanded Eeyou options for pursuing mixed economic strategies – it is possible to hold a steady job in the village yet travel to family hunting territories for weekend and vacation hunting, or even after-hours hunting for those with access to family lands nearer the village. It is also easier for families to maintain a level of surveillance of parts of their customary territories through frequent visits, whereas in the past (and still today for some families) this could only be accomplished by living on the territories most months of the year.[4]

By the same token, however, the opportunity for surveillance has suffered in areas more isolated from road networks. Elmer's extended family has a large territory, running some one hundred kilometres on an east to west gradient, and averaging perhaps forty kilometres in width from north to south. The western end of the territory is not transected by hydro corridors or roads. To get to that end of Elmer's territory, we have travelled the length of a very large lake, Sakami Lake, a journey of some eighty kilometres by freighter canoe, then proceeded upriver to reach a smaller (but still major) lake on the family territory. At one point, freighter canoes must be lined up rapids, and the journey continues on an intermediate lake, beyond which impassable rapids dictate a long portage and switching to a smaller canoe. Not surprisingly, outsiders rarely venture this far, due to the time, the strenuous work, and the dangers involved. Sakami Lake itself became a hydro diversion corridor when Hydro-Quebec implemented electrical generation. It is mostly uncharted, and it contains a great deal of floating timber, much of it waterlogged and invisible below the surface, thirty-odd years after flooding associated with the diversion. Between driftwood hazards and submerged shoals, both capable of wrecking outboard engines, the lake, where big waves are routine on windy days, has become a less preferred travel route even for many local Eeyouch.

Accordingly, Elmer was optimistic, in leading us on this route two years ago, that we would find abundant moose who had experienced very little hunting pressure when we reached the western end of his family's territory. We were, however, surprised and disappointed, upon reaching the long portage that led to the large lake – where his parents and grandparents had often made their winter camp – to hear an outboard engine. During two days of hunting on the lake we saw no moose, and on the first of those days we learned the reason. On a distant shore we spotted an ample cabin built by sport hunters, and through binoculars we were able to make out several forty-five-gallon drums of fuel near the beach: it was a fly-in camp reached by float plane. The lake had been well worked over prior to our arrival, and any moose we would get that trip would have to come from below the rapids or from smaller upland lakes, where the sport hunters would not have troubled to venture.

Let me explain, parenthetically, that Eeyou hunters should not be dismissed as alarmists for perceiving the influx of sport hunters and fishermen onto their territories as a serious problem. In Canada there is a long history of displacement of Indigenous communities from prime hunting and fishing grounds in favour of sport hunters, even where "Indian treaties" had promised that Indigenous inhabitants would not be interfered with in the pursuit of their hunting, fishing, and gathering pursuits. In the case of the Eeyouch's own comprehensive claims settlement, the James Bay and Northern Quebec Agreement (1975), Eeyouch have been disappointed by the inadequate fulfilment of provisions in the JBNQA intended to guarantee greater Eeyou control of sport hunting and fishing activities, through the recognition of Eeyou family hunting territory stewards as game wardens, the development of a robust network of Eeyou conservation officers to be employed by the Quebec government, and the channelling of sport hunters and fishers through Eeyou-owned outfitting businesses. Unfortunately, a large and politically powerful lobby of sport hunters and fishermen in Quebec, in a context of declining habitats and relatively depleted big game populations in many southern regions, has pressed successfully for a greater measure of "public access" to the James Bay territory than was contemplated in JBNQA negotiations. They are especially present from late spring through fall for the sport fishing season, during September and October for the moose hunting season, and during mid-winter for caribou hunting.[5] Many Québécois people have a historical and cultural attachment to hunting and fishing, and it is fair to say that, for many, coming to the James Bay region for hunting and fishing also resonates as an aspect of a nationalistic project to occupy the north – one regarded by members of the Cree Nation and their Indigenous neighbours with considerable caution.

Rough weather prevented us crossing the lake in our small craft to visit the sport hunters' camp that first year, but we determined to do so the year following. The next fall, we equipped ourselves with a larger canoe and engine that cost us considerable effort to portage into the big lake. Our timing was a bit late, however. As we reached the lower end of the portage into the lake, we were inspected by a float plane that circled us, then returned in the direction of the big lake. Before landing at the sport hunters' camp, it could be heard contouring the shoreline of the big lake for fifteen or twenty minutes. We thought initially that the pilot must be trying to spot moose, perhaps for a later hunt. But we learned two days later, when we were able to reach their camp, that its occupants had departed on the same plane that had buzzed us. It then seemed more likely that the protracted flight around the shores of the lake was intended to frighten moose into the bush, in anticipation of our arrival. Some Eeyouch have stories of sport hunters from the south who, after a couple of years in a locale, assume a proprietary attitude, even presuming to warn away Eeyouch who have been in the area for generations.

Notwithstanding the ecological damage caused by industrial resource extraction – and it takes several forms: hydroelectricity, mining, and, further south, forestry – there are still animals to be hunted, fished, and trapped. The animals have adapted and endured more and less well, according to species and circumstance; and Eeyou relations with them endure – forms of ritual practice and ritual respect, dreaming about animals, feasting, recounting narratives of quotidian and extraordinary encounters and interactions with animals, et cetera (Preston 2002 [1975]; Tanner 1979; Feit 1992; Scott 2005). At the same time, new demands of cooperation and competition with other hunters have to be contended with. Eeyou hunters and sport hunters, with access to similar technologies, are subject to similar practical constraints on the ground and on the water. It may not be as satisfying to take a moose or a bear on a transmission corridor within rifle range of a pick-up truck, but it is a lot less work. Of course, only a small proportion of harvestable moose are so fortuitously located. In this connection, it was interesting to witness at our camp in 2011, at the road-accessible eastern end of their territory, that my Eeyou friends were now, in effect, assisting some Hydro-Quebec workers resident in the region to hunt moose successfully along the service road, even if it meant that we ourselves had to work harder to make our own kills further upriver and deeper into the bush. There is a particular logic to this. First, one must understand that, legally, Eeyouch cannot prohibit non-aboriginal sport hunters and fishers from using most of Eeyou traditional land. Therefore, Eeyouch enter into a strategic relationality with a few sport hunters who are amenable to forming friendships. Eeyouch understand that these individuals have a certain territorial etiquette among themselves; once a group of Québécois sport hunters have established themselves in an area, others are more reluctant to traverse the same area – for reasons of both mutual courtesy (a courtesy not automatically extended to Eeyouch) and practical success. By selectively cultivating friendship with a group of "guest" hunters, visibly camped along easy points of access to their territories, Eeyouch are able, to some extent, to discourage others. Befriended hunters are advised where best to get their moose, a reasonable price to pay for the many more moose that might be lost without these hunters' help in limiting access by others. At the same time, Eeyouch are careful not to reveal to guest hunters routes into more remote parts of family hunting territories. As long as the guests are locally successful with limited effort, they invest less energy in discovering for themselves how to use the larger territory, which would negate their value as doorkeepers. Eeyouch establish their own base camps on points of easy access to their territories, not only for their own practical convenience in hunting but also to cultivate these relationships with selected outsiders and to keep an eye on the comings and goings of others. But their superior knowledge of the territory enables them, at the same time, to direct their own effort to the use of secondary camps deep in the bush. It is strenuous, but effective.

These strategies are tailored, as well, to the limited window that recreational hunters are given to make their harvests – roughly a three-week season from late September to mid-October. Most recreational hunters come for a week to ten days, preferring the early season when bull moose tend to be in peak rut and more responsive to calls. Plastic bottles of estrous cow urine, with wicks dispensing scent to attract bulls, are hung by sport hunters along the hydro service road. I remarked that they were still there after these hunters had left, and it was explained to me that Elmer and Wilfred had asked their recreational hunting "guests" to leave them hanging when they departed. This was less to assist the Eeyou hunters (I have not seen Elmer or his brother use cow urine in hunting) than to signal to subsequent potential sport hunters that the area was still in use.

These strategies depend, too, on the relative remoteness of Wemindji's family territories, compared to those of more southerly Eeyou communities living in proximity to larger non-Indigenous settlements. At the community of Waswanipi, for example, the camps of recreational hunters and fishers outnumber those of Eeyou hunters by a ratio of ten to one on some family territories. There, the enormous proliferation of secondary and tertiary forestry roads over the past three decades, together with clear-cutting of large areas (Feit and Beaulieu 2001), has vastly increased access to recreationalists; the closer proximity of non-Indigenous towns has meant that many more recreational hunters and fishers have had opportunity to build up knowledge of the territory.

However, remoteness is only relative, and sport hunters with money to afford airplanes and to fly in construction material and equipment for their camps can turn up literally anywhere there is a large enough piece of water to land a float plane. Such hunters are less accessible to, and less likely to welcome, the cooperation of the Eeyou customary owners and managers of their family territories. Perhaps, having less routine interaction with local Eeyouch, they are more likely than those who arrive by road to try to assert the primacy of their own hunting rights in the area reachable from their camps, notwithstanding their brief history. The Grand Council of the Crees of Eeyou Istchee managed, about four years ago, to secure the government of Quebec's agreement to a moratorium against new recreational cabin permits on Cree territory. However, this does not prevent sport hunters and fishers from establishing temporary seasonal camps throughout Category 3 lands,[6] which are the majority of Eeyou territory. And in the case of the cabin that we discovered with Elmer, it turned out that the occupants had displayed through a windowpane an apparently valid permit obtained from the Quebec government the year prior to the moratorium. There was an important irregularity, however; the permit had been issued for a neighbouring, smaller lake – doubtless a less desirable location for the permit holders and builders of the cabin. A remedy for this apparent flouting of the rules has yet to be reached between Wemindji leadership and the Quebec regulatory authority.

In other instances on neighbouring Eeyou family territories, sport hunters, under restriction of the moratorium, have been testing the limits of what might be considered a "cabin" requiring a permit. Some have recently constructed elevated moose hunting "blinds" that are in effect mini-cabins on stilts, equipped with sleeping and kitchen facilities, no doubt thinking to fly under the radar of the regulation against recreational cabins without permits. The pressure on Eeyou lands is unrelenting, strategies on all sides are creative, and the stakes are high for maintaining some sort of Eeyou control of harvesting access and levels.

On a neighbouring family territory at Wemindji, sport hunters have gained access to and knowledge of an area on which are situated both an important hydroelectric installation and a new gold mine. Two years ago, sport hunters removed a total of seventy moose from this locale in one fall season, a rate of harvest considered by local Eeyou stewards to be unsustainable. Moose hunting seasons and quotas for sport hunts are determined zone by zone, with Wemindji's territories lying within two large zones that also include portions of neighbouring Eeyou communities' territories. From the perspective of government wildlife managers, sustainability is calculated on the basis of kills reported for large regions. The problem is that transportation infrastructure on the ground focuses the great majority of sport hunting pressure on more accessible areas – those along road corridors with easily navigable adjoining waterways. Hence, particular family territories, or specific portions of family territories, come in for disproportionate sport hunting pressure. Moose are relatively sedentary animals, so a local area, once exhausted, takes time to recover – even if the moose population regionally is considered "healthy" from the viewpoint of government biologist-planners.

The kinds of strategies engaged by Elmer's family are quite typical on other family territories at Wemindji exposed to sport hunter access. Various political strategies at the level of Eeyou participation in regional governmental structures, such as recourse to the wildlife co-management mechanisms under the James Bay and Northern Quebec Agreement (1975), are employed. But there is no substitute for Eeyou presence and vigilance on-territory, where constructive relationship building with newcomers on an interpersonal level, to the extent possible, makes the best of a situation in which these newcomers are legally entitled, in the eyes of the state, to hunt and fish over the majority of Eeyou territory.

Conclusion

The reproduction of Eeyou relationality on the land has adapted to nearly forty years of change since the coming of Hydro-Quebec and roads, in the span of my time on the territory. Elmer and I, youngsters in our twenties when we first knew one another, will soon be the elder generation. A career police officer and part-time hunter, Elmer has faced external challenges in managing relations with animals and with other humans on his territory that his parents – consummate occupational hunters – only began to know in their declining years. These changes include not only a more diverse set of relations with non-Eeyouch but also a more complex set of relations internal to Eeyou society. If hunting remains, as Speck (1935) characterized it some eighty years ago, a "holy occupation," it has become a part-time occupation for most Eeyouch. After hours, on weekends, in vacation time, and during "goose breaks" and "moose breaks" built into the employment year, hunting is a major preoccupation. And for people like Elmer who deliberately take retirement early enough to afford some years with strength and good health to devote to the hunting life, and to encourage and mentor younger people in the occupation, it is a return to what matters most about one's place and activity in the world.

The relational micro-politics that I have described play out in an important but very local arena of collective life projects (Blaser, Feit, and McRae 2004), but at the same time extend from the level of family hunting territories, to Eeyou villages and councils, to the Cree Nation and the Grand Council of the Crees of Eeyou Istchee. Family hunting territories are the primary locus of the communities of life, and the practices of reciprocity linking hunters and animals are understood to maintain these communities of life. Hence, the collective life projects of Eeyou politicians and bureaucrats (some avid hunters and some less so) are also significantly shaped by these ontological commitments. As in various Latin American contexts where life projects or *planes de vida* are hitched to ontologically conditioned criteria for "living well," or *buen vivir* (Huanacuni 2010; Gudynas 2011), so, within Eeyou polity, "development" must represent something more than simple "economic justice" in monetary terms, through a better share of revenues from resource extractive revenues. It should be noted that Eeyouch have been extraordinarily successful at achieving justice in these terms. A Cree Nation of sixteen thousand souls, in the so-called *Paix des braves* agreement, has negotiated a minimum guaranteed revenue of $3.5 billion from the Quebec government to be paid out between 2002 and 2052 based on current levels of hydro, mining, and forestry resource extraction – an amount to be indexed in proportion to any increases in the productivity of these sectors, and renewable in 2052 (Anonymous 2002; Scott 2005). More recently, the Grand Council has negotiated a $1.5 billion settlement from the Canadian federal government (Anonymous 2008).

But monetary justice is at best only a partial fulfilment of Eeyou relationality, whether human-to-human or human-to-animal. Living well, *miiyuu pimaatsiiun* (Adelson 2000), demands the ability to undertake activities on the land, to eat "strong" food from the land, and simply to enjoy being on the land. Eeyouch, with their growing population and thorough imbrication in the wage and entrepreneurial economy, face in their own way the internal contradictions of "sustainable development." This takes the form, if you will, of an ethical, at once ontological, contradiction that resembles the dilemma described by Ichikawa (2013), of hunters participating in new economic opportunities while attempting to maintain Indigenous institutions: the difficulty of reconciling the acquisitive and "natural resource" extractive values and premises of market participation with the egalitarian values and premises of a regime of reciprocity that embraces, ontologically, relations with "the natural world." As in the larger society, the "environmentalist" goals of Eeyouch increasingly take the form of attempting to set aside protected areas where high-impact industrial development is restricted, while accepting industrial activities on other parts of their territory as necessary components of the contemporary mixed economy. This is occurring, however, within a nascent conservation strategy (Cree Nation Government 2014) for the whole of Eeyou Istchee, as Crees refer to their territory. Consistent with a commitment to the larger community of life, Eeyouch continue to demand, politically, a much higher standard of environmental protection for their territory than is supported by the Quebec and Canadian mainstream populations.

Perhaps it is impossible to foresee what future will emerge from the aforementioned ethical/ontological contest, a signal instance of entangled "structures of conjuncture." But to conclude with a reflection on the embedded and persistent qualities of Cree relationality, I turn again to Elmer's crooning to his great-nephew, *nituuhuu iiyiyiu*, to consider the terms in that phrase. *Nituuhuu* is only poorly captured by the English term "hunting," for the former evokes notions, simultaneously, of procurement and the nurturance of all forms of life that are hunted and gathered. *Iiyiyiu* (Eeyou), for its part, is an ethnonym that enfolds a vital message. As Nurit Bird-David (2013) notes, ethnonyms are important windows on peoples' understanding of their own pluralities. They certainly, then, shape collective life projects. To be sure, *iiyiyiu* evokes a sense of shared language, culture, and territory – indeed, Eeyou naming of their territory, Eeyou Istchee (*iiyiyiu aschii*), can be translated as "the people's land." This formalization of territory suggests something responding to an ideological model of objective nationhood. But a full unpacking of the Eeyou instance reveals something less expected ... because *iiyiyiu* does not refer just to an Eastern Cree person (though it can, in context). It refers also to *all* humans as opposed to other forms of life, but not only these; it refers as well to all living entities, to the entire community of life, which is the world, which is *aschii*. *That* is a community of life incontrovertibly bound by rules of reciprocity, whether positive in egalitarian practice, or negative in exploitation. *Iiyiyiu*, in fact, expresses an "ontological model of plurality" not only as an ethnonym of national detachment – though strategically it must sometimes be this. The ethnonym *iiyiyiu* simultaneously holds out the implicit possibility, indeed the inevitability, of inclusion. Eeyouch invite all of us to recognize the truth of our status as *iiyiyiuch*, as reciprocating beings in relation with other humans and with all other life forms. This posture, I suggest, is a vital aspect of "taking seriously" what hunters tell us (Nadasdy 2007:26; Poirier 2013:50); of understanding their "openness ... flexibility ... creativity, resistance and agency ... the transformative continuity of their cosmopolitics" (Poirier 2013:51–2). What is at stake, for Eeyouch, and no less for us all, is the recognition that theirs is not just one in a plurality of ontologies and worlds. It asserts reality in the more classical philosophical sense of ontology – fundamental truth about relationships comprising the ground of being shared by us all.

It is a story embedded in the ground of being and reality of relationship, as far as my Eeyou friends are concerned, typical perhaps of human narratives generated over a hundred thousand years of experience as hunters. In our time, it is a story that seems quaintly out of step with the premises and power relations of capitalist expansion. Yet it is rejoined by a globalizing narrative of respect for the planet. It remains to be seen whether the fulfilment of this ontological imperative will be one of catastrophic negative reciprocity, or the rediscovery of respectful relationships to mend increasingly endangered forms, modes, and communities of life.

ACKNOWLEDGMENTS

I am profoundly grateful for the generosity of the late Clifford and Emily Georgekish, who gave me the opportunity to experience the beauty of life on the land that was their home, and to their children Elmer, Frances, Johnny, Gerda, Wilfred, and other siblings who have continued to welcome me as a brother. This chapter is set on their family territory. Other Wemindji friends and family too numerous to name individually, many of whom have also invited me to their family territories and hunting camps, have contributed to my understanding of the issues addressed herein. The Cree Nation of Wemindji Council, the Cree Trappers' Association, and the Grand Council of the Crees (Eeyou Istchee) have been ready and supportive partners in the larger work of which this chapter is a part. My thanks and admiration go to colleagues Françoise Dussart and Sylvie Poirier for their vision and energy in bringing the present volume to fruition, as well as my sincere appreciation of our co-contributors at CHAGS-10 (Conference on Hunting and Gathering Societies) at the University of Liverpool in 2013. I also wish to acknowledge with thanks the support of the Fonds Québécois de la Recherche sur la Société et la Culture, Soutien aux équipes de recherche.

NOTES

1 Poirier (2013:53) puts it succinctly: "The ontological turn allows us to investigate not so much the diversity of worldviews – that is varying representations of the same world – but the multiplicity of worlds."
2 The term "Cree" has been applied and extended, in the course of colonial history, to a broad swath of communities speaking several dialects of a single Algonquian language (Cree-Tête de Boule [Atikamekw]-Montagnais-Naskapi) stretching from the Atlantic coast of Labrador in the east to the Rocky Mountains in the west. This chapter concerns, more particularly, the Crees of Eeyou Istchee of the eastern and southern watersheds of James and Hudson Bays, lying mainly in the modern jurisdiction of Quebec. The Cree Nation of Eeyou Istchee is a federation of ten communities who refer to themselves, in local dialects, as either *Iiyiyiuch* or *Iinuuch*, as linguists render these ethnonyms. I will use the colloquial spellings *Eeyou* (singular) and *Eeyouch* (plural).
3 See also the work of Debbie Rose (1999) on the ecology and ethics of "connection."
4 The family hunting territory system is an Algonkian institution of considerable antiquity, observed by Hudson's Bay Company personnel in the early decades of their presence in the James Bay area (Francis and Morantz 1983: 96). The origins and evolution of the family hunting territory system have been a focus of controversies too complicated to

address here (see Feit 1991 for an overview). It is clear, however, that it has been a remarkably enduring institution to the present day in the Eeyou communities east of James Bay, that such territories have commonly been associated with the same family lines over many generations (Morantz 2002:172–3), and that the system organizes a diversity of hunting, fishing, and trapping activities (Scott 1986).

5 But in recent years, a cyclical decline in caribou numbers has severely curtailed the numbers of sport hunters permitted to take caribou, either autonomously on permits drawn by lottery or through professional outfitting operations.

6 The JBNQA (1975) defined a three-part land regime. Category 1 lands are relatively small areas around each village (about 5,500 square kilometres, or 1.5 per cent of traditional lands) to which Eeyou communities have ownership in collective fee simple. Category 2 lands comprise an additional 65,000 square kilometres (17.3 per cent of Eeyou territory), where Eeyouch have exclusive rights to hunting, fishing, trapping, and other traditional subsistence resources. Category 3 lands (over 80 per cent of traditional Eeyou lands) are deemed public lands under constant pressure by the government of Quebec to be treated like public lands elsewhere in the province for purposes of sport hunting and fishing regulation. However, under the JBNQA, Eeyouch do retain preferential rights to subsistence resources in general, as well as exclusive rights to fur animals and certain other species.

REFERENCES

Adelson, Naomi. 2000. *"Being Alive Well": Health and the Politics of Cree Well-Being*. Toronto: University of Toronto Press.
Anonymous. 2002. *Agreement Concerning a New Relationship between Le Gouvernement du Québec and the Crees of Québec*. Cree Regional Authority/Gouvernement du Québec.
Anonymous. 2008. *Agreement Concerning a New Relationship between the Government of Canada and the Cree of Eeyou Istchee*. Grand Council of the Crees/Government of Canada.
Bird-David, Nurit. 2013. Plenary panel remarks, "Taking Stock." 10th Conference on Hunting and Gathering Societies. Liverpool, 25–8 June.
Blaser, Mario, Harvey A. Feit, and Glenn McRae, eds. 2004. *In the Way of Development: Indigenous Peoples, Life Projects and Globalization*. London and New York: Zed Books and Ottawa: Canadian International Development Research Centre.

Cree Nation Government. 2014. *Cree Regional Conservation Strategy*. Nemaska.

Feit, Harvey. 1991. "The Construction of Algonquian Hunting Territories: Private Property as Moral Lesson, Policy Advocacy and Ethnographic Error." In *Colonial Situations: Essays on the Contextualization of Ethnographic Knowledge*, ed. George W. Stocking, 109–34. Madison: University of Wisconsin Press.

Feit, Harvey. 1992. "Waswanipi Cree Management of Land and Wildlife: Cree Ethno-Ecology Revisited." In *Native People, Native Lands: Canadian Indians, Inuit and Metis*, ed. Bruce Cox, 75–91. Ottawa: Carleton University Press.

Feit, Harvey. 2004. "James Bay Crees' Life Projects and Politics: Histories of Place, Animal Partners and Enduring Relationships." In *In the Way of Development: Indigenous Peoples, Life Projects and Globalization*, ed. Mario Blaser, Harvey Feit, and Glen McRae, 92–110. London and New York : Zed Books and Ottawa: Canadian International Development Research Centre.

Feit, Harvey, and Robert Beaulieu. 2001. "Voices from a Disappearing Forest: Government, Corporate, and Cree Participatory Forestry Management Practices." In *Aboriginal Autonomy and Development in the Canadian Provincial North*, ed. Colin Scott, 119–48. Vancouver: University of British Columbia Press.

Francis, Daniel, and Toby Morantz. 1983. *Partners in Furs: A History of the Fur Trade in Eastern James Bay 1600–1870*. Montreal and Kingston: McGill-Queen's University Press.

Gudynas, Eduardo. 2011. "Buen Vivir: Today's Tomorrow." *Development* 54 (4): 441–7. http://dx.doi.org/10.1057/dev.2011.86.

Huanacuni, Fernando. 2010. *Vivir bien/Buen vivir. Filosofía, políticas, estrategias y experiencias regionales*. La Paz: Instituto Internacional de Integración.

Ichikawa, Mitsuo. 2013. Plenary panel remarks, "Taking Stock." 10th Conference on Hunting and Gathering Societies. Liverpool, 25–8 June.

The James Bay and Northern Québec Agreement. 1975. Éditeur officiel du Québec.

Kohn, Eduardo. 2013. *How Forests Think: Toward an Anthropology beyond the Human*. Berkeley and Los Angeles: University of California Press. http://dx.doi.org/10.1525/california/9780520276109.001.0001.

Morantz, Toby. 2002. *The White Man's Gonna Getcha: The Colonial Challenge to the Crees in Quebec*. Montreal and Kingston: McGill-Queen's University Press.

Mulrennan, Monica, Rodney Mark, and Colin Scott. 2012. "Revamping Community-Based Conservation through Participatory Research." *Canadian Geographer* 56 (2): 243–59. http://dx.doi.org/10.1111/j.1541-0064.2012.00415.x.

Mulrennan, Monica, Colin Scott, and Katherine Scott, eds. Forthcoming. *Partnerships, Politics and Perspectives: Protected Area Creation in Wemindji Cree Territory.* Submitted and under review.

Nadasdy, Paul. 2007. "The Gift in the Animal: The Ontology of Hunting and Human-Animal Sociality." *American Ethnologist* 34 (1): 25–43. http://dx.doi.org/10.1525/ae.2007.34.1.25.

Poirier, Sylvie. 2013. "The Dynamic Reproduction of Hunter-Gatherers' Ontologies and Values." In *A Companion to the Anthropology of Religion,* ed. Janice Boddy and Michael Lambek, 50–68. Hoboken, NJ: John Wiley and Sons. http://dx.doi.org/10.1002/9781118605936.ch2.

Preston, Richard. 2002 (1975). *Cree Narrative: Expressing the Personal Meaning of Events.* Montreal and Kingston: McGill-Queen's University Press.

Rose, Deborah. 1999. "Indigenous Ecologies and an Ethic of Connection." In *Global Ethics for the 21st Century,* ed. N. Low, 175–86. London: Routledge.

Scott, Colin. 1986. "Hunting Territories, Hunting Bosses and Communal Production among Coastal James Bay Cree." In "Who Owns the Beaver? Northern Algonquian Land Tenure Reconsidered." Special issue ed. Toby Morantz and Charles Bishop, *Anthropologica* n.s. 18 (1–2): 163–73. http://dx.doi.org/10.2307/25605197.

Scott, Colin. 2005. "Co-Management and the Politics of Aboriginal Consent to Resource Development: The Agreement Concerning a New Relationship between Le Gouvernement du Quebec and the Crees of Quebec (2002)." In *Canada: The State of the Federation 2003: Reconfiguring Aboriginal-State Relations,* ed. Michael Murphy, 133–63. Montreal and Kingston: McGill-Queen's University Press.

Scott, Colin. 2013a. "Ontology and Ethics in Cree Hunting: Animism, Totemism and Practical Knowledge." In *The Handbook of Contemporary Animism,* ed. Graham Harvey, 159–66. Durham: Acumen.

Scott, Colin. 2013b. "Le partage des ressources au Québec: perspectives et stratégies autochtones" [The Sharing of Resources in Quebec: Indigenous Perspectives and Strategies]. In *Les Autochtones et le Québec: Des premiers contacts au Plan Nord* [Indigenous People and Quebec: From First Contact to Plan Nord], ed. Alain Beaulieu, Stéphan Gervais, and Martin Papillon, 363–84. Montréal: Les Presses de l'Université de Montréal, collection Paramètres.

Scott, Colin, Peter Brown, and Jessica Labrecque, eds. Forthcoming. *Dialoguing Knowledges: Finding Our Way to Respect and Relationship.* Submitted and under review.

Speck, Frank. 1935. *Naskapi: The Savage Hunters of the Labrador Peninsula.* Norman: University of Oklahoma Press.

Tanner, Adrian. 1979. *Bringing Home Animals: Religious Ideology and Mode of Production of the Mistassini Cree Hunters*. St John's: Institute of Social and Economic Research, Memorial University.

Tsing, Anna. 2015. *The Mushroom at the End of the World: On the Possibility of Life in Capitalist Ruins*. Princeton: Princeton University Press.

4 Australia's Indigenous Protected Areas: Resistance, Articulation, and Entanglement in the Context of Natural Resource Management

FRANCES MORPHY

Introduction

We are still searching for what is the best way to live and survive, what is the best way to develop ourselves in our own country, on our own stage. The reason I want to say like that [is] because I am from homeland and I am also a ranger from the IPA, the Indigenous Protected Area, I work for ranger and that is why I need to manage the Yolŋu way and also the modern way ... we are putting together so that we can balance the Whiteman's society *ga* (and) Yolŋu society ... We are still learning, because we are living in technology now. We can see a new journey ... But the culture, don't forget the culture, that's important for us – the land, the *djalkiri*, where the songlines start, where the stories are, where the ancestors [are], that is the important [thing].

This is an extract from a speech by Yinimala Gumana, a Yolŋu man now in his early thirties from the community of Gäṉgaṉ in northeast Arnhem Land in the Northern Territory of Australia.[1] Yinimala was speaking during a gallery talk following the presentation of the 2011 Western Australia Indigenous Arts Award. The winner of the A$50,000 prize was Gunybi Ganambarr, his classificatory mother's brother, who also lives at Gäṉgaṉ. For Yolŋu, their artistic production has been a site of resistance, articulation, and entanglement with the encapsulating Euro-Australian society almost from first contact (see e.g. Berndt 1962; H. Morphy 2000, 2008).

The Laynhapuy Indigenous Protected Area (IPA), and the Yirralka Ranger Program to which Yinimala refers, operate over a large area of northeast Arnhem Land within the region of the Yolŋu-speaking peoples (figure 4.1). The headquarters are at the community of Yirrkala at the Laynhapuy Homelands Aboriginal Corporation. This is the service organization for the small outlying communities known as "homelands" where the majority of the sixty or more Yirralka Rangers live (represented by the stars on the map in figure 4.1).[2] A Management Plan for Stage 2 of the IPA, which will see it expand to cover the majority of the Laynhapuy homelands and the larger community of Gapuwiyak, was nearly complete at the time of writing. This IPA is, in turn, almost surrounded by other IPAs and potential IPAs: if all these are declared, most of Arnhem Land will be included within the IPA system.

In writing about the response of Indigenous peoples to their enforced incorporation within the Australian state, anthropologists and historians have debated how to characterize it.[3] The theme of resistance has been explicitly elaborated in the work of anthropologists Gillian Cowlishaw and Barry Morris (see, e.g., Cowlishaw 1988; Morris 1989), and historians have documented episodes of resistance in its most overt form, that is, physical resistance, at various places and times (e.g., Pedersen and Woorunmurra 2011; Reynolds 1982). The nature of the articulation between Indigenous and Euro-Australian societies has not as yet often been conceptualized in terms of entanglement, although the notion of the intercultural (Merlan 1998; Hinkson and Smith 2005), with its emphasis on relationality and the co-production of contemporary Indigenous sociality, certainly implies an entanglement of the Indigenous in the non-Indigenous. A recent paper (Morphy and Morphy 2013) puts forward a different way of conceptualizing the relationship, in terms of relative autonomy, which posits an articulation between distinct, but not impermeably bounded, sociocultural systems, each with its own trajectory through time. It pays attention to those sites of articulation where actors from the different systems meet, interact, and influence one another. Indigenous Protected Areas are such a site.

Both the intercultural and the relative autonomy approaches acknowledge the differentials of power that are at play, which lead to more influence from non-Indigenous on Indigenous systems than vice versa. Where they differ is in the emphasis on the site and the role of value-creation processes within Indigenous systems. The "intercultural" seems ultimately to predict a convergence, an eventual assimilation of Indigenous ways of being, thinking, and believing into the "mainstream." Relative autonomy, on the other hand, points to the persistence of "territories of difference" (Escobar 2008), where influences

Figure 4.1 The major communities and homelands of the northeastern Yolŋu region

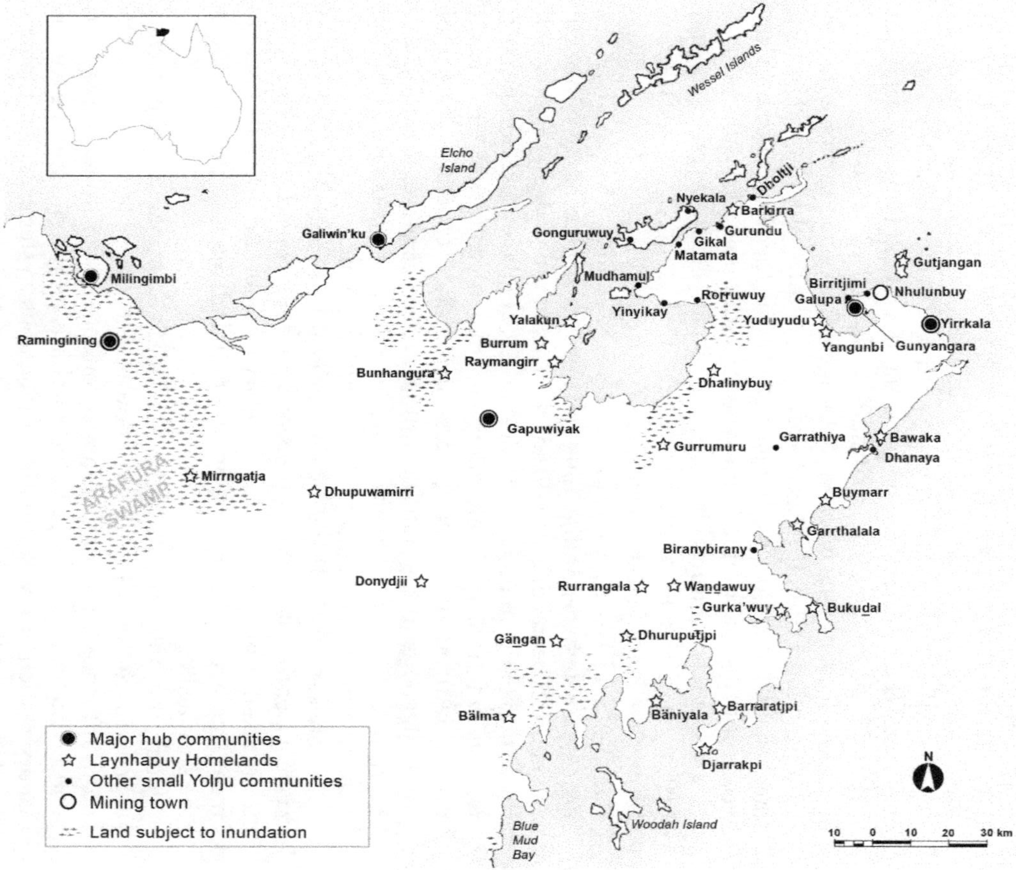

Major hub communities
Laynhapuy Homelands
Other small Yolŋu communities
Mining town
Land subject to inundation

from the more politically powerful mainstream are absorbed and transmuted according to local schemes of value. If this process is to be characterized as entanglement, it is in the sense set out by Dussart and Poirier in this volume: "Each thread-entity-agent-world involved in the entanglement keeps its identity, relative autonomy, and potentiality, while the spatial and temporal interactions ... do bring transformations to each one of them" (p. 5).

In this chapter I put forward a case for viewing the IPA movement as just the latest context for an ongoing Yolŋu project that has been pursued with a well-documented consistency since the arrival of Methodist missionaries in Yolŋu country in the 1920s and 1930s (see, e.g., Berndt 1962; F. Morphy 2009; H. Morphy 2000, 2005, 2006; Thornell 1986; Williams 1986). All the key elements are found in Yinimala's statement in 2011: the insistence that everything rests on Yolŋu ontology, and the recognition of a degree of necessary (mutual) entanglement in the course of the articulation of the Yolŋu life-world with the wider society.

What exactly is an IPA; why have IPAs become so popular with Indigenous groups throughout the continent; what, in settler Australian law, is the connection (if any) with the existing legal framework of rights in land? To answer this final question, it is necessary to outline briefly the history and current status of Indigenous legal interests in land in Australia in general and in northeast Arnhem Land in particular.

Indigenous Interests in Land: Land Rights and Native Title

The history of land rights in Australia differs markedly from that of other "settler" colonial states such as New Zealand, Canada, and the USA. From first settlement (with rare exceptions), the colonists acted on the assumption that Indigenous people did not own the land; the doctrine of Terra Nullius, asserting that the land had "belonged to no one" prior to its accession by the British Crown, was formalized in 1835 through a proclamation issued by the governor of the colony of New South Wales, Sir Richard Bourke. In many parts of the continent from the 1830s onwards, many dispossessed Indigenous people were encouraged or forced to move to specially created reserves, government stations, or mission stations. For much of this period, the "Crown Land" of Arnhem Land remained beyond the colonial frontier, and the Yolŋu clans retained possession and full use of their land and sea estates. In 1931, when the colonial frontier had finally impinged on Arnhem Land, it was declared as an Aboriginal Reserve, covering an area of 960,000 square kilometres. But its status as Crown Land was thereby unaffected. There was already missionary presence in the west of the Yolŋu region, with the establishment of Milingimbi in 1923 by the Methodist Overseas Mission. Yirrkala and Galiwin'ku (Elcho Island) Missions followed, in 1935 and 1942 respectively.[4]

The beginning of land rights for Indigenous people in Australia is often dated to 1976, with the passing of the Commonwealth Aboriginal Land Rights (Northern Territory) Act (ALRA) by the Federal Parliament. But the ALRA had complex antecedents, some of which involved the Yolŋu clans of the Yirrkala area and surrounding regions.[5] In the mid-1950s, the Commonwealth government granted mining exploration licences over the large bauxite reserves on the Gove Peninsula, where Yirrkala stands. The local Yolŋu were not informed, much less consulted. In 1963, when exploration activities became obvious, Yolŋu leaders sent a series of petitions, known collectively as the Bark Petition, to the Federal Parliament, asking for a Parliamentary Inquiry into recognition of Yolŋu rights to their traditional lands.[6] When the petition failed, the Yolŋu challenged the government and the mining company in the Supreme Court of the Northern Territory.[7] The case also failed, with Mr Justice Blackburn finding in 1971 that the relationship of the Yolŋu to their lands, although complex and of great antiquity, could not be construed as property rights under the Australian system of law.[8]

This case had a significant effect on the thinking of senior members of the Labor Party, who were then in opposition at the national level.[9] During the campaign for the national election of 1972, the party leader, Gough Whitlam, pledged support for land rights. In 1973, having come to office, Whitlam instituted a Commission of Inquiry under Mr Justice Woodward, who had been the barrister representing the Yolŋu in the Gove case. In his final report, handed down the following year, Justice Woodward recommended that gazetted Aboriginal Reserves in the Northern Territory should be granted to their traditional owners under inalienable freehold title in fee simple – the strongest available form of freehold – and that a land commissioner be appointed to hear claims by their traditional owners to all other areas of unalienated Crown Land in the Territory.[10] These recommendations resulted in the ALRA, which was finally passed by the Frazer Coalition government in 1976.

It is important to emphasize that the passing of the ALRA did not acknowledge prior native title. However, it was an implicit recognition that the doctrine of Terra Nullius was a convenient fiction, and it paved the way conceptually for the recognition of native title – the recognition that Indigenous peoples had some form of title over the continent prior to European occupation. But this recognition did not come until the 1990s.

The Native Title Act (NTA), passed by the Commonwealth government in 1993, had its origins in the *Mabo* decision of 1992, when the High Court of Australia recognized that the Meriam people of Torres Strait held native title over part of their traditional lands. This decision overturned the doctrine of Terra Nullius as embodied in Blackburn's 1971 finding in the Gove case, and created a state of radical uncertainty on the matter of land title in Australia. It became necessary to draft national legislation to reconcile potential native title claims with Australian common law relating to property rights.

The extent and limits of native title have been delineated progressively through case law, and there is no space to trace these developments here. The salient points to note are that native title has come to be conceived of as a bundle of rights that are liable to extinguishment severally, or as a whole, by past or future actions of government. For example, the granting of freehold title to another party in the past, before the existence of the NTA, is deemed to have extinguished the native title of the original Indigenous owning group. "Future acts" may include such events as the granting of an exploration licence to a mining company. In such cases, particularly with reference to "future acts," native title holders who have met the necessary standard of proof are entitled to be consulted and to negotiate compensation for the extinguishment of some or all of their native title rights.[11]

A Brief History of Indigenous Protected Areas in Australia

The Indigenous Protected Area program was initiated by the federal government in 1997 to provide a framework for Indigenous owned lands to be managed as part of the National Reserve System. Much of the "Indigenous Estate" consists of areas of high, or very high "wilderness quality."[12] It is important to note that the IPA regime has no legal effect on title. Aboriginal groups who live on Aboriginal land, such as the Yolŋu, simply enter into an agreement with the federal government to manage their land as an IPA, and for this they receive a certain amount of funding, including for ranger positions. In "settled" Australia, many IPAs are on land purchased on behalf of Aboriginal groups by the Indigenous Land Corporation, a statutory body established in 1995 under the Commonwealth ATSI (Aboriginal and Torres Strait Islanders) Act, initially to aid groups whose native title had been extinguished. In such cases the group negotiates an Indigenous Land Use Agreement with the government, agreeing to manage their land as an IPA.

From the beginning, a key feature of the program was that Indigenous groups could approach government with a proposal for an IPA, and there was an enthusiastic response. By May 2007 there were "23 declared IPAs covering 190,000 square kilometres and a further 15 IPAs in the process of development" (Altman, Buchanan, and Larsen 2007), representing 2.5 per cent of Australia's land mass. By 2012 there were 51 declared IPAs, and a further 43 in the pipeline; declared IPAs then covered 364,427 square kilometres (Altman and Markham 2012: 7). Declaration of new IPAs continues apace.[13]

Why so much enthusiasm and uptake? The answer lies in part in the idea of Indigenous life projects (see Blaser, Feit, and McRae 2004). In the Australian context, Nicolas Peterson has characterized these as projects in which Indigenous people "seek autonomy in deciding the meaning of their life independently of projects promoted by the state and the market" (2005: 7). Peterson describes the outstation movement as a clear-cut Australian example of this phenomenon, and IPAs with their associated ranger programs can be seen as a second example, particularly in the early days, as far as the motivations of Indigenous actors are concerned. They seemed to offer a greater degree of autonomy than joint management arrangements in the National Park system, and a space in which people could reaffirm, or even re-establish, their stewardship of their country.[14] Although, from the first, IPA plans of management included projects that spoke to Western conservation values and often involved cooperative arrangements with non-Indigenous agencies, both the rhetoric and the practice, in the early days, put the Indigenous group in the driving seat. In 2003, writing about the Nantawarrina IPA in the Flinders Ranges (the first to be declared), Samantha Muller titles her article "Towards Decolonisation of Australia's Protected Area Management" and ends on a hopeful note:

> Successful management achieved under Aboriginal control may be the "symbol" that Western managers need to fully appreciate the significance of Indigenous land management. When this significance becomes acknowledged on a wider scale, Protected Areas in Australia may truly become decolonised. (Muller 2003: 41)

In hindsight, a decade on, Muller's provisional optimism is not warranted. In the case of the outstation movement, the sustainability of small outstation communities became increasingly dependent on state grant funding (for housing and infrastructure) and state welfare transfers. In the case of the IPA system, the state was always a partner. In neither case, therefore, could the "life project" be autonomously sustained, and decolonization, in the sense of disarticulation from the state, was never a possibility, in either case.

Seán Kerins (2012) charts the shift that has occurred in political discourse about Indigenous environmental resource management, from "Caring for Country" with the establishment of the Northern Land Council's Caring for Country Unit in 1995 (which preceded the establishment of the IPA system), to "Working on Country," a term coined in 2007, which was "promoted by the Australian Government as part of its mainstream environmental Caring for our Country initiative" (Kerins 2012: 41). The shift from "Country" to "our Country" has a significance that might escape many readers, especially those who are not from Australia. In the varieties of English spoken by Indigenous people, "Country" has a very particular meaning. It denotes not merely a landscape and its ecology, but the land, seas, and waters as they are imbued with the spiritual forces from which people derive their identity. In coining the phrase "Caring for our Country," government was referencing the Indigenous meaning of Country while at the same time rather deliberately reappropriating the term for application to all Australians. When speaking of "my" or "our" Country, Indigenous Australians will be referring to a specific area from which they derive their identity, whereas other Australians speaking of "our country" are usually referring to the whole of the Australian continent.

Kerins argues that the shift in discourse is correlated with a shift from the original funding of ranger groups according to a participatory development model, in which local values received (at least in theory) as much weight as Western conservation values, to a top-down directive model in which government increasingly sets the priorities for the activities of ranger groups both on and off IPAs: "To continue to receive state funding, caring for country practitioners must now 'play by the rules' set by outsiders and report on outcomes articulated by the state for its support" (Kerins 2012: 42).

This shift has occurred in the context of a wider shift in the Indigenous Affairs policy framework over the same time-span, from the

Howard Coalition government's focus on "Practical Reconciliation," through the shock of the Northern Territory Emergency Response and on into the Rudd and then Gillard Labor governments' era of "Closing the Gaps" and "Stronger Futures."[15] These terms still frame the debate under the current Abbott Coalition government.[16] The emphasis has been, increasingly, on achieving statistical equality at the expense, if necessary, of cultural diversity. For a while these shifts occurred in parallel, both reflecting the spirit of the times. But recently, Indigenous natural resource management has been rebadged as part of the all-encompassing "Closing the Gap," as attested by the 2013 definition of "Indigenous Protected Area" on the website of the (then) Department of Sustainability, Environment, Water, Population, and Communities (SEWPaC):

> An Indigenous Protected Area is an area of Indigenous-owned land or sea where traditional owners have entered into an agreement with the Australian Government to promote biodiversity and cultural resource conservation. Indigenous Protected Areas protect Australia's biodiversity while providing training and employment for Aboriginal people on their own country. *The Indigenous Protected Areas are helping to close the gap of Indigenous disadvantage, with communities reporting better health, social cohesion and higher school attendance.* (Emphasis added)[17]

So far, so innocuous, one might say: it is surely a good thing that communities are reporting such outcomes from the IPA program. However, this statement has to be interpreted in the context of the details of the "Closing the Gap" measures, with their emphasis on recentralizing the Aboriginal population in remote Australia into "growth towns," where, it is imagined, they will be trained to join the "mainstream" workforce. The smaller homelands where the Yirralka Rangers live have been squeezed for some time: for example, there is currently no government support, nor any prospect of it, for building new housing on the homelands. The Community Development Employment Program, which was the mainstay of homelands economies for over thirty years, and without which it would have been impossible for ranger programs to get off the ground, has recently been replaced by the Remote Jobs and Communities Program. The change in title is significant: whereas CDEP, at least in its title, put community development first, the RJCP focuses on individuals as job seekers to be serviced by "providers," and tacks on communities in a rather underspecified way. It is very unclear if this new program can be delivered successfully on the home-lands, and whether it will be adequately resourced for the logistical hurdles that will be involved in administering a program designed for the growth towns to the inhabitants of small and scattered homelands.[18] Moreover the change in direction, not simply a change in name, creates discontinuity and uncertainty. It is unclear nationally or regionally how existing programs, such as ranger programs, will articulate with the new system. Ironically the very process of its introduction, rather than closing a gap, creates one in policy and praxis.

The Yirralka Rangers Program is not under immediate threat: most ranger positions are now grant-funded rather than being CDEP posi-tions.[19] However, the viability of the very communities where the rang-ers live *is* under threat, and they are operating, as Kerins notes, under increasingly constrained conditions. It is relatively easy to acquire funding for projects that government considers important, and to enter contractual arrangements with government agencies for work that is considered valuable to the nation (such as monitoring the coastline for illegal fishing activity, or the control of exotic weeds and pests). It is much harder to find sources of funding for projects that Yolŋu might wish to prioritize. This point leads to a consideration, finally, of how the Yolŋu navigate this IPA space.

Resistance and Articulation

The Yolŋu have a long and distinguished history of engagement with wider Australia: the Elcho Island adjustment movement (Berndt 1962) and the Yirrkala Church Panels (Morphy 2000) testify to their early efforts to reconcile Christianity with the Yolŋu ontological system, and, as noted earlier, through the Bark Petition and the *Milirrpum* (Gove land rights) case that followed, they can be credited with help-ing to initiate the land rights movement that saw the passing of the ALRA in 1976. Much later, in the 2000s, they fought the Blue Mud Bay case[20] that led to the High Court ruling on the status of the waters of the intertidal zone under the ALRA – a ruling that saw the ALRA permit system unequivocally extended to the intertidal waters over 80 per cent of the Northern Territory's coastline. Many of the appli-cants in that case were the children and grandchildren of the litigants in *Milirrpum*.

The idea of instigating the Laynhapuy IPA came from Milirrpum's son Wanyubi Marika, and this not only is no coincidence but also firmly links the Laynhapuy IPA, in Yolŋu thinking, to the land and sea rights agenda. Waka Munuŋgurr, one of the witnesses in the Blue Mud Bay case, made the connection explicit:

Yo, dhuwal ŋunhi ŋanapurr märraŋal nhawi Ranger ... Djälthin ŋanapurr dhiyakuw wäŋaw ŋoyŋu gapu ga diltji malanyŋuw. Yo ŋunhiyinydhi bili yätj malanya ŋanapurr yukurran nhäŋal dhiyal ŋäthil gurra. Guya djämamirr mala warku'yuna dhuwal wäŋa, liya-wawu marrtjinya ... Bala ŋanapurr gärrinyamaraŋal [courtlil]. Dhiyaŋuny bala nhakun ŋayi dhuwal bilin, bala ŋanapurr djälthinan Ranger programgu. Rangermirriyawnha dhiyak wäŋaw ŋoynha gapuwuy dapmaranharaw djäkaw ga diltjiw. Dhiyaŋuy ŋunhi gämurruy ŋunhi sea righttja, ŋanapurr claimingdja dhiyaŋuy gämurruy.

Yes, it was for this that we established the Rangers ... We wanted to have them [care] for the country, the sea and the inland together. Yes, this was needed because we have seen some bad things happen here before. [Professional] fishermen despoiled this country, they came in ignorantly ...Then we provided evidence [to the Blue Mud Bay court hearing]. Because of this, we then wanted a Ranger program. The Rangers will patrol and monitor the places in the sea and care for the land. This is the reason why we undertook that sea rights claim. (Waka Munuŋgurr, cited in Laynhapuy Homelands Association Incorporated 2006: 6, 9)

In an earlier paper on the Blue Mud Bay case (F. Morphy 2008), I made the argument that Yolŋu see themselves as encapsulated but not colonized; and that many of their actions and statements in the case could be interpreted as a discourse about the sovereignty of Yolŋu *rom* (law). The judge in the case, Justice Selway, while naturally not recognizing that argument, nevertheless understood that for the Yolŋu the case was "merely the latest aspect of a more protracted campaign" (Selway 2005: 213, cited in F. Morphy 2009: 104). But if we are to understand the Yolŋu view in terms of resistance, we have to see the site of that resistance in the ontology of *rom* itself. This is the way that Yolŋu view the situation: unlike Australian settler law, which is manifestly always changing through human actions, the tenets of *rom* are inaccessible to human agency. Humans have no sovereignty over the ancestral forces that created *rom*, and in this sense Australian law, which is humanly made, can never have sovereignty over *rom*, no matter what mundane power relations hold between the settler society and the Yolŋu.

But *rom*'s Achilles heel is that it comes from the land and sea, which are imbued with ancestral forces. Damage to country, particularly to the *djalkiri* (foundation) places where the ancestors transformed themselves or were transformed into features of the landscape, damages the foundation of *rom* and the people whose *birrimbirr* (animating essence) comes from those places. Yolŋu reason therefore that if they are to remain healthy and strong they need to protect those places. And this is where ranger programs and the IPA system become another part of the protracted campaign to protect *rom*. *Rom* resists, by its very nature, but its living representatives must find ways to articulate with the encompassing world to protect it, and therefore themselves.

Although Waka does not mention it in the quotation given above, he has in mind an incident that galvanized the Yolŋu of the coastal clans into producing the Saltwater collection of over eighty bark paintings that are now in the collection of the National Maritime Museum in Sydney and which contributed to the push for hearing the Blue Mud Bay case. Waka is a senior *djuŋgayi* (ceremonial manager) for his mother's clan, Maḏarrpa, whose country includes the crocodile nesting site at Garraŋali. Bäru (crocodile) is the ancestor of the Maḏarrpa clan, and this nesting site is a *djalkiri wäŋa*, a major source of conception spirits for Maḏarrpa. Out fishing one day, Waka came across an abandoned fishermen's camp, illegally situated close to Garraŋali, and found the remains of a butchered crocodile. When he speaks of despoiling the country, and ignorance, this is what he has in mind. Fishermen were also routinely despoiling another site created through the actions of the ancestral crocodile, by staking their nets into the sand in the intertidal zone at Yathikpa. During the court hearing, persons unknown killed another crocodile and strung its head up in a tree at Yathikpa.

Despite such malevolence on the part of some local non-Yolŋu, Yolŋu continue to welcome visitors to their country, because they see the necessity for articulation, but they look for opportunities where articulation can be on Yolŋu terms. There are parallels here with the way in which Cree people attempt to control sport hunters on their land through "strategic relationality with a few ... who are amenable to forming friendships" (see Scott in this volume, p. 59; see also Poirier in this volume). Yolŋu want to create contexts in which to deploy the politics of persuasion (see F. Morphy 2008; H. Morphy 2006). Here again the IPA is relevant, for one possible activity on the IPA is to set up sites for visitors, carefully placed away from *djalkiri* areas, and another is to develop guided walks. In this way, visitors can be welcomed and educated, but their movement through the landscape can be controlled.

At the time of writing, I was part of the team of consultants who were assisting the Yirralka Rangers to put together a management plan for Stage 2 of the Laynhapuy IPA. My role was to assist in the process of consulting the Yolŋu of the region about their priorities for the IPA. It will come as no surprise that the protection of *djalkiri wäŋa*, and the development of systems to welcome but also control visitors, both on land and sea, figured prominently in people's thinking. People prioritized these over the more conventional, and in government thinking more central, roles such as the control of weeds and feral animals.[21]

Many of those consulted were also insistent on the urgent need for cultural mapping. Unlike the Warlpiri as described by Peterson in this volume, many Yolŋu are living in the homelands "on country," and pursuing hunting and gathering activities on a daily basis. But older people who grew up ranging widely on foot are aware that younger people, accustomed to travelling by vehicle to favoured hunting, fishing, and gathering sites, know their country and its names in less minute detail than their elders – they have less "embodied knowledge" of much of their country, in Peterson's terms. They may know the names of many places through the songs that they hear in ceremony, but they have never visited them. The activity of the rangers is resulting in a renewed acquaintance with the details of the physical landscape, but this new form of embodied experience needs to be coupled, in the opinion of old and young alike, with a simultaneous reconnection to the names and meanings held in the songs. Here the technology of GPS and Cybertracker, with which the rangers are now familiar, becomes a useful new tool in the "reproduction of ontological relationships to land," rather than being, as Peterson suggests (p. 248), simply a reflection of "our" culture of literacy. Another very interesting line of thinking also became apparent during the consultations. It was clear at the outset that senior Yolŋu living in the Laynhapuy IPA had been having serious conversations for some time about "cross-border" cooperation with the ranger groups of surrounding IPAs. As one man put it: "We see lines as links, not boundaries." The areas of "shared management agreements" that will figure in the finished plan are the result of this Yolŋu insistence on taking a regional view.

Because there are no consequences in Australian law for the status of IPA land, the state does not see these boundary lines as political in any way, and so it is relaxed about the prospect of boundaries being shifted around. It can even countenance the prospect of overlapping boundaries. Paradoxically, this gives Yolŋu the space to be very political. For this region of Arnhem Land has ambitions for regional autonomy, which surface periodically in attempts to break away from the Northern Land Council and set up a separate land council for the Yolŋu region. Such attempts have been thwarted in the past by the unwillingness of government to support and underwrite such a move, and by internal political rivalries. Although no one is saying so explicitly, I think it likely that some Yolŋu leaders see the declaration of IPAs across the region as the opportunity to forge a regional polity on the basis of an uncontentious issue, caring for country. All Yolŋu are united in their desire to have more control over what happens on their land and in their sea country.

Conclusion: Articulation or Entanglement?

I have already played with the meaning of "resistance" in speaking of the ontology of *rom*. In conclusion I look more closely at the idea of entanglement, drawing on ideas in a recent co-authored paper (Morphy and Morphy 2013). In that paper, as noted earlier, Howard Morphy and I develop an analytical framework based on the idea of the relative autonomy of social systems and subsystems. This has consequences for the nature of the articulation within and between such systems.

Yolŋu have a term for a kind of negative entanglement – *mämuy*. They evoke it in describing the effects on individuals, and on the social fabric of Yolŋu society, of addiction to alcohol, or gambling, or other introduced substances (including money itself). They do not use it when talking about such things as the ranger program, or the kind of knowledge that the rangers acquire in the course of their training.

This is not to deny the relevance of many of the points made by Elodie Fache (this volume) about the power asymmetry between Indigenous and non-Indigenous knowledge systems in the IPA context. But there are important local differences between the cases in the two chapters. The Yirralka rangers are more numerous than the Yugul Mangi Rangers discussed by Fache, and because the majority live on homelands rather than in the hub settlement of Yirrkala, their contact with the non-Indigenous staff of the IPA is more intermittent. Much of their day-to-day work is self-directed, giving scope for Yolŋu priorities and concerns to come to the fore. They are able to see much of the introduced system of knowledge and its technologies as an adjunct to their own, as an articulation that does not necessarily imply entanglement. The inequalities of power that concern them are at the level of influence (or lack of it) that they have over access to sources of funding for major projects that they would themselves prioritize.

We were attracted to relative autonomy as a model in part because it resonates with how Yolŋu themselves conceptualize the articulation between their system and that of the encapsulating settler society. Because of their belief in the autonomy of *rom*, they see no contradiction in incorporating new ideas and technologies, particularly if they can be used to increase the capacity of Yolŋu to protect and look after their country, and to strengthen the economic base of the homelands. They see this as articulation, but not as entanglement.

But are they right? The answer may be that they are right for as long as they believe themselves to be. They are right for as long as the ontology of *rom* prevails in their thinking about their identity as Yolŋu. They are right so long as they can continue to manoeuvre within the IPA space to pursue their own agenda. But this is dependent on the IPA remaining the kind of space where the Yolŋu "two-way" view of articulation can sit beside the essentially monocultural impulses of their paymasters. There is no doubt that forces from the settler world constantly put pressure on the Yolŋu world view, and potentially constrain the potential for such manoeuvring. The government view of the IPAs as being primarily concerned with resource management has funding implications. It is hard to get funding and resources for projects that Yolŋu regard as foundational, such as cultural mapping, and it is likely that government will become increasingly prescriptive about what counts as "valuable" work for rangers.

Arguably the rangers themselves are taking on some "mainstream" attitudes as they acquire the knowledge and skills to put mainstream programs into effect. They are beginning to value rangering as "work." This is potentially a source of tension between the rangers, as a newly professionalized group, and the senior leaders of their communities. Those tensions occasionally surface when senior community members want the rangers to undertake tasks that the rangers do not see as "ranger work." But while Yinimala Gumana is simultaneously an apprentice *djirrikay* (regional ritual specialist) and a senior ranger, and sees these as complementary roles, these tensions will remain manageable, and negotiable. Indeed the Yirralka Rangers have a paid group of people, titled "Senior Cultural Advisors," precisely to fulfil a mediating role between the rangers and their community leaders. For the moment, both the rangers and their seniors see the IPA and the ranger program as a space where "technology" and "culture" can be mutually reinforcing. Wanyubi Marika put this view succinctly in response to a suggestion that people would be surprised to know he was a ranger as well as a prominent artist (Annandale Galleries in association with Buku-Larrnggay Mulka 2008). Wanyubi replied: "It's the same thing. Protecting the country through the *gamunuŋgu* [sacred designs] is the same thing as protecting the land physically as a Ranger. There is no difference."

ACKNOWLEDGMENTS

I would like to thank Helen Frazer, Seán Kerins, and Howard Morphy, and the indefatigable editors of this volume, Françoise Dussart and Sylvie Poirier, for suggestions that vastly improved this chapter. To the Yirralka Rangers and senior members of the Laynhapuy homelands communities, whose views I hope I have reflected accurately, I express my admiration for their resilience and commitment to always remaining Yolŋu in a changing world. All errors of fact or interpretation are my responsibility alone.

NOTES

1 The full speech, recorded on 7 September 2011, may be viewed at https://www.youtube.com/watch?v=2Ni5rACaDxA; the extract begins eleven minutes into the recording.
2 The homelands movement, which saw many Aboriginal people leaving mission stations and government settlements to re-establish small communities on their own "country," began in the 1960s and gathered force in the 1970s. It was facilitated by the policy of self-determination initiated by the Whitlam Labor government when it came to power in 1972, but the impetus towards decentralization had preceded the 1972 election. People's reasons for wanting to move varied from place to place; in the case of eastern Yolŋu clans, a major factor was the establishment of a mining township on the Gove Peninsula close to the then Methodist mission at Yirrkala. For a brief history of the homelands movement in this area see F. Morphy (2008).

3   For some time the term "Indigenous" (with initial captital letter) has been the conventional means of denoting the Aboriginal and Torres Strait Islander peoples whose lands and seas fall within the boundaries of the Australian state. There are signs that the terms "First Peoples" and "First Nations" are beginning to supplant it.

4   There is a large literature on this period of missionization and the events that led to it, by both missionaries (see, e.g., Thornell 1986) and anthropologists (see, e.g., Berndt 1962; Williams 1986); a detailed account is beyond the scope of this chapter. See also Sachiko Kubota's chapter (in this volume) on more recent developments at Galiwin'ku.

5   The ALRA was preceded in 1966 and 1970 by two other Acts, passed by the states of South Australia and Victoria respectively, which converted Aboriginal Reserves in those two states into Land Trusts held by statutory authorities on behalf of the Aboriginal traditional owners of the relevant regions.

6   These consisted of written petitions in the Gumatj dialect of Yolŋu Matha (Yolŋu language) with English translations pasted onto sheets of stringy bark. The borders of the barks were painted with designs belonging to the clans of the affected area (see H. Morphy 2000).

7   The case, popularly known as the Gove land rights case, was *Milirrpum v. Nabalco and the Commonwealth of Australia* (1971) 17 FLR 141.

8   For a detailed analysis and account of the case and its aftermath see Williams (1986).

9   Also significant was the seven-year strike by Gurindji cattle station workers who walked off Wave Hill Station in 1966 in protest at their wages and conditions. They set up a community at Daguragu (Wattie Creek), where their struggle developed into a call for the return of their lands. The Gurindji cause attracted considerable public support, particularly from the trade union movement and elements of the Labor party. For an advocate's view of the Gurindji walkoff, written at the time, see Hardy (1968) (the original edition of his *The Unlucky Australians*; latest edition published in 2006). For an overview of land rights from a historian's point of view see Attwood (2003).

10 See F. Morphy (2009) for a more detailed summary.

11 There is a voluminous literature on native title as it has developed since the 1990s, tracing both its legal aspects and the social effects of the claim process on Indigenous groups. For a series of case studies concerning the latter see Smith and Morphy (2007).

12 See Altman, Buchanan, and Larsen (2007) for an extended discussion and a series of illuminating maps.

13 However, in 2012 the Australian government ceased providing funding for a further expansion of the program. See e.g. https://www.wilderness.org.au/campaigns/Indigenous-conservation/new-Indigenous-protected-areas-announced-in-the-kimberley, accessed 12 June 2013.

14 There is a large literature on Indigenous involvement in various forms of land management, including joint management arrangements. For a summary of systems of joint management see chapter 2 of Bauman and Smyth (2007).

15 The Northern Territory Emergency Response (also known as the Intervention) was a series of draconian measures introduced in the Northern Territory by the Howard Coalition government in 2007. For critical commentary on the Intervention see Altman (2007); Morphy and Morphy (2013).

16 Since the time of writing, the Coalition government has changed its leader. The current prime minister is Malcolm Turnbull. The framing of the debate remains as it was.

17 From www.environment.gov.au/Indigenous/index.html, accessed 12 June 2013. Since this chapter was written, the responsibility for IPAS has moved to another government department.

18 The RJCP indeed proved to be a problematic program (see Fowkes and Sanders 2016). Since the time of writing it has been replaced by yet another program: the Community Development Program (CDP).

19 This may no longer be entirely true. The Abbott government has shifted responsibility for Indigenous programs almost entirely into the Department of Prime Minister and Cabinet, and the IPA program is no longer the responsibility of the (variously named over time) department of the environment. At the time of writing the fate of the IPA program was very unclear, and it remains so under the Turnbull government.

20 *Northern Territory of Australia & Anor v. Arnhem Land Aboriginal Land Trust & Ors* (2008) HCA 29 (Blue Mud Bay Case).

21 It could be argued that feral water buffalo are to the Yolŋu what camels are to the peoples of central Australia (see Petronella Vaarzon-Morel in this volume); their management raises very similar tensions and dilemmas around questions of ontology and relationality. Unfortunately there is no space to expand on this topic here.

REFERENCES

Altman, Jon C., ed. 2007. *Coercive Reconciliation: Stabilise, Normalise, Exit Aboriginal Australia*. Melbourne: Arena Publications.

Altman, Jon C., Geoff Buchanan, and Libby Larsen. 2007. "The Environmental Significance of the Indigenous Estate: Natural Resource Management as Development in Remote Australia." CAEPR Discussion Paper 286. Canberra: Centre for Aboriginal Economic Policy Research, The Australian National University.

Altman, Jon C., and Francis Markham. 2012. Submission to the House of Representatives Standing Committee on Aboriginal and Torres Strait Islander Affairs Inquiry into the Native Title Amendment Bill 2012. Electronic document. http://www.aph.gov.au/Help/404?item=%2fparliamentary-business%2fbills-legislation%2fbd%2fb d1213a%2f13bd1&user=extranet%5cAnonymous&site=website, accessed 13 June 2013.

Annandale Galleries in association with Buku-Larrnggay Mulka. 2008. *Wanyubi Marika & Young Guns II*. Sydney: Annandale Galleries.

Attwood, Bain M. 2003. *Rights for Aborigines*. Sydney: Allen and Unwin.

Bauman, Toni, and Dermott Smyth. 2007. *Indigenous Partnerships in Protected Area Management in Australia: Three Case Studies*. Canberra: Australian Institute for Aboriginal and Torres Strait Islander Studies.

Berndt, Ronald M. 1962. "An Adjustment Movement in Arnhem Land, Northern Territory of Australia." *Cahiers de L'Homme* 2.

Blaser, Mario, Harvey A. Feit, and Glenn McRae, eds. 2004. *In the Way of Development: Indigenous Peoples, Life Projects and Globalization*. London and New York: Zed Books and Ottawa: Canadian International Development Research Centre.

Cowlishaw, Gillian. 1988. *Black, White or Brindle: Race in Rural Australia*. Cambridge: Cambridge University Press.

Escobar, Arturo. 2008. *Territories of Difference: Place, Movements, Life, Redes*. Durham, NC: Duke University Press. http://dx.doi.org/10.1215/9780822389439.

Fowkes, Lisa, and William Sanders. 2016. "Financial Penalties under the Remote Jobs and Communities Program." CAEPR Working Paper 108. Canberra: Centre for Aboriginal Economic Policy Research, the Australian National University.

Hardy, Frank J. 1968. *The Unlucky Australians*. Melbourne: Nelson. Republished in 2006 by One Day Hill, Camberwell, Vic.

Hinkson, Melinda, and Benjamin R. Smith, eds. 2005. "Figuring the Intercultural in Aboriginal Australia." *Oceania* 75 (3): 209–21.

Kerins, Seán. 2012. "Caring for Country to Working on Country." In *People on Country: Vital Landscapes, Indigenous Futures*, ed. Jon C. Altman and Seán Kerins, 26–44. Sydney: Federation Press.

Laynhapuy Homelands Association Incorporated. 2006. Laynhapuy Indigenous Protected Area: Management Plan, April 2006. Unpublished draft version 11 April 2006. Yirrkala, NT: Laynhapuy Homelands Association Incorporated.

Merlan, Francesca. 1998. *Caging the Rainbow: Places, Politics and Aborigines in a North Australian Town.* Honolulu: University of Hawai'i Press.

Morphy, Frances. 2008 "Whose Governance, for Whose Good? The Laynhapuy Homelands Association and the Neo-Assimilationist Turn in Indigenous Policy." In *Contested Governance: Culture, Power and Institutions in Indigenous Australia,* ed. Janet Hunt, Diane Smith, Stephanie Garling, and Will Sanders, 113–51. CAEPR Research Monograph 29. Canberra: ANU ePress.

Morphy, Frances. 2009. "Enacting Sovereignty in a Colonized Space: The Yolngu of Blue Mud Bay Meet the Native Title Process." In *The Rights and Wrongs of Land Restitution: Restoring What Was Ours,* ed. Derek Fay and Deborah James, 99–122. New York: Routledge-Cavendish.

Morphy, Frances, and Howard Morphy. 2013. "Anthropological Theory and Government Policy in Australia's Northern Territory: The Hegemony of the 'Mainstream'." *American Anthropologist* 115 (2): 174–87. http://dx.doi.org/10.1111/aman.12002.

Morphy, Howard. 2000. "Art and Politics: The Bark Petition and the Barunga Statement." In *The Oxford Companion to Aboriginal Art and Culture,* ed. Sylvia Kleinert and Margo Neale, 100. Melbourne: Oxford University Press.

Morphy, Howard. 2005. "Mutual Conversion? The Methodist Church and the Yolngu, with Particular Reference to Yirrkala." *Humanities Research* 12 (1): 41–53.

Morphy, Howard. 2006. "Sites of Persuasion: Yingapungapu at the National Museum of Australia." In *Museum Frictions: Public Cultures/Global Transformations,* ed. Ivan Karp, Corinne A. Kratz, Lynn Szwatja, and Tomas Ybarra-Frausto, 469–99. Durham, NC: Duke University Press. http://dx.doi.org/10.1215/9780822388296-023.

Morphy, Howard. 2008. *Becoming Art: Exploring Cross-Cultural Categories.* Sydney: University of New South Wales Press.

Morris, Barry. 1989. *Domesticating Resistance: The Dhan-Gadi Aborigines and the Australian State.* Oxford: Berg.

Muller, Samantha. 2003. "Towards Decolonisation of Australia's Protected Area Management: The Nantawarrina Indigenous Protected Area Experience." *Australian Geographical Studies* 41 (1): 29–43. http://dx.doi.org/10.1111/1467-8470.00190.

Pedersen, Howard, with Banjo Woorunmurra. 2011. *Jandamarra and the Bunuba Resistance*. Broome: Magabala Books.

Peterson, Nicolas. 2005. "What Can Pre-Colonial and Frontier Economies Tell Us about Engagement with the Real Economy? Indigenous Life Projects and the Conditions for Development." In *Culture, Economy and Governance in Aboriginal Australia*, ed. Diane Austin-Broos and Gaynor MacDonald, 7–18. Sydney: Sydney University Press.

Reynolds, Henry. 1982. *The Other Side of the Frontier: Aboriginal Resistance to the European Invasion of Australia*. Sydney: Penguin Books.

Selway, J. 2005. The "Blue Mud Decision." *Gumana v Northern Territory of Australia* [2005] FCA 50.

Smith, Benjamin R., and Frances Morphy, eds. 2007. *The Social Effects of Native Title: Recognition, Translation, Coexistence*. CAEPR Research Monograph 27. Canberra: ANU ePress.

Thornell, Harold. 1986. *A Bridge over Time: Living in Arnhem Land with the Aborigines 1938–1944, As Told to Estelle Thomson*. Melbourne: J.M. Dent.

Williams, Nancy. 1986. *The Yolngu and Their Land: A System of Land Tenure and the Fight for Its Recognition*. Canberra: Australian Institute of Aboriginal Studies.

5 Mediation between Indigenous and Non-Indigenous Knowledge Systems: Another Analysis of "Two-Way" Conservation in Northern Australia

ELODIE FACHE

Introduction

Since the 1990s, international discourse has recognized that Indigenous peoples "have developed over many generations a holistic traditional scientific knowledge of their lands, natural resources and environment" (United Nations 1992: 279). The valuable contribution that this knowledge can make in achieving sustainable development has also been emphasized. Community-based natural resource management policies and projects in particular reflect this perspective by implying that Indigenous peoples hold "knowledge that the world needs" (Tsing et al. 2005: 7). In this context, concepts of "traditional ecological knowledge" (TEK), "Indigenous ecological knowledge" (IEK), and simply "Indigenous knowledge" (IK) have emerged. However, no consensus has been established with regard to the definition of these concepts. Non-Indigenous people generally use them to refer to "a body of environmental knowledge accumulated over hundreds of generations" (e.g., Ens et al. 2012a: 101). Yet from an Indigenous perspective, these concepts involve a "way of life" rather than just "a body of knowledge," and knowledge has to be understood holistically rather than being reduced to its "ecological" aspects (see McGregor 2004: 79–80; Nadasdy 2003a: 60–113).

Increased appreciation for "traditional ecological knowledge" has led to efforts to combine it with Western science in the domains of environmental management and conservation. Scholars are progressively analysing the multidimensional challenges and issues inherent in this process of knowledge entanglement. For instance, on the basis of Canadian case studies, Paul Nadasdy (1999, 2003a, 2003b) has demonstrated how initiatives aiming to integrate "traditional ecological knowledge" with Western science do, in practice, extend mainstream modes of environmental management as well as state power within Indigenous communities. Despite such critical analyses, Indigenous Australians aspire to jointly use their own knowledge systems and Western science in the context of land and sea management (e.g., Ens 2012; Muller 2012).

I address such matters here with regard to the "two-way approach" policy enacted in the Northern Territory of Australia. This policy promotes the combination of Indigenous and non-Indigenous knowledge systems for conservation purposes. Its implementation relies on Indigenous "rangers" who carry out day-to-day duties of land and sea management around their community on behalf of the wider group(s) having rights and responsibilities over the area (see also Kerins 2012: 33).[1] Ranger jobs are mainly funded by the Australian government, which assumes that environmental conservation is a pathway towards Indigenous economic development. In Ngukurr, a community located in the Northern Territory where I conducted field research between 2007 and 2010, Indigenous rangers have been operating a formalized land and sea management program for more than ten years. As one of these rangers explained, this program contributes to "bringing Indigenous culture and non-Indigenous culture together" (personal communication, 28 April 2009).

With its emphasis on a combination of Indigenous and non-Indigenous knowledge systems, the so-called "two-way approach" presents a particularly intricate form of entanglement of the Indigenous world in the non-Indigenous world and vice versa. In this chapter, I illustrate that this approach involves the three characteristics of entanglement highlighted by Françoise Dussart and Sylvie Poirier in this volume: inevitability (here, even promotion) of correlations, uncertainty of outcomes, and unintended consequences. As suggested by my ethnographic examples focused on "weed" and "feral animal" control within the Ngukurr region, some of these unintended consequences include an increasing non-Indigenous influence in land and sea management activities conducted on Indigenous-owned lands and, more generally, the reproduction of power asymmetries between Indigenous and non-Indigenous knowledge systems and actors.

Furthermore, I argue that the concept of mediation, as a corollary of the notion of entanglement, is a heuristic avenue for analysing some of the assumptions, mechanisms, and side effects of the "two-way approach."

While the notion of entanglement draws attention to the dialectical and dialogical dimensions of encounters between Indigenous and non-Indigenous knowledge systems (see Dussart and Poirier in this volume), the concept of mediation sheds light on the practical implications of such encounters. It therefore allows inquiry into the epistemological, ontological, social, and political issues inherent in the interactions between Indigenous and non-Indigenous knowledge holders involved side by side in specific "two-way" projects.

The Community of Ngukurr and Its Ranger Program

Under the Australian Indigenous self-determination policy, the Roper River Mission, which had been run by the Church Missionary Society from 1908 to 1968, became the community of Ngukurr in the 1970s.[2] Seven main language groups (Alawa, Marra, Ngalakgan, Ngandi, Nunggubuyu, Ritharrngu, and Wandarrang) were represented on the mission and are now collectively named "Yugul Mangi" in Ngukurr. This community, which counts more than one thousand people, is located in Arnhem Land, an Aboriginal reserve that the government returned to its "traditional owners" under the Aboriginal Land Rights Act (Northern Territory) Act 1976 (for further details on these contextual elements, see Sachiko Kubota, Frances Morphy, and Nicolas Peterson in this volume). The people settled in Ngukurr participated in the decentralization or so-called "outstation movement" that followed the adoption of this act (see Poirier and Sachel 1992): they established small settlements or "outstations" within their homelands throughout the Ngukurr region. However, these outstations are no longer inhabited, and only limited transport is available for those who are willing to regularly visit these places in order to fish, hunt, collect bush foods or medicinal plants, and, more generally, care for their country.

In Indigenous Australia, the term "country" refers to the multidimensional and reciprocal relationships between a group of people, their land and sea estate, the mythical beings that have shaped this estate, and all the other non-humans connected with it: animals, plants, waters, minerals, stars, etc. Indeed, Indigenous people do not conceive the world through the prism of the Western opposition between "nature" and "culture." Their ontology – that is to say their philosophy about the world and being-in-the-world, which has actual implications in their everyday life – is rather relational, meaning that between

Figure 5.1. Ngukurr, its outstations, and the area of operation of its ranger group (author's adaptation of a map by Taylor et al. 2000: 20)

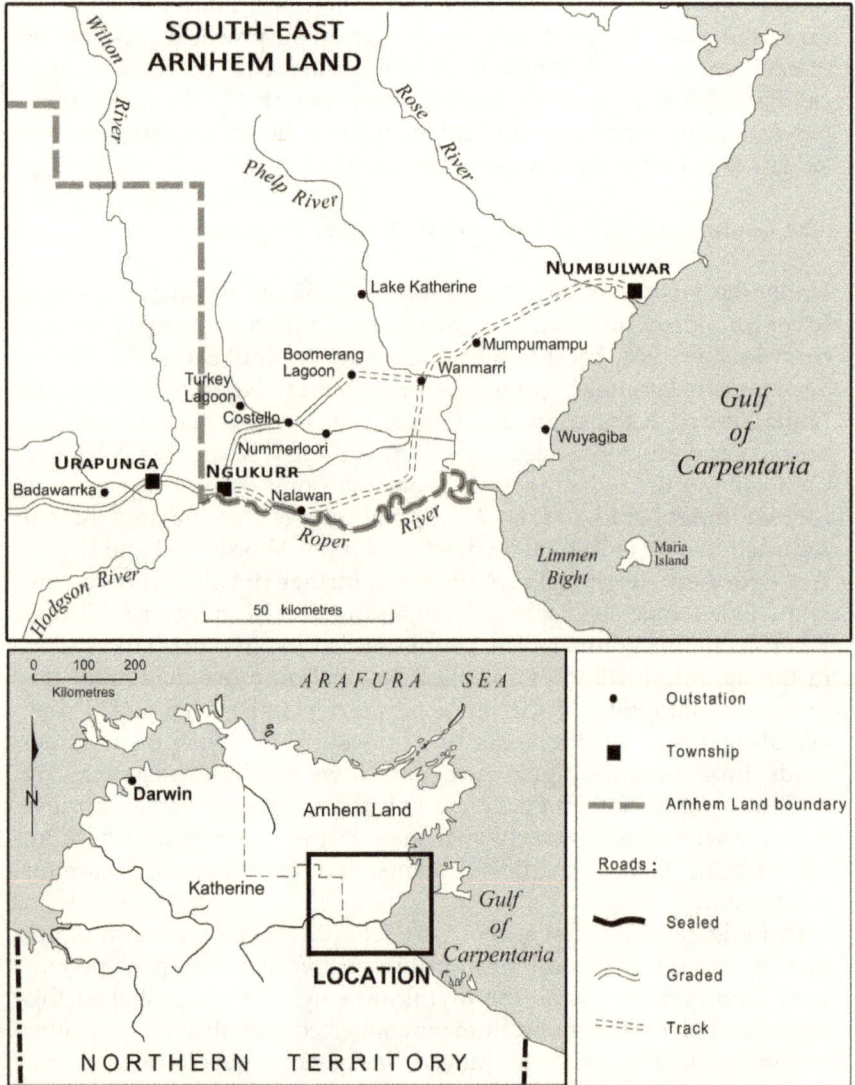

humans and non-humans boundaries are permeable and relations are negotiable (see Poirier in this volume).

In Ngukurr, rights and responsibilities for country are shared between complementary and interdependent groups of people: *mingirringgi* ("owners"), *junggayi* ("managers"), and *darlnyin* ("backups" or "supervisors"), although the Australian legal system only recognizes the *mingirringgi* as "traditional owners." A *mingirringgi* has specific rights and responsibilities on his or her country, but the *junggayi* and *darlnyin* hold the right to "talk for" that country. *Mingirringgi*, *junggayi*, and *darlnyin* are also supposed to carry out the management and protection of "sacred sites" (meaning sites created by mythical beings) in close collaboration with each other (see Fache 2015). As Seán Kerins explains below, caring for such sites and the country in which they are embedded involves physical as well as ritual and social practices:

> [C]aring for country constitutes something far greater than a person, or group of people, having a job and physically managing a geographic area by dealing with the problems created by weeds and feral animals. Caring for country encompasses being spiritually bound to country through intimate connections with ancestral beings still present in the land and waters. For Aboriginal people, caring for country is first and foremost about looking after these powerful and sacred places; protecting their values, ceremonies, songs and stories, as well as associated processes of spiritual renewal, connecting with ancestors, food provision and maintaining language, law, knowledge systems and, importantly, kin relations. (Kerins 2012: 29).

Since the creation of the local ranger program in 2002, the financial and technical means available to care for country have tended to be monopolized by Indigenous rangers, a situation that some community members consider to be problematic.

This ranger program was initially created by and for Indigenous women only. Several men who had been involved in a landcare project in the 1990s and who occasionally worked with the women rangers officially joined the program in 2007. During my fieldwork in Ngukurr in 2009 and 2010, the core of the ranger group was composed of four women and four men, between thirty and sixty-five years old,[3] who lived in and were strongly attached to Ngukurr. The Northern Land Council under the government-funded Working on Country program employed these rangers.[4] Among them, one woman and one man had the status of "senior rangers" and, from the end of 2009 onwards, one man was the "coordinator" of the group, a role that had beforehand always been assigned to non-Indigenous people. Up to four additional community members, selected by the rangers themselves, also occasionally joined the team (under the Community Development Employment Projects scheme).

The official purpose of the ranger group was "to assist Traditional Owners to care for their land and sea country" under the auspices of the Yugul Mangi Land and Sea Management Aboriginal Corporation established in 2008. This governing body included a board of directors whose members represented the seven language groups historically associated with Ngukurr. Yet this body reflected the process of bureaucratic participation that, as I have shown elsewhere (Fache 2013, 2014), is intrinsically associated with the ranger system.

The rangers' area of operation covered several thousand square kilometres in the tropical savanna zone that spans the northern third of Australia. This area may become a major part of the southeast Arnhem Land Indigenous Protected Area (IPA), which was proposed in 2010 and was in a consultation stage in July 2015. The idea of proposing this IPA did not come from the rangers or their local community, but rather from the non-Indigenous spouse of the then female Government Business Manager (GBM). GBM positions were introduced in Ngukurr and other Indigenous communities of the Northern Territory in 2007 to support the implementation and monitoring of the Howard Coalition government's Northern Territory Emergency Response (also known as the Intervention). If the southeast Arnhem Land IPA is finally declared, it would be interesting to investigate whether the analysis of IPAs offered by Frances Morphy in this volume is also relevant in this case.

At the time of my fieldwork, the rangers' activities included the controlled burning of landscapes (see Fache and Moizo 2015), the control of weeds and feral animals (see below), the removal of marine debris (such as fishnets) accumulated on beaches, fee-for-service work as part of the Northern Australia Quarantine Strategy (such as collecting ants and mosquito larvae), the harvesting of wildlife products for commercial purposes (such as crocodile eggs), and collaborative ecological research projects. Ceremonies were not recognized as an integral component of the rangers' remunerated tasks under the Working on Country program.

The "Two-Way Approach"

In northern Australia, the "two-way approach" – also known as "two-way learning," "two-way transmission," "both ways approach," or "two-toolbox approach" – was originally developed in the 1970s in the context of bilingual education programs designed for Indigenous children in some Northern Territory communities (Ens et al. 2012a: 102–3; Muller 2012: 62; Preuss and Dixon 2012: 3). "Two-way education" aims to ensure that children are partly taught in their own language and that their own knowledge system is incorporated in the school curriculum alongside Western science; it "provides the context in which both pupils and teachers can interrogate the differences and similarities between the 'two' systems of knowledge and develop the ability and understanding to apply them jointly in particular contexts" (Morphy 2002: 8).

From the 1990s onwards, the term "two-way" has increasingly been used to describe collaborative ecological research and joint methods of environmental management and conservation. It presupposes that Indigenous and non-Indigenous Australians actively share their complementary knowledge and skills in order to achieve common goals in these domains.

Joe Morrison, whose heritage is Dagoman (Northern Territory) and Torres Strait Islander, raises "the question of whether the two paradigms, of Western science and Indigenous knowledge, can be productively combined, or whether we will see a continuation of paternalistic colonial dominance of the first Australians in our supposedly postcolonial era" (2007: 254). Recent studies on the joint use of Indigenous and non-Indigenous knowledge systems for conservation purposes, referred to as the "two-way approach," have also demonstrated that this question has to be addressed very carefully.[5]

While the "two-way approach" promotes the equal valuation and use of Indigenous knowledge and Western science, its real-world implementation through ranger programs tends to result in scientific paradigms overshadowing Indigenous knowledge. Ranger groups, in northern Australia and beyond, "acknowledge that they apply Western knowledge more than IK [Indigenous Knowledge] because of the nature of the problems being addressed" or because "they are not currently holders of the [Indigenous] knowledge" (Sithole and Hunter-Xenie 2007: 56–7, 76). They also tend to regret that, in their training activities, greater weight is given to the acquisition of licences and post-secondary qualifications than to intergenerational transmission of Indigenous knowledge, whose holders are now few and aging (see also Hunt 2010: 38).

In addition, the involvement of Indigenous people should ideally be significant in all stages of "two-way" projects, but that is not systematically the case in practice. In collaborative ecological research, for instance, Wayne Barbour and Christine Schlesinger highlight how non-Indigenous ecologists struggle with "the challenge of relinquishing [to their Indigenous colleagues] ultimate control of what is done, why it is done, when and how it is done, and what is done with the information" (2012: 37); as a result, the research process may be "incompatible with the more holistic nature of Indigenous ecological knowledge and Indigenous ideas about research" (2012: 38).

In Ngukurr, the Indigenous rangers undertake land and sea management on behalf of the "traditional owners" of the region rather than in association with them, meaning that these "traditional owners" as well as the other community members[6] are *de facto* excluded from the rangers' activities. At the same time, non-Indigenous actors – scientists, agents of the Northern Land Council, staff of government agencies (such as Bushfires NT) and NGOs (such as Greening Australia), and others (such as instructors) – are involved in each of the rangers' projects. As we shall now illustrate, this situation influences the categories and paradigms that emerge from the ranger program.

The "Two-Way Approach" in Action: The Ideology of Ecological Purity

The control of "weeds" and "feral animals" is a major task for many Indigenous ranger groups throughout northern Australia. It consists, for instance, in spraying a patch of plants classified as "weeds" with chemicals to eradicate them, or in culling a number of pigs or horses to take blood samples or undertake post-mortem analyses. These activities are generally based on the "two-way approach" and therefore involve diverse governmental or non-governmental agencies and non-Indigenous actors alongside Indigenous rangers. The implementation of these activities around Ngukurr highlights how the non-Indigenous actors who use their scientific background to support Indigenous rangers introduce the latter and their community to – or even tend to impose on them – concepts, priorities, and practices grounded on a non-Indigenous understanding of the "natural" environment.

Through their involvement in the management of "weeds" and "feral animals," these non-Indigenous actors convey an ideology of ecological purity, which differs from the views and aspirations expressed by Indigenous community members.

"Weeds" are presented as one of the most significant environmental threats in the Northern Territory (e.g., NLC 2004: 17). Indigenous rangers' tasks include the control or eradication of several plant species classified as "weeds of national significance," such as *Mimosa pigra* and *Parkinsonia aculeata*. During my field research in 2009 and 2010, the Indigenous rangers based in Ngukurr defined "weeds" as exogenous plants (coming from Africa, Asia, or America) that were introduced in Australia "a long time ago" and that have become "pests," meaning invasive plants that compete with and therefore threaten "native plants and trees."

During conversations and interviews, the rangers explained that they had learnt about "weeds" and associated environmental issues during their professional training delivered by instructors or governmental or non-governmental agents, as well as through booklets these actors left behind them. Some of the rangers had also developed their knowledge and skills in this domain by way of their land management courses and certificates. They pointed out that previous generations, like themselves before they became rangers, were not aware of the impacts of "weeds."

The rangers also endeavoured to pass on information about these plants to family members, especially about poisonous "weeds" such as Bellyache Bush (*Jatropha gossypiifolia*), whose fruits and seeds are toxic when ingested. Some community members regarded the rangers, who could identify such plants and attempted to control them, as being "specialists" or "experts" in "weeds." Such an expertise focuses on a well-defined component of the environment rather than considering that everything is interconnected in a holistic way. Such an expertise also is recognized on the basis of professional status and skills, while knowledge about the flora is usually shared – and sometimes restricted – on the basis of social belonging (language group, clan membership, moiety, semi-moiety, subsection),[7] kinship position, gender, and age.

Yet community members' knowledge of "weeds" remained fragmentary. As was also highlighted by Barbour and Schlesinger, "some Indigenous people, generally those who have been exposed to Western concepts of NRM [natural resource management], share the Western conservationist view that weeds are undesirable, foreign, invasive species, while others, who may not have been exposed to these ideas, do not know what a weed is" (2012: 38). For younger generations in particular, "weed" was a synonym for "ganja," a word used in *Kriol* to refer to cannabis.

Interestingly, the oldest community members first and foremost associated the "weeds" category with an aquatic plant species growing in permanent ponds, also known as billabongs. They classified this plant as a "weed" because they had observed its increasing spread during the last twenty years, and from their own perspective this was a major source of concern, especially with regard to the health of fish species and water lilies. Nevertheless, governmental agencies and Western ecologists did not recognize this plant as a "weed," and the Indigenous rangers therefore neither identified it as a "weed" nor tried to control its spread. Some community members did attempt to persuade the rangers (and, via the rangers, the institutions involved in broader environmental governance and conservation) that their concerns were well founded, and that the unrecognized "weed" should be included in weed management activities. For instance, a woman in her fifties asked me to photograph the aquatic plant and a wounded fish (according to her, the wound was caused by the plant), hoping that the rangers would intervene after seeing this evidence, but without success.

This particular case illustrates well the existence of "partial connections" (Strathern 1991; see also Dussart and Poirier in this volume) between local uses of the "weeds" category and the official definition of a "weed," that is, "any plant growing out of place and [that] can be both a symptom and a cause of land degradation," and, therefore, "any plant that requires some form of action to reduce its effect on the economy, the environment, human health and amenity."[8] It also demonstrates that the rangers' perspectives and agendas are not necessarily consistent with the concerns expressed by other community members. This observation reflects a tension inherent in local understandings of what the ranger program provides the community. While community members tended to see this program as a means to "properly" care for the entire region where outstations are no longer inhabited, they also described it as "a new system introduced by the government" and as interfering with the way land and sea management should be organized. The rangers were indeed supposed to comply with local expectations and bureaucratic requirements at the same time (see Fache 2013, 2014).

Barbour and Schlesinger invite "ecological scientists" to consider whether they can "justify imposing their views about weeds on Indigenous land managers, without giving them the right to decide for themselves" (2012: 38–9). Another issue also should be noted: Indigenous rangers tend to impose their own views about weeds within their community, instead of taking account of local understandings and concerns.

Such questions resonate with issues raised by "two-way" research and management activities focused on "feral animals." "Feral animals" is a generic category referring to introduced animal species, initially domesticated but returned to an untamed state. According to the Northern Land Council, Aboriginal landowners in the region under its authority – the Top End of the Northern Territory – "are generally concerned about the environmental damage caused by large vertebrates, cane toads and insects" (NLC 2004: 19). In this region, the large vertebrates are buffalo (*Bubalus bubalis*), pigs (*Sus scrofa*), horses (*Equus caballus*), and, to a lesser extent, donkeys (*Equus asinus*), while in Central Australia they are mainly camels (*Camelus dromedarius*), which Petronella Vaarzon-Morel covers in this volume. These ungulates in southeast Arnhem Land are classified by the government (at the national level as well as in the Northern Territory) as "feral animals," and are thereby recognized as threats to native fauna and flora.[9]

In 2009 and 2010, the Indigenous rangers based in Ngukurr were involved with a non-Indigenous ecologist based in Canberra in a "two-way ecological research" on the impacts of ungulates in wetlands (see Ens 2009, 2012; Ens et al. 2012b; Fache 2013). The project consisted of excluding so-called "feral animals" from three fenced freshwater billabongs, which were to be monitored for five years to compare their health status with unfenced areas. The main purpose was to "demonstrate the damage that feral animals have on country" to the "traditional owners" of the region (Ens 2009: 1) so that they could make informed decisions about the fate of these animals. The "traditional owners" were presented with several options, phrased as follows:

Do we want to:
- Keep feral animals (pigs, buffalo and horses) and let them damage country?
- Control them to a certain level of acceptable damage?
- Cull them all and help restore the country to how it used to be before the feral animals came? (Ens 2009: 2)

Each option suggests that the "feral animals" category is consensual and homogeneous, and that its constituent species are pests damaging the environment. In fact, the research aimed to convince "traditional owners" and the other community members that "feral animals" were causing major ecological problems and that these problems could be fixed by partial or total culling, even if culling was generally perceived as cruel and wasteful from an Indigenous perspective (see Vaarzon-Morel in this volume).

During my field research in Ngukurr, I observed that the Indigenous rangers themselves had adopted this discourse. However, the other community members' perspectives on buffalo, pigs, horses, and donkeys were diverse and more complex. These different species were perceived neither as belonging to a generic category nor systematically as an environmental threat. For instance, a male elder of the community was of the opinion that "They don't do any damage. Some people might think they do. I don't know. I think they are just animals that were unfortunate that, you know, they got stuck here or travelled a long way to be up here" (personal communication, 5 August 2009). Some other community members had never considered the impacts of these animals on country because they had not been able to visit their outstations for a long time and were therefore unaware of changes in the landscapes. This was the case with a middle-aged woman who informed me that she had heard and thought about the matter for the first time when she joined the ranger group for a few months in 2009.

Furthermore, community members who believed that buffalo, pigs, horses, and donkeys did damage their country also conveyed positive views of these animals, especially with regard to economic benefits derived from their commercial exploitation. Buffalo, they explained, can be exploited for human consumption or valued as game in the context of tourist safaris. Horses can be used in the cattle industry and their meat can be sold for pet consumption. Aesthetic, symbolic, and social considerations were also expressed. The beauty of horses was generally admired, and, like camels in Central Australia, donkeys were associated with Christianity. Horses, buffalo, and pigs were sometimes treated as pets, having names and sometimes skin names.[10] While camels are classified as "feral animals" by the Australian government and Western ecologists, the Ngaatjatjarra people in the Western Desert associate each individual camel, perceived as showing emotions and empathy, with a personal name and genealogy. For them, camels and dogs are indeed the only animals having the capacity to engage in social relationships with human beings (Dousset 2014: 146–51; see also Vaarzon-Morel in this volume). Similarly, in Ngukurr, it seems that so-called "feral" horses, buffalo, and pigs can individually obtain a social status and engage in relationships with human beings in a way that no animals other than dogs can experience.[11]

In addition, for community members who did perceive buffalo, pigs, horses, and donkeys as environmental threats, none of the generic options suggested above was relevant. They accepted the idea of culling buffalo and pigs but dismissed the idea of culling horses and donkeys as inappropriate. And because they did not want animals to be killed "for nothing," they rather contemplated the option – regardless of its practical feasibility – of relocating them in their country of origin.

Such Indigenous perspectives do not fit well with the Western perspective that "feral animals" have disturbed the formerly untouched state of the environment, remain exogenous, and should all be removed so that the environment can recover its so-called integrity. Yet the rangers conveyed these ideas through their "two-way ecological research."

Processes of Mediation

Drawing on my ethnography, I consider that one can better understand the practices and challenges inherent in the "two-way approach" when one analyses them using the concept of mediation.[12] Like the notion of entanglement (see Dussart and Poirier in this volume), the concept of mediation evokes the complex relations between connectedness and distinctiveness faced by Indigenous peoples under policies of partial recognition. Indeed, this concept refers to the process of connecting and establishing communication between what are perceived as two dynamically distinct worlds, systems of meaning, and cultures (see Blundo 1995: 77). Such a process involves the transformation of the meaning of things and practices so that they become relevant within both universes. In the context of the "two-way approach," mediation is focused on integrating Indigenous knowledge applied to natural resource management (or "traditional ecological knowledge") with Western science; each system of knowledge is dynamic rather than monolithic. Mediation involves the building of cross-cultural categories – such as "weeds" and "feral animals" – that are supposed to become, in Howard Morphy's words, both "a basis for inclusion of disparate social and cultural phenomena within the same conceptual framework and a means of creating a framework for expressing difference" (2002: 5).

However, I privilege here the concept of mediation over the notion of entanglement in order to draw attention to the actors who take on an intermediate position between Indigenous and non-Indigenous knowledge systems in order to facilitate their encounter and allow their correlation. As understood here, mediation requires that identified knowledge holders establish a dialogue and undertake a work of mutual translation. Indigenous rangers and their non-Indigenous collaborators (scientists, agents of land councils, staff of governmental agencies and NGOs, instructors, etc.) involved in joint projects assume this role of knowledge holder. Indigenous rangers are promoted to the status of custodians and spokespersons of "traditional ecological knowledge" on the basis of their professional function, at least in the context of formalized land and sea management, even if they have not yet necessarily acquired such a status in the eyes of other community members. They are thus entrusted with the intricate responsibility to mediate between local "traditional ecological knowledge" and their non-Indigenous collaborators' technical-scientific knowledge, meaning to co-produce cross-cultural categories in dialogue with these collaborators. Their main challenge is to ensure that their knowledge, and thereby their beliefs, values, social relations, and practices, are not simply subsumed into their non-Indigenous collaborators' categories, nor distorted to become compatible with bureaucratic modes of environmental management (see Nadasdy 2003b: 369).

Michael Howard (1978), John Von Sturmer (1982), Hans Dagmar (1990), and Philip Batty (2005), among others, have highlighted that Indigenous Australians who act as mediators or brokers between their local community and "the non-Aboriginal world of mining companies and government" or "the wider society" have to face complex situations. Acting as a mediator or broker tends to be a mechanism of disassociation and isolation from the local community (Dagmar 1990: 113; Howard 1978: 29). According to Von Sturmer, Indigenous mediators or brokers "may be courted, feared, but are never acknowledged as 'bosses' ... of the knowledge, the information which legitimates their power base" (1982: 95). In addition, their local community can accuse them of exploiting their role for personal gain, or even request them to prove their legitimacy, that is to say their affiliations with specific groups of belonging and areas of land, their connections with certain "traditions," their "Aboriginality" (Batty 2005: 219). Similarly, Indigenous rangers have an ambiguous position within their own community, at least in Ngukurr. They are both community members and, because of their mediation role, the interface – or even gatekeepers – between the local population and the diverse non-Indigenous actors who are involved in formalized land and sea management within their area of operation. Furthermore, they are supposed to be custodians of local "traditions" with regard to caring for country while trying to combine these "traditions" with ecological concepts, priorities, and practices. They are therefore continuously caught in "double bind" situations: as mediators, they face injunctions that are extremely difficult (or impossible?) to satisfy at the same time.

Non-Indigenous collaborators also occupy an intricate role in "two-way" projects. They introduce Indigenous rangers to Western scientific paradigms and protocols. At the same time, they endeavour to integrate Indigenous world views, land and sea management practices, and preferred methods of work in such paradigms and protocols. For instance, in the the "two-way" research on "feral animals" presented above, the monitoring of fenced and unfenced billabongs associated non-Indigenous quantitative methods (such as collecting data about the ground surface and ground cover along one-hundred-metre long transects, and testing the temperature, pH, conductivity, and turbidity of water using electronic water quality metres) with "'traditional' Indigenous observational analysis of change" (Ens et al. 2012b: 28–9). Nevertheless, local views of so-called "feral animals" were not included in the project when it was first developed.

One of the corollaries of this analysis is that non-Indigenous actors are increasingly and actively involved in creating the domain of "natural (and cultural) resource management" within Indigenous-owned lands. The "two-way approach" transfers to them a significant number of local responsibilities for country (see also Fache 2014; Fache and Moizo 2015). Therefore, encouraging "two-way" initiatives is tantamount to endorsing the decrease of community members' control of their own affairs under the guise of, as phrased by Ens (2012: 63), "empower[ing] local Indigenous people so they can regain control of the management of their ancestral lands." This situation echoes the ambiguities of the Indigenous self-determination policy developed by the Australian government in the 1970s: Indigenous people's power to run their own affairs was to be restored through building an Indigenous bureaucracy modelled on, and linked to, the state bureaucracy (see Batty 2005; Rowse 1992). This policy paradoxically implied that "further dependence was required to achieve independence; management by whites was needed to realize self-management" (Cowlishaw 1999: 234).

It is worth stressing that the "two-way approach" requires real-world encounters between Indigenous and non-Indigenous social actors who have divergent as well as changeable rationales. Their interactions therefore involve misunderstandings and negotiations, gaps between agreed purposes and practical operations, asymmetries of power, and tensions or conflicts. For instance, during my field research in Ngukurr, I observed that the Indigenous rangers did not work on the "two-way" research on "feral animals" outside the one- or two-week working sessions organized by their non-Indigenous collaborator, who was a woman in her thirties. Even during these sessions, when the non-Indigenous ecologist was on site, the involvement of the rangers, particularly the men, was limited, and had to be negotiated. The rangers' time and efforts could be shared between this research and another project such as "fire management" (controlled burning of landscapes), a core aspect of caring for country responsibilities to which the men gave priority over the control of so-called "feral animals." Some rangers also did not wish to be involved in the monitoring of fenced and unfenced billabongs. In a context where personal feelings were recognized as legitimate reasons for action or for "not doing something" (see Burbank 2006: 6–7), the rangers did not feel like being involved in monitoring activities because they faced family problems during the working sessions, they considered the process of data collection "boring," or they were a posteriori dissatisfied with some of the arrangements decided with their non-Indigenous collaborator.

Because the "two-way approach" implies complex interactions between social actors of different cultural backgrounds, rather than just between disembodied knowledge systems and geographically distant institutions, it raises important issues regarding the sharing of knowledge (see also Sithole and Hunter-Xenie 2007: 55–7).

First, Indigenous rangers' and their non-Indigenous collaborators' capacity for mediation would ideally be based on pre-existing, extensive understanding of each other's knowledge systems. In practice, however, the stage of mutual learning is rarely, if ever, completed. One of the main purposes of the "two-way approach" is the learning of mainstream ecological knowledge and natural resource management knowledge by Indigenous rangers and, through them, land-owning groups. The non-Indigenous actors in charge of facilitating the learning process have themselves acquired such knowledge through many years of educational and professional experience. Their knowledge is associated with their mastering of specialized categories (such as "weeds" and "feral animals"), their understanding of Western institutions, and their own world view and set of values. The extent of this background, coupled with limited funding, which restricts the social interactions required for knowledge sharing, renders this learning process very challenging.

For their part, Indigenous people see the "two-way approach" as an opportunity to document their "traditional ecological knowledge" and thereby facilitate intergenerational transmission (on the commitment to transmit knowledge to younger generations, see Poirier in this volume for a Canadian example). When in 2007 I first met the women rangers of Ngukurr, then led by a sixty-five-year-old doyenne, they wanted my own research to focus on water lilies in order to provide an opportunity to get young girls involved in "traditional knowledge" about these plants. They were particularly willing to teach them the way to grind water-lily seeds and use the flour to make flatbreads, a know-how that only a few "old women" still held. The women rangers finally gave up on the project for several reasons that I cannot detail here. However, this project illustrates their broader ambition to teach young girls about the food, medicinal, and craft uses of plants, and thereby contribute to the maintenance of these girls' relationships with country. It also reveals that they deemed the support of non-Indigenous collaborators necessary to achieve such an ambition.

Some Indigenous people, however, are reluctant to share knowledge with non-Indigenous people. One major reason behind this reluctance relates to the issue of knowledge repatriation. Non-Indigenous people dealing with "traditional ecological knowledge," especially in the domains of natural resource management and research, are now expected to respect intellectual property rights. Best practices include "the return of any knowledge, in the form of data,[13] that has been removed from the location from which it was obtained," and this in compliance with local protocols (see Holcombe 2009: 18–19). In the (sometimes recent) past, however, ethnoscience research did not systematically involve a process of knowledge repatriation. As a result, some Indigenous people are still not confident that the knowledge they share with non-Indigenous people will be returned to them.[14]

Another source of concern pertains to questions of legitimacy. In Indigenous Australia, knowledge cannot be transferred to anybody or by anybody. A significant part of Indigenous knowledge is considered to be sacred and secret. Such knowledge is held only by initiated men or women who have specific relationships with the sites, mythical beings, and rituals concerned, and is passed on in the context of highly codified ceremonial activities. More generally, Indigenous knowledge is gender specific, dependent on social and genealogical positions, and progressively acquired through active involvement in religious and other arenas. The sharing of Indigenous knowledge with non-Indigenous people is therefore fundamentally controlled.

As far as non-restricted (meaning non-sacred and non-secret) knowledge of country is concerned, it is supposed to be passed on to outsiders by people having customary responsibilities and rights for country, entitled to talk for and about country. In Ngukurr, as we have seen, such people have the status of *mingirringgi* ("owners"), *junggayi* ("managers"), and *darlnyin* ("backups" or "supervisors"). The "two-way approach" does not always comply with this protocol. Indigenous rangers are invited to share knowledge related to the entire region with outsiders in contexts that do not systematically allow the right persons' involvement or previous permission. Furthermore, the persons having customary responsibilities and rights for country may not be regarded by all as worthy holders of "traditional ecological knowledge." Indeed, the most knowledgeable people often die before having completed the process of intergenerational transmission, and younger people are not always available (e.g., because of schooling), able (e.g., because of language loss), or willing (e.g., because knowledge means responsibilities) to learn from them.

Although knowledge sharing is at the core of the "two-way approach," this very expression suggests that a compartmentalization is maintained between what would be fundamentally Indigenous and what would be fundamentally non-Indigenous knowledge systems. Yet since the colonial period, there have been mutual – even if unequal – influences between these knowledge systems and the associated world views (see Morphy 2002). For instance, as illustrated by the case of so-called "feral animals," the Indigenous Australians' holistic understanding of caring for country highlighted by Kerins (2012: 29; quoted above) is not devoid of Christian beliefs, ecological concerns, and hopes for economic development.

Since the mid-1990s, ranger programs in northern Australia have become a key context in which Indigenous and non-Indigenous actors are supposed to create, through their social interactions and dialogues, new ways of thinking about and caring for the environment that make the most of their diverging perspectives and produce a context-specific entanglement. The knowledge systems involved, as well as the corresponding ways of thinking human/non-human relationships, are indeed not hermetic: hybridizations between them have preceded and are broader than, but are still amplified by, the "two-way approach." Nevertheless, both Indigenous and non-Indigenous actors conceive their knowledge sharing as a juxtaposition of separate Indigenous and non-Indigenous components which preserves the specificity and encapsulatedness of divergent world views (see the notion of "relative autonomy" introduced by Morphy in this volume).

Conclusion

While epistemological, ontological, social, and political challenges are increasingly recognized, the "two-way approach" continues to be presented by Indigenous and non-Indigenous, governmental and non-governmental actors alike as necessary for effective research, management, and conservation of the environment in the Northern Territory. This approach aims to offer an alternative to the integration of Indigenous knowledge in scientific protocols pre-established through top-down processes. Under the "two-way approach" framework, Indigenous and non-Indigenous knowledge systems are supposed to be recognized and used on an equitable basis through bottom-up collaborations. Yet asymmetries of power are still embedded in, and reproduced by, these "two-way" initiatives. There have been some attempts to consolidate the foundations of such initiatives to ensure that they create "a language of equals between Indigenous and non-Indigenous sciences" (Muller 2012: 76; e.g., Ens et al. 2012a; e.g., Preuss and Dixon 2012: 12–14). However, the very idea that knowledge combination is necessary reveals that Indigenous knowledge is not valued in its own terms, but only validated when correlated with Western science. The "two-way approach" thus has to be reshaped if the next step is to further promote Indigenous ways of knowing.

Using the concept of mediation, my analysis emphasizes that this "two-way approach" aims to connect Indigenous knowledge and Western science, but is founded on – and reproduces – the assumption that these knowledge systems are and will remain fundamentally distinct and rooted in an "ontological divide" (Muller 2012). It also demonstrates that our attention should no longer focus solely on this ongoing disctinctiveness, but rather on how knowledge entanglements are performed, that is to say on the social interactions and dialogues (or the "sites of articulation"; see Morphy in this volume) between Indigenous and non-Indigenous actors acting as mediators.

The "weed" and "feral animal" control cases discussed in this chapter reveal some of the politics and challenges involved in the building of cross-cultural categories for conservation purposes. They also raise important questions of legitimacy with regard to knowledge sharing. Above all, because of their mediation role, Indigenous rangers have to continuously negotiate their legitimacy in the eyes of both their local community and their non-Indigenous collaborators, whose expectations and aspirations are not necessarily similar. They thereby contribute to the organization of new modes of knowledge transmission in which their role is central. Such a role provides them with a new power base, a status of specialists in the domain of formalized land and sea management, and material and immaterial resources (such as jobs and salaries, vehicles and driving licences, training and certificates, attendance at meetings and events throughout Australia, etc.). At the same time, their credentials may be challenged whenever they do not manage to comply with the diverging demands they face.

For their part, non-Indigenous actors involved in "two-way" initiatives generally aim to respond to Indigenous people's aspirations "to be valued and to have ownership of the research and management that is occurring on their country" (Barbour and Schlesinger 2012: 38). Paradoxically, their involvement in the projects of Indigenous rangers means that the latter and their local community do not fully control the ecological research and land and sea management activities conducted within their territory.

ACKNOWLEDGMENTS

This chapter is based on research funded through a PhD scholarship granted by Aix-Marseille University (2008–11) and smaller grants from CREDO (Centre for Research and Documentation on Oceania, France). I am grateful to the scholars who have contributed to my work on this topic through discussions and comments, in particular Jon Altman, Seán Kerins, Julian Gorman, and Laurent Dousset. My deepest thanks go to the people of Ngukurr, especially the Yugul Mangi Rangers.

NOTES

1 Since the 1970s, Indigenous land rights have been recognized by the Australian government through specific legislation such as the Aboriginal Land Rights (Northern Territory) Act 1976, and some Indigenous groups have obtained collective titles over defined areas that had been confiscated during the colonial period. These land-owning groups are commonly referred to as "traditional owners," a statutory category applied to "a local descent group of Aboriginals who: (a) have common spiritual affiliations to a site on the land, being affiliations that place the group under a primary spiritual responsibility for that site and for the land; and (b) are entitled by Aboriginal tradition to forage as of right over that land" (Holcombe 2004: 65)

2 For a detailed presentation of the ethnographic and theoretical context of my research, see Fache 2013, 2014.

3 Three were over fifty years old, and three around forty years old.

4 The Northern Land Council is "an independent statutory authority of the Commonwealth." Established in the 1970s, it is "responsible for assisting Aboriginal peoples in the Top End of the Northern Territory to acquire and manage their traditional lands and seas." See http://www.nlc.org.au/ (accessed 9 September 2014).

5 See for example the journal *Ecological Management and Restoration*'s special issue on "Indigenous land and sea management in remote Australia" (2012), http://onlinelibrary.wiley.com/doi/10.1111/emr.2012.13.issue-1/issuetoc (accessed 4 June 2014).

6 Including the board of the Yugul Mangi Land and Sea Management Aboriginal Corporation.

7 In Ngukurr, the system of social organization is based on the complementary moieties Duwa and Yirritja (every human and non-human belongs to one of these two categories) as well as semi-moieties and named subsections.

8 See "Weeds" on the website of the Northern Territory Government's Department of Land Resource Management, https://landresources.nt.gov. au/weeds (accessed 12 June 2014), and "Weeds in Australia" on the website of the federal government's Department of the Environment, http://www. environment.gov.au/biodiversity/invasive/weeds/weeds/what.html (accessed 11 September 2014). The way the non-Indigenous actors involved in the rangers' activities and training understand the concept of "weed" may vary from this definition.

9 See "Feral Animals" on the website of the Northern Territory Government's Department of Land Resource Management, https://landresources.nt.gov.au/ feral (accessed 13 June 2014), and "Feral Animals in Australia" on the website

of the federal government's Department of the Environment, http://www.
environment.gov.au/biodiversity/invasive-species/feral-animals-australia
(accessed 13 June 2014).

10 Skin names classify the concerned animals in the local social organization,
in the same subsection as the pet owners' children.

11 I have not observed situations in which donkeys become pets, probably
because they are less common than horses, buffalo, and pigs in the
Ngukurr region.

12 This analysis is inspired by the literature on "local development brokers"
in contemporary Africa (see for instance Bierschenk et al. 2000; Blundo
1995; Olivier de Sardan 1995).

13 For instance, maps, audiovisual materials, or lists of names and uses for
local plant species.

14 Sithole and Hunter-Xenie reported that "many of the Traditional Owners"
interviewed in the context of their community-driven evaluation of
Aboriginal land and sea management in the Top End of the Northern
Territory observed that "some IK [Indigenous Knowledge] has been
passed on to researchers (scientists and anthropologists) and communities
are finding it hard to get that knowledge back" (2007: 55–6).

REFERENCES

Barbour, Wayne, and Christine Schlesinger. 2012. "Who's the Boss? Post-
Colonialism, Ecological Research and Conservation Management on
Australian Indigenous Lands." *Ecological Management & Restoration* 13 (1):
36–41. http://dx.doi.org/10.1111/j.1442-8903.2011.00632.x.

Batty, Philip. 2005. "Private Politics, Public Strategies: White Advisers and
Their Aboriginal Subjects." *Oceania* 75 (3): 209–21. http://dx.doi.org/
10.1002/j.1834-4461.2005.tb02881.x.

Bierschenk, Thomas, Jean-Pierre Chauveau, and Jean-Pierre Olivier de Sardan,
eds. 2000. *Courtiers en développement: Les villages africains en quête de projets*
[Development Brokers: African Villages in Search of Projects]. Paris: APAD,
Karthala.

Blundo, Giorgio. 1995. "Les Courtiers du développement en milieu rural
sénégalais" [Development Brokers in Rural Senegal]. *Cahiers d'Etudes
Africaines* 35 (137): 73–99. http://dx.doi.org/10.3406/cea.1995.2024.

Burbank, Victoria. 2006. "From Bedtime to on Time: Why Many Aboriginal People
Don't Especially Like Participating in Western Institutions." *Anthropological
Forum* 16 (1): 3–20. http://dx.doi.org/10.1080/00664670600572330.

Cowlishaw, Gillian. 1999. *Rednecks, Eggheads, and Blackfellas: A Study of Racial Power and Intimacy in Australia*. Ann Arbor: University of Michigan Press.

Dagmar, Hans. 1990. "Development and Politics in an Interethnic Field: Aboriginal Interest Associations." In *Going It Alone: Prospects for Aboriginal Autonomy: Essays in Honour of Ronald and Catherine Berndt*, ed. Robert Tonkinson and Michael Howard, 99–123. Canberra: Aboriginal Studies Press.

Dousset, Laurent. 2014. "Pour une anthropologie de l'incertitude: Une autre introduction aux Aborigènes d'Australie" [For an Anthropology of Uncertainty: Another Introduction to Indigenous Australians]. HRD dissertation, Department of Social Anthropology, University of Strasbourg.

Ens, Emilie Jane. 2009. Freshwater Billabong Monitoring and Protection from Feral Animals. Report prepared with Yugul Mangi Rangers for Community and Greening Australia NT. Canberra: ANU, CAEPR. http://caepr.anu.edu.au/Freshwater-Billabong-Monitoring-and-Protection-Feral-Animals.php

Ens, Emilie Jane. 2012. "Conducting Two-Way Ecological Research." In *People on Country, Vital Landscapes, Indigenous Futures*, ed. Jon Altman and Seán Kerins, 45–64. Sydney: Federation Press.

Ens, Emilie Jane, Max Finlayson, Karissa Preuss, Sue Jackson, and Sarah Holcombe. 2012a. "Australian Approaches for Managing 'Country' Using Indigenous and Non-Indigenous Knowledge." *Ecological Management and Restoration* 13 (1): 100–7. http://dx.doi.org/10.1111/j.1442-8903.2011.00634.x.

Ens, Emilie Jane, Gillian M. Towler, Cherry Daniels, the Yugul Mangi Rangers, and the Manwurrk Rangers. 2012b. "Looking Back to Move Forward: Collaborative Ecological Monitoring in Remote Arnhem Land." *Ecological Management and Restoration* 13 (1): 26–35. http://dx.doi.org/10.1111/j.1442-8903.2011.00627.x.

Fache, Elodie. 2013. "Impérialisme écologique ou développement? Les acteurs de la gestion des ressources naturelles à Ngukurr en Australie" [Ecological Imperialism or Development? The Actors of Natural Resource Management in Ngukurr, Australia]. PhD dissertation, Department of Social Anthropology, Aix-Marseille University.

Fache, Elodie. 2014. "Caring for Country, a Form of Bureaucratic Participation: Conservation, Development and Neoliberalism in Indigenous Australia." *Anthropological Forum* 24 (3): 267–86.

Fache, Elodie. 2015. "Les droits et responsabilités aborigènes envers la terre à Ngukurr (Terre d'Arnhem, Australie du Nord) sont-ils 'reconnus'?" [Are Aboriginal Land Rights and Responsibilities "Recognized" in Ngukurr (Arnhem Land, Northern Australia)?]. In *Les conceptions de la propriété foncière à l'épreuve des revendications autochtones: Possession, propriété et leurs avatars* [Conceptions of Land Ownership in the Context of Indigenous Land

Claims: Possession, Property and Their Avatars], ed. Maïa Ponsonnet and Céline Travési, 119–42. Marseille: Pacific-Credo Publications.

Fache, Elodie, and Bernard Moizo. 2015. "Do Burning Practices Contribute to Caring for Country? Contemporary Uses of Fire for Conservation Purposes in Indigenous Australia." *Journal of Ethnobiology* 35 (1): 163–82. http://dx.doi.org/10.2993/0278-0771-35.1.163.

Holcombe, Sarah. 2004. "Traditional Owners and 'Community-Country' Anangu: Distinctions and Dilemmas." *Australian Aboriginal Studies* 2: 64–71.

Holcombe, Sarah. 2009. *Indigenous Ecological Knowledge and Natural Resources in the Northern Territory: Guidelines for Indigenous Ecological Knowledge Management (Including Archiving and Repatriation).* Darwin: Natural Resources Management Board.

Howard, Michael C. 1978. "Aboriginal 'Leadership' in the Southwest of Western Australia." In *Whitefella Business: Aborigines in Australian Politics,* ed. Michael Howard, 13–36. Philadelphia: Institute for the Study of Human Issues.

Hunt, Janet. 2010. "Looking after Country in New South Wales: Two Case Studies of Socioeconomic Benefits for Aboriginal People." CAEPR Working Paper 75. Canberra: ANU.

Kerins, Seán. 2012. "Caring for Country to Working on Country." In *People on Country, Vital Landscapes, Indigenous Futures,* ed. Jon Altman and Seán Kerins, 26–44. Sydney: Federation Press.

McGregor, Deborah. 2004. "Traditional Ecological Knowledge and Sustainable Development: Towards Coexistence." In *In the Way of Development: Indigenous Peoples, Life Projects, and Globalization,* ed. Mario Blaser, Harvey A. Feit, and Glenn McRae, 72–91. London and New York: Zed Books and Ottawa: Canadian International Development Research Centre.

Morphy, Howard. 2002. "Cross-Cultural Categories: Yolngu Science and Local Discourses." Paper presented at the 9th International Conference on Hunting and Gathering Societies, Edinburgh, 9–13 September, http://livingknowledge.anu.edu.au/html/background/discussions/morphy_yolnguscience.htm, accessed 9 September 2014.

Morrison, Joe. 2007. "Caring for Country." In *Coercive Reconciliation: Stabilise, Normalise, Exit Aboriginal Australia,* ed. Jon Altman and Melinda Hinkson, 249–61. North Carlton, Vic.: Arena Publications Association.

Muller, Samantha. 2012. "'Two Ways': Bringing Indigenous and Non-Indigenous Knowledges Together." In *Country, Native Title and Ecology,* ed. Jessica K. Weir, 59–79. Canberra: ANU e-Press.

Nadasdy, Paul. 1999. "The Politics of TEK: Power and the 'Integration' of Knowledge." *Arctic Anthropology* 36 (1–2): 1–18.

Nadasdy, Paul. 2003a. *Hunters and Bureaucrats: Power, Knowledge, and Aboriginal-State Relations in the Southwest Yukon.* Vancouver: University of British Columbia Press.

Nadasdy, Paul. 2003b. "Reevaluating the Co-Management Success Story." *Arctic* 56 (4): 367–80. http://dx.doi.org/10.14430/arctic634.

NLC (Northern Land Council). 2004. Environmental Management Status Reports for Aboriginal Lands in the Northern Land Council Region: A Supporting Document to the Caring for Country Strategy 2003–2006. Darwin: NLC, Caring for Country Unit.

Olivier de Sardan, Jean-Pierre. 1995. *Anthropologie et développement: Essai en socio-anthropologie du changement social* [Anthropology and Development: An Essay in Socio-Anthropology of Social Change]. Paris: Karthala, APAD.

Poirier, Sylvie, and Alain Sachel. 1992. "Le mouvement des outstations australiennes" [The Australian Outstation Movement]. *Anthropologie et Sociétés* 16 (3): 119–26. http://dx.doi.org/10.7202/015236ar.

Preuss, Karissa, and Madeline Dixon. 2012. "'Looking after Country Two-Ways': Insights into Indigenous Community-Based Conservation from the Southern Tanami." *Ecological Management and Restoration* 13 (1): 2–15. http://dx.doi.org/10.1111/j.1442-8903.2011.00631.x.

Rowse, Tim. 1992. *Remote Possibilities: The Aboriginal Domain and the Administrative Imagination.* Darwin: North Australia Research Unit, ANU.

Sithole, Bevlyne, and Hmalan Hunter-Xenie (with the collaboration of Lorraine Williams, Jonnie Saegenschnitter, Dean Yibarbuk, Matthew Ryan, Otto Campion, Balupalu Yunupingu, Mona Liddy, Elaine Watts, Cherry Daniels, Grace Daniels, Peter Christophersen, Victor Cubillo, Eddie Phillips, Wanyubi Marika, Donna Jackson, and Wayne Barbour). 2007. *Aboriginal Land and Sea Management in the Top End: A Community-Driven Evaluation.* Darwin: CSIRO.

Strathern, Marilyn. 1991. *Partial Connections.* Lanham, MD: Rowman and Littlefield Publishers.

Taylor, John, John E. Bern, and Kate Senior. 2000. *Ngukurr at the Millennium: A Baseline Profile for Social Impact Planning in South-East Arnhem Land.* CAEPR Research Monograph 18. Canberra: ANU.

Tsing, Anna Lowenhaupt, J. Peter Brosius, and Charles Zerner. 2005. "Introduction: Raising Questions about Communities and Conservation." In *Communities and Conservation: Histories and Politics of Community-Based Natural Resource Management*, ed. J. Peter Brosius, Anna Lowenhaupt Tsing, and Charles Zerner, 1–34. Lanham, MD: AltaMira Press.

United Nations. 1992. Agenda 21. Results of the United Nations Conference on Environment and Development, Rio de Janeiro, Brazil, 3–14 June. https://sustainabledevelopment.un.org/content/documents/Agenda21. pdf, accessed 9 September 2014.

Von Sturmer, John. 1982. "Aborigines in the Uranium Industry: Towards Self-Management in the Alligator River Region?" In *Aboriginal Sites, Rights and Resource Development*, ed. R.M. Berndt, 69–116. Nedlands: University of Western Australia Press.

6 Cultural Politics of Land and Animals in Treaty 8 Territory (Northern Alberta, Canada)

CLINTON N. WESTMAN

Introduction

In this chapter, I will focus on entanglements between the land, the animals, and the Indigenous Peoples of northern Alberta, specifically the cultural politics of the land and animals for members of semi-isolated Cree-Métis communities during the contemporary period. The data I am drawing on is based on my mixed-method ethnographic, linguistic, and policy research in northern Alberta since 1996. Specifically, I am drawing on both ethnographic observations of hunting and policy-based discussions of a land claim settlement. The dual focus is appropriate given the volume's focus on multiple forms of engagement and entanglement. My geographical area of interest is a swampy, forested region of northwestern Canada, between the Peace and Athabasca rivers (inhabited mainly by Aboriginal people, but still subject to land claims and jurisdictional debates as they seek to assert their right to self-determination), until recently at the epicentre of an oil boom. I document the lived vitality of Aboriginal politics, identity, ontology, and livelihood in what has been, and likely will again be, a very busy part of the boreal forest.

Contemporary Cree people of northern Alberta struggle to maintain their engagement with the land in multiple settings and contexts, including the following: land claims negotiations and implementation processes; legally mandated consultations with oil, gas, and forestry interests; animist and Christian rituals oriented to the land; and the hunting/gathering life in general. These "worlds" convey different epistemological and ontological principles, though many Cree move between them fluidly (Ghostkeeper 1996; Westman 2015). Frequently such engagement reflects an animist relational ontology, which remains vitally important for many if not most Cree people, and which for them animates the hunting/gathering life in terms of its spiritual importance. Such engagements and entanglements reflect a strong desire for a stable and legally recognized connection to their home territory, exemplified and enacted by hunting, trapping, fishing, and gathering pursuits, as well as through ritual practices. For First Nations people in the Prairie Provinces who signed historical treaties with the Crown, their aspirations, engagements, and entanglements are frequently expressed in terms of treaty rights and in terms of their identity as Treaty Indians. This is problematic, as the Crown has a quite different perspective on both the legal nature of treaty agreements and the political-ontological basis of these sacred agreements.

The Anthropological Engagement of Ontology

Recently, anthropologists have given a renewed focus to the importance of animist relational ontologies in considering the cultural politics and life-worlds of contemporary Indigenous peoples. Such ontological frames are political (see Françoise Dussart and Sylvie Poirier in this volume), not only in the sense that nation-states have historically tried to deny and suppress them, but also in the sense that, as values and lived experience, they tend to collide with state aspirations and imperatives towards limitless growth based on the "development" of "natural resources" found on Indigenous peoples' territories. The entanglements on traditional lands that I am describing are multifaceted and presuppose political-ontological (Blaser 2013) and/or cosmopolitical (Poirier 2008) engagements of diverse kinds. Indeed, Harvey Feit (2014 and in this volume, pp. 25–50) has shown that a "quest for power" is implicated on several levels of development politics, including the following: attempts of state and industrial actors to exploit power or energy inherent in natural resources; efforts by Indigenous people to claim rights or decision-making authority through negotiation, legal struggle, advocacy, and other means; and last but not least, the ontological and cosmological circuits and relations whereby some Indigenous people gain special powers or insights from the spirit world, specifically through hunting, such as (in this chapter) the power to turn into a moose and fly away, or, less dramatically, to find and call moose and other animals easily – perhaps through a combination of ritual power and practical knowledge.

In this respect, hunting and its ontological frames, no less than energy exploitation or land claims negotiations, are also replete with political significance. In effect, as Feit writes, hunting exemplifies a quest for power on Indigenous people's terms. Considering hunting as politically and ontologically significant helps us to understand better the significance of other forms of power relations impinging on Indigenous peoples. Such highly localized "life projects" (Blaser 2004) are critical to the articulation of Indigenous peoples' agency and identity in the face of energy exploitation and other capitalist projects nationally and globally. These political and ontological entanglements are a continuing reminder of the radical alterity of Indigenous worlds (Povinelli 2002), posing critical challenges to the mechanisms of recognition and inclusion in neoliberal, settler-colonial states. Moreover, such engagements and epistemologies provide the basis for a strong normative critique of capitalist development and industrial predation (Westman 2013b), while daily practices grounded in Indigenous ontologies embrace and uphold a different temporality and teleology from those of the mainstream societies, in which Indigenous peoples' rights to resources and impacts specific to Indigenous peoples are assessed (Westman 2013a).

At least since Frank Speck described hunting as a "holy occupation" (1935) for the Naskapi (Innu), studies of Cree and other Northern Algonquian peoples have been fundamental in establishing the political nature of such ontological entanglements (e.g., Poirier 2001). The central tenets of Northern Cree ontology and relational practices have been discussed by a range of Indigenous and non-Indigenous scholars (see Brightman 1993; Ghostkeeper 1996; Tanner 1979; Vandersteene 1960; Waugh 2001; Westman 2015). Such literature is also connected to a renewed global interest in animist ontologies (Clammer, Poirier, and Schwimmer 2004; Laugrand and Oosten 2007). Significantly, many scholars concerned with the "ontological turn" in social science (e.g., Descola 2013), including its phenomenological wing (e.g., Ingold 2000), engage more or less heavily with and are at least partially inspired by the work of Algonquianist scholars of the Canadian sub-Arctic, chiefly that of A. Irving Hallowell (2010). This is fitting, as Hallowell's work on questions of ontology among the Northern Ojibwe of Manitoba and Ontario was innovative and significant. Like his mentor, Speck, Hallowell was concerned about the psychic reality of the behavioural environment for the Ojibwe, framing such questions in ontological rather than epistemological terms (Darnell and Murray 2010). It is critical that we understand the degree to which Indigenous people may share their world with unseen forces, including the spirits of animals (Darnell 1991). In this sense, Hallowell's work remains important to understanding the ontological entanglements of Northern Algonquian peoples such as the Ojibwe and the Cree, and quite likely other Indigenous peoples further afield as well.

For Hallowell and for many Cree and Ojibwe people, animals and other entities may be seen as persons – potentially with spiritual power – who can grant or withhold their support. Considering this matrix of entanglement, spiritual power in Algonquian hunting societies correlates with success and efficacy at hunting (or gathering) and with leadership and authority. Through observance of ritual, taboo, sacrifice, speech, silence, and intentionality, hunting is a contemplative – even religious – act, replete with significance. While the complex practices underpinning these observations are variable and in flux, they remain essential and normative to many people. The bush is also important for those with Christian commitments. As Hallowell noted, and as my own research reflects, many Christians continue to feel the reality of and engage with non-human persons, including animal spirits. Some Christians, particularly Evangelicals and Pentecostals, may eschew the ritual aspect of bush life, but still talk to animals and feel a profound spiritual connection in nature, as the best place to talk to God (manitow: the same word is used in animist contexts).

Rights to land and livelihood as upheld by Treaty 8 (c. 1899) are an important reference point for contemporary discussions of engagement with land. Indeed, the historical "numbered" treaties are a major touchstone in the identity and political aspirations of First Nations in Canada's Prairie Provinces generally. Further underpinning its connection to both historical and contemporary politics, the treaty itself is sacralized through ritual – the use of the pipe connotes an offering and communication with spiritual entities – and is recognized by First Nations people as a sacred agreement to enter into kin-like relations and to share the land (Cardinal and Hildebrandt 2000). On the other hand, the Canadian state continues to view the treaties as legalistic land surrenders that entail a limited number of contemporary obligations on the part of federal and, to a lesser extent, provincial governments.

The Politics of Practice

Indigenous people in northern Alberta were already enmeshed in global markets by the time the treaty was signed; nevertheless, hunting, fishing, and trapping continued as the main way of life in most areas well into the postwar period (Asch 1990; Brody 1988; Westman 2016). Beginning in the 1950s in some regions, and expanding across much of northern Alberta and northeastern British Columbia by the 1970s, rapid growth of oil and gas exploration and extraction began to threaten Indigenous people's land-based practices. This has been even more the case over the past twenty years with the continued expansion of bitumen (oil/tar sands), heavy oil, fracking, and other unconventional energy sources (Westman 2013a, 2013b).

Particularly since 2011, I have been studying the impacts and benefits of Aboriginal engagements with state and corporate actors around energy issues (principally bitumen, oil, and natural gas). The political economic imperative for development is clear; however, the reach and effects of its benefits to Aboriginal communities are less clear. While most Aboriginal men who participate in the regional labour force earn a significant portion of their income from resource industries, overall labour force participation in Aboriginal communities remains well below national and provincial averages. Unemployment is high, even among labour force participants, and many jobs open to Aboriginal people are short-term or relatively unskilled and low-paid. Moreover, the benefits of high-wage industrial work do not always extend to women, who typically work in service or caring roles, sometimes dealing professionally with the fallout from industrial labour and its impact, while also raising families with frequently absent working partners. During busts in the commodity cycles, families and communities reliant on industry salaries for a relatively large portion of their income are highly vulnerable. Hunting and fishing – and to a lesser extent trapping – provide an important food security buffer (or income in the case of trapping) that may act as a hedge in communities with high food costs and poor selection of nutritious foods.

Cree people in the central part of northern Alberta maintain their engagement with the land principally on two interrelated levels: by negotiating with the state and with corporations for jurisdiction and benefits, and through their hunting practices. Their traditional hunting land base (where many elders were born) is mainly controlled by the provincial government and leased to industry, with smaller Indian Reserve lands nominally under federal jurisdiction but held in trust for particular First Nations (Indian Bands). Most of the "Crown" (provincial) land is subject to overlapping pulp, timber, oil, gas, bitumen, and mineral concessions regulating exploration and exploitation. Informal roads, cutlines, and well-pad sites score the bush. In this context, one can question the degree to which the hunting, fishing, trapping, and gathering rights guaranteed in the treaty are being upheld (Ross 2003). Individuals may have rights to fur management areas (trap lines) where their interest in the land is registered, but hunting rights are more diffuse and their loss is less quantifiable. One Cree leader described the loss of traditional lands to industry as a "tsunami," while another compared it to "a dream." Such remarks reflect the extensive extraction activities on the land in recent decades throughout northern Alberta. Nevertheless, many people profess a desire to *both* live a traditional life *and* benefit from the economic growth related to oil and forestry operations. This is similar to the connection to land and animals seen among Quebec Cree and other Indigenous peoples in many other chapters in this volume.

Describing the politics of land claims and energy consultations to set the stage for a discussion of the lived experience of a hunting trip necessitates different tones and approaches in this chapter. Nevertheless, such dissonance is not so different from that navigated by local people in their efforts to assert and live out their territorial jurisdiction and political authority, in accordance with relational commitments. For instance, Mike Beaver, the elder who invited me hunting, lives and leads in these different contexts, based on his knowledge of bush practice and its spiritual principles, as well as his skill in communicating with outsiders and his own people as a sort of cultural broker. As an elder, former chief, and former council member of Bigstone Cree Nation (BCN: one of Canada's largest First Nations, in terms of membership), Mike was involved in promoting the settlement of the recent land claim through a series of videos, which he narrated in English and Cree, explaining the settlement in order to "get the vote out" for its successful conclusion. He also participated in another video project, produced by an oil company, to express the company's commitment to engaging with BCN respectfully and promoting Cree cultural values and knowledge. Mike is involved in training and representing trappers and is a member of Bigstone's Health Board. I have been working with Mike for well over ten years. Although he is not the only elder I work with, this particular chapter was written with Mike's support and approval, largely based on information he provided during my research at his hunting camp.

In order to come to a fuller understanding of contemporary cultural politics of bush life among First Nations peoples, it is useful to consider the many competencies displayed by such individuals as Mike in their daily lives. In addition to his political leadership and hunting knowledge of the bush, Mike is a key ceremonialist in both Catholic and animist contexts, and the person who has taught me most about Cree rituals, including the *wihkohtowin* ceremony (Westman 2015). I have seen him lead these ceremonies, singing, drumming, and praying before dozens of people in the oblong lodge. I have also seen him lead thousands of Aboriginal and non-Aboriginal pilgrims in prayer at Lac Ste Anne, a major Catholic pilgrimage site (and Aboriginal holy place) in Plains Cree territory near Edmonton, hundreds of kilometres from Wabasca-Desmarais, his home community. Contemporary aspirations, rights, negotiations, and hunting practices should similarly be seen as potentially engaging a relational ontology or sentient ecology.

The Treaty Land Entitlement of the Bigstone Cree Nation

Relational interactions with animals through hunting are political and are intimately related to rights upheld through treaty negotiations. When Cree and Dene peoples negotiated Treaty 8 with representatives of Canada (symbolically with the British Crown), beginning in 1899, they indicated that their first priority was to protect the people's right to hunt, fish, and trap on their lands; the treaty affirmed that this right was protected on unoccupied Crown lands. We can infer with confidence that such activities meant far more than just "subsistence" (see Westman 2016 for a critical discussion of this term): it was a way of life (*pimâtisowin*), with all the social, cultural, ritual, and cosmological dimensions attached to such a value-laden concept (cognate terms are used by other Algonquian nations discussed in this volume). By contrast to hunting rights, acquiring reserve land was initially a secondary objective for most northern Aboriginal people.[1] Crucially, in the case of Bigstone and many other bands, the initial allotment of reserve land was less than the combined entitlement of those recognized as band members.

Drawing on oral traditions, most First Nations view the treaties as a sacred agreement to share the land while respecting one another's autonomy. By contrast, governments have focused their concern on the Crown's legal obligations (and attendant certainty over Crown land for the Crown's industrial stakeholders), based on the written text of the treaty (Canada 1966). This vision also indicates a particular ontological and quasi-mythological orientation towards the land, one which is apparent in other accounts of the Canadian state appearing in this volume. Such a narrow vision of land claims and a minimalist approach to hunting and livelihood rights on the part of state agents have contributed to the protracted land claims dispute I describe below. Moreover, the terms of the settlement for this dispute do not fully address Cree aspirations or understandings of the treaty, but rather represent a pragmatic attempt to secure land, funding, and services for a largely impoverished and isolated regional population.

The Bigstone Cree Nation's legal agreement with Canada and Alberta to address its land claim (treaty land entitlement) is the largest *Specific Claim* settlement in Canada's history. In Canada's land claims policy, specific claims differ from *Comprehensive Claims* in that the former result from a specific breach by the Crown of an identifiable lawful obligation, whereas the latter result from a global claim of rights flowing out of unextinguished Aboriginal title (as with the Quebec and BC examples discussed in this volume). Typically, Comprehensive Claims have not been negotiated in jurisdictions, such as Alberta, where historic treaties were previously signed; the Comprehensive Claim settlements in the Northwest Territories (on Treaty 8 and Treaty 11 lands) provide an exception to this rule.

In March 2010, thirty years after beginning research into early treaty pay lists, church records, and ethno-historical data on regional population dynamics, and over a decade after beginning negotiations, members and affiliates of the Bigstone Cree Nation ratified a Treaty Land Entitlement (TLE, a type of Specific Claim) claim settlement.[2] The main issues were cash compensation, reserve lands, and (particularly in isolated northern communities that had previously lacked a reserve land base and received minimal services or programs) community infrastructure. Polling occurred in many large and small communities across northern Alberta; an absolute majority of electors voted in favour of an agreement that Bigstone's council had negotiated with the governments of Canada and Alberta to fulfil treaty obligations.

The treaty had provided for a square mile of reserve land per family of five, to be held in trust for the collective good of the band. For complex historical reasons, the Treaty Land Entitlement of key ancestral BCN families and individuals, during the early twentieth century, had not been fulfilled, largely because of the sheer number of individuals and small bands of individuals involved, moving seasonally through a vast northern forest. Decades later, in a new political climate, after a number of historical contingencies and policy changes had fallen into place, BCN was able to negotiate a significant financial settlement and land transfer to rectify the breach of treaty.

As the largest Specific Claim settlement in Canadian history – and one of the most complex in that it also creates a new First Nation for two communities and a new governance arrangement within Bigstone's remaining communities – the Bigstone claim is worthy of study.[3] It differs significantly from the Comprehensive Claim settlements and negotiations that are more widely studied across Canada (including in this volume); however, the BCN claim is also unique among Specific Claim settlements, owing to Bigstone's complex history. I observed and participated in land claims negotiation and strategy sessions around this claim between 2000 and 2006, and draw on my contextual knowledge in this discussion.

The settlement acknowledges Canada's failure since 1899 to provide adequate lands, services, and ancillary benefits to Bigstone's membership, as agreed in Treaty 8. It also has the effect of conferring Indian Reserves and new communities for three historically isolated settlements. The resulting compensation in land (about 567 square kilometres) and cash ($249 million) compares somewhat favourably to the land and cash allotments in many Comprehensive Claim settlements or proposals, and is well in excess of other Specific Claim settlement on both fronts. The money and land value of the claim reflects not only the size of the land entitlement and the number of historical individuals involved in it, but also a range of discrete and somewhat unrelated historical legal breaches (i.e., other Specific Claims concerning ancillary treaty benefits that were not provided, such as ammunition, twine, and farming implements), which were then "rolled up" into the settlement. It is also based on a ratcheting effect drawn from comparisons with two previous multimillion-dollar settlements in the region with related issues (Woodland Cree First Nation and Loon River Cree First Nation), as well as from comparison with federal and provincial offers to settle the longstanding (and similar) claim of the Lubicon Nation (Goddard 1991; Martin-Hill 2008; Westman 2010).

Importantly, the BCN settlement set the stage for the recognition of a new First Nation (Peerless Trout First Nation, PTFN) and allocation of reserve lands around the hamlets of Trout Lake and Peerless Lake, as well as the construction of new communities and facilities at Trout Lake and Peerless Lake. This is in fulfilment of decades of community aspirations, which included organizing a legal action initiated by elders. Moreover, while remaining within Bigstone, the communities of Chipewyan Lake and Calling Lake also receive reserve lands, new community infrastructure, and a new governance arrangement assuring these smaller communities representation on the BCN council. Land will be set aside as Indian Reserves at each of these formerly landless isolated communities associated with BCN/PTFN and in other regions throughout the territory, notably a number of small lakes, prairies, and cemeteries that were once habitation sites, which are connected by trails and are still part of people's repertoire of hunting and spiritual places. The main BCN communities around Wabasca-Desmarais also receive expanded reserve lands in their immediate vicinity.

While Comprehensive Claim settlements, as discussed by Colin Scott and Harvey Feit in this volume, can give significant control over land and resources in a broader area, Specific Claims do not. The Bigstone settlement does not address aspirations for self-government, compensation for development, or management of off-reserve lands and wildlife, though some of these remain BCN aspirations. Many other features associated with Comprehensive Claims are also missing, including fee simple ownership of land, major legislative change, and the ability to provide most services to off-reserve members. This may explain in part why a small number of voters organized against the settlement, with many more (approximately 40 per cent) failing to vote.

Moreover, the settlement does not really facilitate or comprehend Cree people's multifold ontological relationships with the land and with animals and nature, except in a narrow legalistic frame. Nor does it fully operationalize Cree understandings of Treaty 8. In this respect it is quite interesting that, while the treaty signatories spoke eloquently about the importance of hunting and animals, the recent regional land claims settlements, such as the TLE agreements providing for new community infrastructure and political status for isolated communities (Woodland Cree First Nation in 1999, Loon River Cree First Nation in 1990, and the Bigstone Cree Nation in 2010), do not typically mention moose or hunting at all.

Moose Hunting and Anthropological Fieldwork

When I asked the late Trout Lake elder Solomon Sinclair, in 2005, about how people had lived in the past, he simply replied in Cree, "*môsak*" (plural moose). The moose is a huge herbivore native to Canadian forests. As such, moose are a focal species for Cree and Métis hunters, the subject of much specialized knowledge and discussion, and the target or subject of rituals, spiritual utterances, and much pragmatic labour and speech. It is common, especially in the fall, to see a group of people working around an outdoor table or rack, butchering and drying moose meat.

The changes from the dogsled days to the current means of accessing the land (generally with trucks, powerboats, snowmobiles, and all-terrain vehicles) have occurred within a single lifetime, as has the explosion of oil workers and infrastructure on the land. Nevertheless, many Cree people continue to hunt, fish, trap, and seek opportunities to spend time in the bush or otherwise enjoy the fruits of these activities. In the communities where I conduct fieldwork (mainly Trout Lake and Peerless Lake), hunting and fishing continue to supply key nutritional resources and remain an important part of family economic strategies. Furthermore, many people spend time at cabins, camp meetings, Bible camps, ceremonies, and cultural retreats held in the bush, where traditional food is often an important part of the overall experience.

In late September 2013 I participated in a week-long moose hunt with Mike Beaver and members of his extended family. While this is not the only hunting trip I have participated in, it provides a range of rich data because of its longer duration, larger number of participants, and successful outcome. The annual family moose hunt is a key cultural activity and is important in maintaining Mike's family members' connections to the land, animals, and tradition. This is particularly the case for those who are not usually active hunters. I will reflect directly on this experience as I discuss the importance of both tradition and renewal. I want to consider how Cree relations with animals are being maintained in this context of cultural, linguistic, and environmental change (see Scott in this volume for a similar discussion).

My approach is quite different from that taken by Robert Jarvenpa and Hetty-Jo Brumbach, another discussion of a high-tech moose hunt in which contemporary sociocultural meanings, changes, and contexts are explicitly *not* the analytical focus (1983: 175). Rather, their search is for cultural ecological and archaeological patterns and proxies. Instead, I favour the approach adopted by Thomas McIlwraith (2012), who considers the camp and its technologies in an ensemble, as a home (see also Sahlins 1999). In this reading, a camp is the locus of labouring, dwelling, and – yes – hunting on the landscape, in a very affective, engaged, and entangling sense.

Bouncing Along on a Cree Hunting Trip

September, 2013: Our hunting camp is just off the road, in a large cut-block that had been cleared in the forest for oil and gas extraction. Indeed, the clearing still featured at its centre a prominent piece of above-ground metal infrastructure, for servicing underground pipelines. I was the first to arrive at the campsite, to which Mike had kindly provided me directions. Located off the gravel road, the large, rough clearing provided access to one or two cutlines for easy bush travel – a perfect site for a hunting camp. There was also a drying rack of wooden rods that Mike had built up near a firepit. I began setting my tent up near the rack, with the late summer sun and clear blue sky promising a most pleasant week in the outdoors. I knew I was in the right place but I contacted Mike on the satellite phone to be sure he was safely on his way (Scott provides a similar discussion of his arrival at a hunting camp in this volume). Although the road-accessible site had been chosen for the convenience of family members and other visitors, the lack of cellular phone service ensured a feeling of remoteness and made the satellite phone a valuable asset for safety and convenience. Upon arriving, after graciously accepting my gift of tobacco, Mike borrowed the phone to call family members en route, to make final arrangements with them, in Cree.

Two motor homes, one travel trailer, several trucks, multiple generators, various all-terrain vehicles, and two or three tents soon stood in the clearing around the drying racks, surrounding a central area with carpeting, tarps, hearths and grill structures, rifles, tools, food, coolers, kids' bikes, gear, screen tents, and lawn chairs. A core group of some fifteen people from four generations (including eight adults) stayed for several nights, while a smaller number of other family members stayed a shorter period or visited at least once. The intergenerational nature of the trip was part of the focus and lent a holiday atmosphere, notwithstanding the seriousness of shared intent. Campers indicated that it was important for children to learn about life in camp and spend time with grandparents and other family members in a camp setting, in spite of having to miss a few school days to do so. The speech I heard was a mix of Cree and English, with those under thirty speaking almost exclusively in English.[4]

Our trip spanned the final days of summer and the first days of fall, as the moose's rutting season began. During this time of year, as Mike said, bull moose especially "live on love." They are more aggressive, so thus easier to stalk and, critically, call. This week also coincided with the opening of the provincially regulated moose-hunting season, meaning that there would also be non-Indigenous hunters around (see Scott and Poirier in this volume). We did indeed see other parties of hunters, and once, the camp was approached by a provincial wildlife officer checking the hunters for Indian Status cards.[5]

Although its participants clearly considered it a very Cree thing to do, the hunt also contained many modern conveniences of the sort described by Marshall Sahlins (1999) in discussing the "Indigenization of Modernity," showing that contemporary northern peoples adopt the modern tools and technologies required to pursue their hunting life with ease (see Dussart and Poirier in this volume for a further discussion of Sahlins's theories regarding cultural entanglements). The study of such changes and continuities is indeed fascinating and reminds one of Pierre Bourdieu's (1982) remark that certain discourses, particularly those of a religious character, are amphibious and can easily take new structures and meanings in different contexts.

Every morning before dawn and every evening before dusk, groups of men would set out in different directions to search for moose along roads or cutlines, or near wetlands. Mike took the time to gather some plants, and hunters also shot a few game birds. Mike and his grandchildren set up a few rabbit snares, but were unsuccessful in that particular pursuit, as far as I know.

Men also kept busy working around the camp, preparing equipment, cutting wood, or digging and framing a pit privy that was described to me as an "Indian toilet." This was accomplished through the use of tools, including a power drill and a chainsaw as well as lumber, hardware, and a shovel, brought along for multipurpose work. Men prepared early breakfasts (the breakfast eaten before going hunting) and some other meals and dishes.

Women generally worked at keeping the camp, preparing food, and minding the youngest children. Teenaged girls occasionally participated in the hunting and trapping activities, as well. Women took charge of the drying and butchering process in camp after the moose kill, although Mike tended the fires after the kill and assisted with the butchering and drying. This is consistent with tradition, given that gender roles in such domestic production were not completely fixed in Cree society. McIlwraith (2012) and Jarvenpa and Brumbach (1983) provide similar examples of gender role flexibility (albeit within limits) in hunting camps.

While occasionally playing with younger children, a fourteen-year-old male youth generally followed the activity patterns of adult males and was praised as a "natural hunter" by female relatives, while enduring the regular teasing of adult male companions, in contrast to the quiet support he received from his grandfather. This young man spends time in the bush regularly and has killed multiple moose to share with family members and others.

Children practised hunting small birds, shooting arrows or pellets for target practice, and setting snares. Many of these activities and learning experiences resembled those described in the ethnographic literature on hunting camps and reflect Cree cultural values and ontological principles. For example, when one child killed a small bird, he was praised for his shooting accuracy but admonished not to "play with" the dead animal.

Children's play patterns also included riding bicycles and small quads, riding horseback when a relative with a horse trailer visited the camp, accompanying adults on short hunting and snaring trips, and playing with toys or watching videos around camp. There was an inflatable bouncing station with a slide – *a bouncy castle* – powered by generator, which was blown up each afternoon for the youngest children to play upon. These children jumped up and down, bouncing along to the noise of quads and generators, to the smell of poplar smoke and moose meat drying. Many anthropologists have described family life in Algonquian hunting camps, but I do not recall any accounts that mentioned the bouncy castle. Yet to these children it all fitted together seamlessly, the bouncing electric playpen as natural a part of the hunting camp as a rabbit snare, a drying rack, a rifle, a motor home, an Indian toilet, a hatchet, a chainsaw, a *Dora* video, a whetstone, or a satellite phone. Here is another example of the multiple worlds in which Cree people participate.

Bringing Home Animals

If the camp is a home to which one brings hunting bounty, it is also characterized by liminal zones where the boundaries of culture and nature blur and must be renegotiated. Anthropologists of the Arctic and sub-Arctic, particularly Adrian Tanner (1979), have richly documented ethnographically the means by which transitions between human and animal spaces and substances are managed socially, referring to inter-species relations manifested through speech, pragmatic labour, ritual practice, and gender politics. This section takes a similar approach in seeking to understand the manner in which animals enter the camp space and the human community.

Mike notices the non-edible animals, not just moose and furbearers. For example, he even takes account of nuisance camp birds like the raven and the grey jay or whisky jack. Both birds, particularly the whisky jack in the Cree context, have a strong association with trickster figures (Westman 2013b), who were integral to setting society and the world in order. Shortly after the first three of us had arrived at the campsite, Mike pointed out the call of the whisky jack, which announced that it too had arrived at the camp to live with us. Similarly, when the first raven flew over croaking, Mike addressed the raven in Cree by speaking the onomatopoeic species name, *kâhkakow*. The first raven to arrive at the camp calls the other ones in, Mike said. Such inherently social birds are companion species with humans and are strongly associated with camps and cabins.

As he looks at the raven, Mike says to me in English, "I wish I could fly." People could fly, he tells me. People in the old days were very powerful. Indeed, Mike's great-grandfather could turn into a moose and then fly. Once someone was tracking Mike's great-grandfather and saw that his human tracks had turned into moose tracks. The moose tracks subsequently disappeared as the moose itself took flight in yet another metamorphosis.[6]

Mike insisted: "Those stories are true." Here we have the linkages between humans and other animals, birds and moose, and shamanic transformation, discussed within an hour of our arrival at camp. Perhaps I was given these remarks because I frequently discuss ceremonies with Mike, or because I had just given Mike tobacco, which he uses in the ceremonies he performs. Subsequently, the next morning, our first in the new campsite, Mike would use some of the tobacco I gave him to say a prayer asking a blessing for his family and for our safety on the hunt.

Such knowledge of relationships between different species and related phenomena reflects a practical knowledge as well as a distinctive ontological frame or world. Hunters use many different clues and signs in their environment to understand their prey. To underscore the linkages between the habits of moose and other species, particularly birds, Mike pointed out that the moose would be moving soon, since he had just seen one of the first Vs of migratory geese overhead, flying south. The migrating season of geese and the rutting season of moose generally overlap. According to some hunters, there is also a linkage to the change in the leaves, although this is less reliable in Mike's view. The beginning of the rut always occurs in September, which is called *onôcihitowipîsim* (mating moon) in Cree. The full moon in late September or early October is thus especially propitious as a time to hunt moose.

Late September is also the time for the *wihkohtowin* feast (Westman 2015). Such collective feasts are led by Mike and many others, giving thanks for the bounty of the summer and praying for success in the winter and renewal the following spring. Moose and other animals play a pivotal role in the *wihkohtowin*, both symbolically and materially, paradoxically as the object or victim of a sacrifice and as the subject or recipient of it. In the old days these thanksgiving feasts were given in oblong lodges at every lake and clearing where people dwelled, to share the meat from fall moose kills. One special food used at such feasts was the bull's rump fat, which today is called Indian Popcorn.

When Mike killed a cow moose, in a hilly aspen grove, on the fifth morning of our hunting trip, he was travelling the cutlines on a quad, all alone, heading to a wetland location that he had scouted previously. I could hear the shot from camp, as could the others present, who spoke of it with muted excitement. When Mike returned to the clearing shortly after, he rode in wordlessly, with little facial expression, and gave me a discreet thumb-up with direct eye contact. His teenaged grandson and I gathered tools to help butcher and pack the animal. As we approached the kill site on a cutline, I rode in a small trailer behind Mike's quad, bouncing along uncomfortably on the uneven ground and awaiting instruction before being able to help. Eventually, with Mike's direction, I participated fully in the field butchering process.

Two other family members, who had been hunting elsewhere, learned of the kill when they returned to camp for breakfast, and came quickly to join us in the work. Parts of the animal were laid in the trailer, on boughs cut for this purpose. Mike drank blood and kept some choice organs. Most of the innards were left by the cutline, along with the hide (traditionally an important part of the bounty). As Mike said, few people make hide anymore, given the labour required to cure it.

Bringing the meat home to camp set the stage for a whirlwind of activity as Mike prepared a large, smouldering fire beneath the drying racks he had built around the secondary hearth. Linda, Mike's wife, leading the other women and girls, as well as Mike, began to process the meat more fully, cutting up large portions and slicing it to set on the racks for drying. It is the air and sun that dry the meat; the smoke mainly flavours it and keeps insects away, so the meat must be sliced very thin. Sharpening knives is a constant undertaking. Drying meat is done in both the camps and the communities. Most camps have a drying rack, which may be covered by a tarp. In the communities, people often use a small outbuilding or tarped tent as a smokeshack.

The family dried hundreds of pounds of muscle meat in three days, as well as some lower leg tendons, and organs including the heart, liver, kidneys, nose, eyes, and tongue. We ate some of the meat at camp in stews and as fried meat, but the vast majority was quickly and efficiently dried over a period of two to three days. Dried meat is a delicacy, and family members keep it to enjoy over a long period as a snack and cultural food; I was also given dry meat to take home to my family. A few weeks later, Mike and his grandson shared the bounty of the young man's subsequent bull kill more widely, because they already had abundant dry meat from our trip. Sharing meat was and is an important aspect of community and reflects a deeper relationship with the slain animal and beyond.

Mike talks about how hard Linda works when their family does dry meat: "She's such a good worker," he says. There was much joking discussion around the fire and drying racks of "tradition," which would require the hunter to sleep naked with his wife the night of a moose kill. But I also heard more serious discussions of the ceremonies and rituals of the season, including questions about whether Mike planned to host any ceremonies that fall. Day and night, Linda presided over many of the discussions with her kind listening and supportive advice.

Afterwards, I spoke to Mike about the spiritual gift of the animal. I had witnessed his means of honouring it, including by hanging the cow's milk sack in a tree (the calf, now several months old, would survive on its own without the cow). Mike also asked me to place a cigarette in the campfire for the moose spirit. He had previously said a prayer of thanks, upon killing the moose.

I have spoken previously to many elders about similar practices, gestures of respect to the spirit world such as suspending or elevating animal parts. Many people had told me that elevation of animal parts was no longer practised, or that they did not understand such things, even while some of the same informants had moose skulls and antlers on their roofs. In this instance, as elsewhere, I have learned to assume that Cree animist ritual practice with its distinct ontological underpinnings is still ongoing and widespread. Indeed, there are a number of experts who enact its relational and symbolic repertoire.

Mike and other elders discuss related narratives of spiritual power, and enact practices such as putting fat in the fire and carrying out pipe ceremonies. These events occur in the community as well as the bush. Indeed, it is significant that during our trip, Mike had to return home to Wabasca-Desmarais for a day to lead a pipe ceremony at a major community ceremonial gathering. His daughter went with him so she could attend the local high school's graduation ceremony, to honour a friend. Teasing out such ritual and social obligations requires knowledge of social and relational contexts that extend well beyond, while also reflecting and affirming the importance of, the hunting camp. Although the camps have been somewhat decentred in Cree ritual and social life (as well as in scholarly analysis), they retain a strong symbolic importance. In most instances there is a tangible physical or wireless connection to the outside world. Nevertheless, one can still find peace and quiet, and honour social relationships of various kinds, in the hunting camp and on the trail of animals.

Conclusion

Cree people in the central region of northern Alberta have endeavoured for more than a century to seek recognition of their rights, and protection of a land base on which to live and hunt. These aspirations have most frequently – and most successfully – been expressed in an idiom of treaty promises. That is the spirit in which people hunt on their lands, which also provide them sustenance. In a similar way, the land claims and consultation/negotiation processes that First Nations enter with corporations and governments may also provide First Nations people with both a means of economic sustenance and a measure of control over their lands. Such processes provide the ground for First Nations people to make important claims in terms of identity and rights vis-à-vis Treaty 8 and the Canadian Constitution. In this sense it is complementary to consider discussions of treaty politics in the same chapter as an ethnographic account of a hunting camp, in order to gain a fuller understanding of Aboriginal peoples' engagement with the land as a hallmark of both practice and identity.

Near the end of our trip, Mike said: "When an elder gives you a story it's just part of it, it's up to you what you do with it. You've got to figure the rest out." I am trying to understand how moose and other species fit into the relational ontology that is the Northern Cree life-world, such as when the moose offer themselves to the hunter, or speak to the shaman from within the shaking tent. Or when a powerful person turns into a moose and flies away. In this chapter I have examined multiple aspects of Cree and Métis people's engagement and entanglement with the land and animals through ontological connections, in the politics of intergovernmental relations, and in the practicalities and pragmatics of everyday life. Such entangled frames of engagement are very important to local people's sense of themselves as Aboriginal, and – at least in Mike and Linda's family – each has its connections and refractions in the hunting camp. The treaty and the hunting camp provide frames of reference for the aspirations and assertions involved in negotiations with industry and government. How to incorporate the more qualitative and experiential aspects of Indigenous peoples' relationships with animals and nature into energy consultations, impacts and benefits discourses, and land claims discussions remains an open question.

ACKNOWLEDGMENTS

Recent research was supported by the Social Science and Humanities Research Council of Canada (Cultural Politics of Energy in Northern Alberta), Aberdeen University and The European Research Council (Arctic Domus: Emplacing Human-Animal Relations in the Circumpolar North), and the University of Saskatchewan. I also acknowledge the support of the Bigstone Cree Nation and the Peerless Trout First Nation, as well as the advice of David Anderson, Melvin Beaver, Mike and Linda Beaver and family, Brian Thom, Christopher Wilson, and Robert Wishart. Other hunters and elders also graciously shared their knowledge. I acknowledge the insights of anonymous reviewers. Finally, I thank the editors for their advice and support.

NOTES

1 Many people chose to accept *scrip* for land or cash, as Métis, rather than accepting treaty benefits including entitlement to reserve land, as Indians. The scrip process was plagued by fraud. Furthermore, many in northern Alberta who initially received Indian status subsequently had it revoked from them or their descendants for various reasons, prior to the 1980s (Goddard 1991). Many such families are now recognized as First Nation members. These regional historical particularities are strongly implicated in the Bigstone claim.

2 See Canada 2000; Narine 2011; Reddekopp 1997.
3 Bigstone Cree Nation's membership included large numbers of people residing in and around the communities of Wabasca-Desmarais, Calling Lake, Chipewyan Lake, Trout Lake, and Peerless Lake (as well as cities and towns in northern Alberta, including Edmonton, the provincial capital). Trout Lake and Peerless Lake now constitute Peerless Trout First Nation (PTFN). Most PTFN members reside at Peerless Lake and Trout Lake.
4 In more northerly "back lakes" communities such as Trout Lake and Peerless Lake, young adults are more fluent in the Cree language. Even teens and children often speak more Cree, particularly in the bush or when doing traditional activities (Westman and Schreyer 2014).
5 First Nation members are issued federal photo identification cards (colloquially known as "Status Cards" or "Treaty Cards"), which function as identification and establish rights to particular federal programs and services. In this instance, the provincial wildlife officers may request Status Cards to establish eligibility for subsistence hunting under provisions of the Indian Act, treaties, and provincial wildlife acts. It is the federal government that issues the cards and maintains a list of eligibility for registration as a Status Indian. Unlike First Nation members, Métis people do not have generalized hunting rights in Alberta; their hunting rights are contested in spite of a series of favourable court judgments. Prior to Canada's adoption of a new constitution in 1982, both federal and provincial governments acted to curtail First Nations hunting rights in various ways. Provincial government scientists and wildlife managers repeatedly advocated the curtailing of treaty rights to hunt moose, based on their largely unsubstantiated view that First Nation hunters were diminishing the resource, but also based on the province's desire to maintain a vigorous hunting industry for both residents and tourists.
6 On the importance of metamorphosis among Algonquian peoples, see Hallowell 2010: 375; Ingold 2000: 92.

REFERENCES

Asch, Michael. 1990. "The Future of Hunting and Trapping and Economic Development in Alberta's North: Some Myths and Facts about Inevitability." In *Proceedings of the Fort Chipewyan and Fort Vermillion Bicentennial Conference*, ed. Patricia McCormack and R. Geoffrey Ironsides, 25–9. Edmonton: Boreal Institute for Northern Studies.

Blaser, Mario. 2004. "Life Projects: Indigenous Peoples' Agency and Development." In *In the Way of Development: Indigenous Peoples, Life Projects and Globalization*, ed. Mario Blaser, Harvey A. Feit, and Glenn McRae, 26–44. London and New York: Zed Books and Ottawa: Canadian International Development Research Centre.

Blaser, Mario. 2013. "Ontological Conflicts and the Stories of Peoples in Spite of Europe: Towards a Conversation on Political Ontology." *Current Anthropology* 54 (5): 547–68. http://dx.doi.org/10.1086/672270.

Bourdieu, Pierre. 1982. *Ce que parler veut dire: l'économie des échanges linguistiques*. Paris: Fayard. Translation 1991. *Language and Symbolic Power*, ed. J.B.Thompson, trans. G. Raymond and M. Adamson. Cambridge: Polity Press.

Brightman, Robert. 1993. *Grateful Prey: Rock Cree Human-Animal Relationships*. Berkeley: University of California Press.

Brody, Hugh. 1988. *Maps and Dreams: Indians and the British Columbia Frontier*. Vancouver: Douglas and McIntyre.

Canada. 1966. Treaty No. 8, Made June 21, 1899 and Adhesions Reports, etc. Ottawa: Queen's Printer.

Canada. 2000. Bigstone Cree Nation Inquiry: Treaty Land Entitlement Claim. Commission of Inquiry (Indian Claims Commission: P.E. James Prentice, co-chair; Daniel Bellegarde, co-chair; Carole T. Corcoran, commissioner). Ottawa: Indian Claims Commission.

Cardinal, Harold, and Walter Hildebrandt. 2000. *Treaty Elders of Saskatchewan: Our Dream Is That Our Peoples Will One Day Be Clearly Recognized as Nations*. Calgary: University of Calgary Press.

Clammer, John, Sylvie Poirier, and Eric Schwimmer, eds. 2004. *Figured Worlds: Ontological Obstacles in Intercultural Relations*. Toronto: University of Toronto Press.

Darnell, Regna. 1991 "Thirty-Nine Postulates of Plains Cree Conversation, 'Power,' and Interaction: A Culture-Specific Model." In *Papers of the Twenty-Second Algonquian Conference*, ed. William Cowan, 89–102. Ottawa: Carleton University Press.

Darnell, Regna, and Stephen O. Murray. 2010 "Series Editors' Introduction." In *A. Irving Hallowell, Contributions to Ojibwe Studies: Essays, 1934–1972*, ed. Jennifer S.H. Brown and Susan Elaine Grey, ix–xi. Critical Studies in the History of Anthropology Series, ed. Regna Darnell and Stephen O. Murray. Lincoln: University of Nebraska Press.

Descola, Philippe. 2013. *Beyond Nature and Culture*. Chicago: University of Chicago Press.

Feit, Harvey. 2014 "Hunting and the Quest for Power: Relationships between James Bay Crees, the Land, and Development." In *Native Peoples: The Canadian*

Experience, 4th ed., ed. C. Roderick Wilson and Christopher Fletcher, 115–45. Don Mills, ON: Oxford.

Ghostkeeper, Elmer. 1996. *Spirit Gifting: The Concept of Spiritual Exchange.* Calgary: Arctic Institute of North America.

Goddard, John. 1991. *Last Stand of the Lubicon Cree.* Madeira Park, BC: Douglas and McIntyre.

Hallowell, A. Irving. 2010. *Contributions to Ojibwe Studies: Essays, 1934–1972*, ed. Jennifer S.H. Brown and Susan Elaine Grey. Critical Studies in the History of Anthropology Series, ed. Regna Darnell and Stephen O. Murray. Lincoln: University of Nebraska Press.

Ingold, Tim. 2000. *The Perception of the Environment: Essays on Livelihood, Dwelling, and Skill.* London and New York: Routledge. http://dx.doi.org/10.4324/9780203466025.

Jarvenpa, Robert, and Hetty Jo Brumbach. 1983. "Ethnoarchaeological Perspectives on an Athapaskan Moose Kill." *Arctic* 36 (2): 174–84. http://dx.doi.org/10.14430/arctic2260.

Laugrand, Frédéric, and Jarich Oosten, eds. 2007. *La nature des esprits dan les cosmologies autochtones* [The Nature of Spirits in Aboriginal Cosmologies]. Quebec: Les Presses de l'Université Laval.

Martin-Hill, Dawn. 2008. *The Lubicon Lake Nation: Indigenous Knowledge and Power.* Toronto: University of Toronto Press.

McIlwraith, Thomas. 2012. "A Camp Is a Home and Other Reasons Why Indigenous Hunting Camps Can't Be Moved Out of the Way of Resource Developments." *Northern Review* 36: 97–126.

Narine, Shari. 2011. "Settlement Restores Some Land and Creates New Nation." *Windspeaker* 29 (7): 11.

Poirier, Sylvie. 2001. "Territories, Identity and Modernity among the Atikamekw (Haut St.-Maurice, Quebec)." In *Aboriginal Autonomy and Development in Northern Quebec and Labrador*, ed. Colin H. Scott, 111–29. Vancouver: University of British Columbia Press.

Poirier, Sylvie. 2008. "Reflections on Indigenous Cosmopolitics/Poetics." *Anthropologica* 50 (1): 75–85.

Povinelli, Elizabeth A. 2002. *The Cunning of Recognition: Indigenous Alterities and the Making of Australian Multiculturalism.* Durham, NC: Duke University Press. http://dx.doi.org/10.1215/9780822383673.

Reddekopp, G. Neil. 1997. "The Treaty Land Entitlement of the Bigstone Cree Nation." Unpublished manuscript. Edmonton: Government of Alberta (Aboriginal Affairs and Northern Development).

Ross, Monique. 2003. "Aboriginal Peoples and Development in Northern Alberta." Occasional Paper 12. Calgary: Canadian Institute of Resource Law.

Sahlins, Marshall. 1999. "What Is Anthropological Enlightenment? Some Lessons of the Twentieth Century." *Annual Review of Anthropology* 28 (1): i–xxiii. http://dx.doi.org/10.1146/annurev.anthro.28.1.0.

Speck, Frank G. 1935. *Naskapi: The Savage Hunters of the Labrador Peninsula.* Norman: University of Oklahoma Press.

Tanner, Adrian. 1979. *Bringing Home Animals: Religious Ideology and Mode of Production of the Mistassini Cree Hunters.* New York: St Martin's Press.

Vandersteene, Roger. 1960. *Wabasca: dix ans de vie indienne* [Wabasca: Ten Years of Indian Life]. Gemmenich, Belgium: Éditions O.M.I.

Waugh, Earle. 2001. "Religious Issues in the Alberta Elders' Cree Dictionary." *International Review for the History of Religions* 48 (4): 468–90.

Westman, Clinton N. 2010. "The Making of Isolated Communities in the Lesser Slave Lake Interior, Alberta." In *Papers of the Rupert's Land Colloquium 2008,* ed. M.A. Lindsay and M.A Richard, 223–41. Winnipeg: Centre for Rupert's Land Studies, University of Winnipeg.

Westman, Clinton N. 2013a. "Social Impact Assessment and the Anthropology of the Future in Canada's Tar Sands." *Human Organization* 72 (2): 111–20. http://dx.doi.org/10.17730/humo.72.2.e0m6426502384675.

Westman, Clinton N. 2013b. "Cautionary Tales: Making and Breaking Community in the Oil Sands Region." *Canadian Journal of Sociology* 38 (2): 211–32.

Westman, Clinton N. 2015. "The wihkohtowin: Ritual Feasting among Cree and Métis Peoples of Northern Alberta." *Anthropologica* 57 (2): 299–314.

Westman, Clinton N. 2016. "Aboriginal Subsistence Practices in an 'Isolated' Region of Northern Alberta." In *Subsistence under Capitalism: Historical and Contemporary Perspectives,* ed. Dean Bavington, James Murton, and Carly Dokis, 162–94. Montreal and Kingston: McGill-Queen's University Press.

Westman, Clinton N., and Christine Schreyer. 2014. "*Înîhiyawîtwâw* 'They Are Speaking Cree': Cree Language Use and Issues in Northern Alberta, Canada." *International Journal of the Sociology of Language* 230: 115–40.

7 Entanglements in Coast Salish Ancestral Territories

BRIAN THOM

The Spirit Snake, Belief and Experience

In 1993, when I was spending my third summer camping out on reserve lands in a Coast Salish community, a fellow my age who had become a friend and guide invited me to the community's winter ceremonial bighouse. After a day out with his relatives fishing sturgeon, we drove up in his truck and went inside the iconic Northwest Coast building. Huge cedar poles supported the structure, which was enclosed with cedar planks and covered by a gabled roof with openings for the two large open fire pits. As we walked on the dirt floor of the quiet building, my friend explained to me for the first time about the winter ceremonies that were held there, about the practices of new initiates to the spirit dance and the powerful transformations of the lives of people who attended (like those described in Amoss 1978; Kew 1990; Bierwert 1996). He told me a particularly vivid story about an event that had just happened late in the previous winter when a huge spirit snake (as he called it), which lived below the building, erupted out of the floor when a dance was fully under way. It moved around the room, disturbing the dancers, putting in danger the new initiates and others who had assembled that night. Several of the older women, who could see the snake clearly and knew what to do, acted together to get it under control, to put it away. My friend, who was generally jovial, turned to me with a very intense and serious look and said: "Do you *believe* anything I just said?" This was clearly an important moment, and I didn't want to give a glib answer. I felt that the bounds of our relationship and the limits of my grasping what it was that he had shared were immediately at stake. What was I able to believe about this important experience from his recent life, one that I'm sure he sensed immediately upon sharing it was far outside my own? Were there bounds on how the worlds we were mutually encountering had begun to be entangled?

Indeed, in that moment, though we had never discussed it, he had read my position correctly. I had grown up in a secular family, which never went to church, and where discussions about "belief" had only seriously come up in my childhood in conversations about the Easter Bunny and Santa Claus. Outside my family, however, I had been sensitized to the social implications of making open declarations of one's beliefs. In my 1980s high school in suburban British Columbia, there was significant peer pressure to join evangelical church youth groups which were then popular and widespread. I had openly spurned youth pastors and recruitment officers of the local Masonic organization (which had active chapters of the Order of DeMolay and Job's Daughters) and as a consequence I had been socially ostracized. As a young man after high school, I had held back from categorically declaring my own personal beliefs, which didn't seem to matter in the same way with my new social cohort. But here I was six years later being confronted with these same questions again. Though I couldn't put my finger on it, the implications this time seemed to be different, and propriety gave me only a moment to respond. "Well, I've never *experienced* anything like that. I don't know what I believe or not, but really, I just have had no experience like this" (fieldnotes, 26 May 1993). My friend smiled wryly, breaking the tension that I felt, and put his arm on my back with a joke about me probably not wanting that kind of experience, unless I was looking to take the difficult and demanding journey of becoming a bighouse initiate.

His question and my answer to it have stayed with me for the twenty years since. Though I could spend my summers sharing experiences fishing, collecting berries and medicinal plants, learning something of the language, undertaking archaeological investigations, that moment demanded I consider the implications of the worlds he was pointing out to me, including the worlds of spiritual and ancestral power that I was otherwise oblivious to and the prerogatives of respectful relations that my presence among them entails. My tentative and unsure answer – which redirected the question from my own beliefs and their corollary, my dis-beliefs and the implied judgments of the value of his actual lived experience – prioritized a way of being over a way of knowing (ontology over epistemology), and for me opened up the possibility of finding ways to share our entangled humanity. It is in these moments when multiple and seemingly irreconcilable views on the world become entangled through mutual experience that the human capacity for coexistence can be probed.

The concept of entanglement (Françoise Dussart and Sylvie Poirier in this volume) is particularly helpful in thinking through the implications and impacts of seemingly disparate elements of multiple worlds connecting. In becoming entangled within Indigenous territories, our worlds connect in unexpected, powerful ways. Though the entangled connections are always partial and situated, grounded in the respective ontologies and senses of responsibility (Colin Scott in this volume), reflecting and acting on the consequences of these mutual encounters positions us to make positive change. In this chapter I investigate contemporary entanglements with the agency of Indigenous ancestors and spirits, continuing to reflect on shared experiences of the world that my Coast Salish friends, teachers, and colleagues have pointed out to me. Like the spirit snake experienced in the bighouse, ancestral power and presence may be encountered in many places in the contemporary Coast Salish landscape, with potentially significant and at times unexpected consequences, from sudden strokes or unfortunate deaths to poverty or business trouble. People work to maintain respectful relations with the ancestors and other powerful non-human persons and places. Doing so is fundamental to leading life well, to being a decent human being.

Maintaining respectful ancestral relations is a fundamental human problem not only for Coast Salish peoples but for all of us living in, sharing, and being entangled with Indigenous territories (Dussart and Poirier in this volume). Drawing attention to the potentiality of ancestral action has political implications and demands consideration by everyone concerned for what it means to live and coexist respectfully within Indigenous territories. This is a particularly critical point in geographies like the British Columbia Lower Mainland and Vancouver Island where Indigenous territories substantively intersect with dense and expanding urban centres or are subject to industrial development, where the potential for encounters is widely shared. What are the possibilities of coexistence and mutual respect in a landscape seemingly prominently defined and shaped by private property land titles (Thom 2014), alongside and sometimes on top of Indigenous ancestral places? What are the ways for living in Indigenous ancestral territories in the twenty-first century?

In drawing our attention to the importance of taking seriously Indigenous ontological categories and experiences, my reflections here are inspired by the insights of anthropologists like Sylvie Poirier (2004; 2013), Paul Nadasdy (2007), Colin Scott (2006), Tim Ingold (1996), Mario Blaser (2012, 2013), Harvey Feit (1986, 2004), and Elisabeth Povinelli (1995). Their works are critical of the conventional discourses in the social and natural sciences (and by extension the underlying logic of colonial governments and the general public in states like Canada and Australia), which reject a priori claims for the agency and personhood of things in the world – that rocks or glaciers cannot actually listen; that long-deceased ancestors cannot physically or materially influence the lives of the living (Povinelli 1995; Cruikshank 2005). Conventional discourse, at best, accepts these assertions as mere beliefs or metaphors, which may in and of themselves be "true" within the social and cultural system, but whose value as truth is relative to all others. This universalizing logic has "worked as a 'neutralizing tool' in our understanding of other people's worlds, other ways of being in the world" (Poirier 2013: 59), where those with the power get to decide what is really "out there" in nature (Blaser 2013: 548) and what can be dismissed as cultural difference.

The approach of these scholars "takes seriously" (Nadasdy 2007: 26) the conceptions and experiences of Indigenous peoples. Tim Ingold, for one, has convincingly argued that Indigenous peoples do not "approach their environment as an external world of nature that has to be 'grasped' conceptually and appropriated symbolically within the terms of an imposed cultural design, as a precondition for effective action … indeed, the separation of mind and nature has no place in their thought and practice" (1996: 120). Others have suggested that we can open up the possibility and potentiality of multiple worlds where humans are not the only meaningful agents (Poirier 2013: 51), where animals, ancestors, spirits, stones, stumps, the weather all have potential agency, and where people exercise their personal autonomy in attending to respectful relations and engaging in reciprocity and sharing with their non-human partners. These Indigenous, "relational ontologies" are not just a "view" or a "perspective" but a total entailment in the world, with tangible consequences for everyone concerned. To approach these multiple ways of being in the world, Sylvie Poirier has suggested that "we need to ask 'how do people see the world' at the same time as 'which world do they see'" (2013: 54), providing an approach that acknowledges the interconnectedness of how we know about the world, what exists in the world, and what is (Dussart and Poirier in this volume). My reflection on encounters in Coast Salish ancestral places reveals ways in which individuals and actors can attend to the nature of relationships and senses of responsibility within these entangled worlds. This essentially anthropological stance opens up the possibility for critical engagement of the outcomes of experiences within these worlds – which are so often interwoven with threads of colonialism – and offers imaginative possibilities for new relationships based in mutual respect without requiring the diverse elements of the entangled systems to become one.

Coast Salish Ancestral Places

In Coast Salish territories – located in the urban and forested watershed and islands around the cities of Vancouver, Victoria, and Seattle – ancestors have a vital and continued presence. Nowhere are the ancestors of Coast Salish peoples more present than at places where remains have been interred. Ancestral agency is readily encountered in these places, having the potential to impact anyone, from those who are vulnerable (children, sickly people, ritual initiates, the elderly) to those who do not take the proper precautions and care to attend to respectful relations. Protocols and teachings about respectful and circumspect behaviour at graveyards and burial sites and near the aggrieved are well known in the Coast Salish community and have long been documented in the ethnographic literature (e.g., Stern 1934: 35–9; Jenness 2016: 89, 110–11; Bierwert 1996: 175–6; Barnett 1955: 218–22). Like a "stored charge" (Bierwert 1996: 169), ancestors may act upon the living through coming into close contact, their effect "coming out of the ground like a power" with the potential to cause harm (Boyd 2009: 716–17). My colleagues and I (McLay et al. 2008) summarized law, protocols, and teachings of Coast Salish peoples which guide their interactions with these ancestors. These follow two broad cultural principles, centred on respect for ancestral places and belongings, and on the maintenance of relations of reciprocity between the living and the dead. We observed that in maintaining relations of respect and reciprocity, Coast Salish customary laws include inherited rights related to knowledge and practice of caring for the dead, and overarching principles of nondisturbance and avoidance (2008: 162). While these laws, protocols, and teachings are well understood in Coast Salish communities today, the obvious challenge has been where individual settler, commercial, or state interests have disrupted, disturbed, or desecrated ancestral places, in spite of Coast Salish legal frameworks (McLay et al. 2008; see also Boyd 2009). As I argue below, the norm of entanglements does not have to continue to be fraught with colonial power, as Coast Salish people have been generous in sharing ways of living and coexisting in these worlds.

Berries in the Graveyard

I encountered the dangerous potential of this stored charge personally when visiting a pioneer cemetery on Gabriola Island in 2001. I was travelling with a small group of elders to pay respects at the grave of "Jane" – a Cowichan woman who lived in the mid-nineteenth century and married an early settler on the Island named Degnan, for whom the island's Degnan Bay is named. The elders I was working with at the time had located Jane as having come from a Cowichan family that several could trace their genealogy to, and wished to honour their ties to her and to the lands and waters of Gabriola Island where she had lived by visiting her grave site.

I was walking around the graveyard, and noticed a ripe trailing blackberry growing on the ground. This native plant has a sweet, flavourful berry and is harder to find than the invasive Himalayan blackberry. I picked a couple of the berries and went to ask one of the younger men who had come to assist the elders if he could remember the Hul'q'umi'num'-language name for it. Abraham C. Joe – a gentleman in his late seventies at that time – walked up to me, grabbed and held my hand. He had seen me pick the berries up and sternly scolded me for having done so. He warned that that if you take food from a graveyard, you can get paralysed. It happened a long time ago to his friend Richard, who picked some food from a graveyard and ended up with a paralysed face, and could never really talk again. Abraham warned it could split you in half – half your face and body would be paralysed. You'd go blind in one eye, deaf in one ear. He said that it was serious business, it was no joke. He then forcefully slapped the berry out of my hand – Abraham was a boxer in his youth – and walked away. The people around me, mostly tribal staff members and a few elders, looked somewhat surprised at how sternly he scolded me. I told his spouse later that I had appreciated the advice and that I wouldn't have known better if he had not told me. She felt bad that Abraham had been so stern and asked him to apologize. Later that day he rejoined me, standing close to my face, with his strong hand on my back, and whispered that there were no hard feelings. He told me again how serious it was, looking me straight and long in the eye. I thanked him. Abraham and I since became good friends. We frequently joked about the time he "punched me in the graveyard." It was for my own good, he would say, it showed that he cared about me.

The seriousness of my near-transgression and its potential consequences has long struck me as important. The potential for ancestors to act was well known to me, but I had not internalized it. I had been to burnings (also described by Barnett 1955: 220–1; Jenness 2016: 94, 125; McHalsie 2007: 118–20) where families offer plates of food to a fire tended by ritual specialists, who in turn receive messages from the deceased that came to feast and hear the prayers of the family who have gathered. I had been to funerals where the remains of the deceased or the items that were involved in their burial were handled with particular care for the safety of all concerned, employing special knowledge handed down in families by people who had the inherited privilege of that kind of work. At one funeral, for instance, where it is customary for the mourners gathered to help bury the dead with a few shovelfuls of soil each, a *thithu* (ritual specialist) reminded everyone that the shovel is *s'xexe* (sacred, taboo, potent), and that the immediate family would not be safe handling it. I have also witnessed families lower their blinds during evening meals to ensure that the deceased do not come looking for food and its essence to take away. However, this was the first time that such ancestral agency struck me so directly and personally. My friend was taking care of me, ensuring that I didn't ignorantly fall victim to the consequences of ancestral power.

Avoiding Ancestral Power at Burial Places

Anthropologist Colleen Boyd (2009) has described similar ancestral agency and the potential for its powerful impact on the living in her discussion of the "ghostly" presence of Coast Salish ancestors at a multimillion-dollar industrial development near Port Townsend, Washington. Her work reveals how dominant discourses of settler society may acknowledge such places as metaphorically "haunted," but that it generally holds Coast Salish narratives of ghostly experiences in sceptical disbelief (2009: 714). Coast Salish peoples, however, do not see encounters with ancestors disturbed by this industrial site as metaphorical hauntings or paranormal beliefs, but as part of the lived, embodied world, entangled with history and concerns for ongoing relationships among humans, places, and ancestors (2009: 703). My own encounters and experiences are consistent with this view. The presence of Coast Salish ancestors and their power and agency in the world is a marked concern wherever there is potential for encountering them, irrespective of how ancient they may be. As the burial places of the ancestors who died even two or three millennia ago are often well preserved in shell-laden cultural soils (along with other archaeological remains), as well as those in caves, on islets, and in forested places, this agency of ancestral presence has the potential to be encountered nearly anywhere in Coast Salish landscape. Given that the ancestors occupied many of the places now coveted by settler society, entanglements continue when governments issue permits for playgrounds, campsites, homes, or industrial sites in these locales, creating conflict with ancestral sites, putting people in danger.

Auggie Sylvester, an elder from Penelakut Tribe, who with his wife, Laura, is often called out to work when there are human remains that must be handled or cared for, once pointed out to me that there is a graveyard under the basketball court at Thetis Island near the ferry landing. This is not a well-known or marked graveyard, but one of many such places that have been covered by non-Aboriginal settlements, now so pervasive throughout the Coast Salish region. He told me that growing up, his grandfather had told him, "Don't you go play there, that's a graveyard" (undated fieldnotes, circa 2005). So, as we boated past that location on Thetis Island watching people moving actively around it, he said that he had never gone there, even when other kids (mostly his non-native neighbours resident on the island) were playing. His observation highlights how settlers so frequently are blithely ignorant of the location of ancestral burial grounds, and of the consequences of not taking care around them. Indeed, while playing games in a cemetery is similarly prohibited by provincial cemeteries legislation, ancient Indigenous grave sites are not afforded such protection. In this elder's estimation, the kids playing there – or at any other of these locations of ancestral graves – are at risk of consequences of ancestral agency.

The potential of this ancestral agency is often clearly brought into focus when the ground-altering activities associated with urban development disturb or disrupt ancient burial places. In 1994, I worked as an archaeologist doing excavations at the Somenos Creek site (DeRw-018) in the municipality of North Cowichan on Vancouver Island.

The site was slated for development into a housing subdivision, and the archaeological work was being done in conjunction with Cowichan Tribes (the nearby First Nation) to mitigate the extensive site disturbance, which was scheduled to follow. The excavation strategy was focused on revealing ancient house structures, which had been detected in test excavations and reinforced through a preliminary ground-penetrating radar survey (Brown 1996). Though we were not looking for them, we encountered many burials – literally several dozen – and it quickly became evident to everyone that this was not only an ancient household landscape but also an ancient mortuary landscape. Elders from Cowichan Tribes who visited the site on a regular basis to advise us and assess our work discussed with us their views on how to proceed as burials were revealed. One woman, an elderly member of Cowichan Tribes' committee, had very serious concerns about the situation that was unfolding. Something like this had happened in her family in the past, and she wanted all of us to learn from her experience. These are my notes of what she said:

> My father was a "powder-monkey" on the Gulf Islands. He was hired by a landowner to blow up stumps on Saltspring Island. He was blowing up one of those stumps to take it out and uncovered the remains of twins. The landowner came and took the skulls. My father protested and asked for the bones back. The landowner refused. A few days later my father came back to the islands to protest again. He couldn't sleep and felt ill. The landowner said these were his bones and he could deal with them as he liked. They were none of my father's concern. He showed my father the two skulls all polished up and sitting on the mantel-piece with a candle inside. My father went home. The next day the landowner called my father up to come to the Island. When he arrived, he saw what was left of the house. It was as if the whole thing had been ransacked. Things were broken everywhere except the two skulls. The landowner said that during the night everything started to fly around and get wrecked. The landowner said he was sorry and wished my father would take back the bones – asked him what he would do. My father said he would take all the bones and take care of them. He took the two skulls and took all the bones left near the stump and wrapped them in blankets and did a re-burial ceremony for them. (Fieldnotes, September 1994)

Through telling this story, though she didn't come right out and say it, she was emphasizing to us the potential consequences for the people who would come to live at this place if the burials were similarly dis-respectfully treated. Properties could be ruined, lives put in disarray. She and her colleagues on the elders' committee were well attuned to these entanglements. They shortly thereafter recommended to chief and council that the archaeological work cease, that all remains that had been uncovered be reburied with the appropriate burning feast for the deceased, and that support be withdrawn for any further land-altering activity at this ancestral site. Weeks later, after archaeological work was halted, a "burning" was held, alighting a feast of traditional foods while a *thithu* worked to restore respectful relations with the disturbed ancestors. While people caring for us and this place were no longer bothered by the dead in their dreams, the land developer faced long-term financial difficulties, as chief and council insisted the high-density residential housing project not proceed. This precipitated a nearly twenty-year dispute over land use for the area, with the property owner having numerous subsequent development and rezoning applications denied by the local municipal government, who to their credit did not want to be disrespectful to their First Nations neighbours so vigorously opposed to the further desecration of the ancient village and burial site (McLay et al. 2009; McLay, Brown, and Oakes 2013). Finally in 2013, the municipality created a series of land buy-backs, restrictive covenants, and zoning bylaws to limit any further development impacts to the burial site.

This encounter highlights the potential implications of taking seriously Indigenous political ontology (Blaser 2013). Reflecting on ancestral experiences inspires action with political power and consequences. Mutually entangled in the world of these ancestors and their living descendants, archaeologists and municipal council respected the agency that they themselves may not have fully understood or "believed," taking a bold stance that transcended their narrower bureaucratic and legal duties. When such a respectful approach to entanglement is not shared, there can be further consequences.

Desecrating Ancestral Graves, Disturbing Ancestral Action

The story of the development and disturbance of ancestral sites is all too familiar in the Coast Salish world (McLay 2004). My notes of a 2009 political meeting of Coast Salish leaders, to discuss the consequences of building and other permits being issued by governments for development on well-documented burial sites in the Gulf Islands, recall one elder from the Songhees community cautioning those gathered about the outcome of ignoring their advice: "Poets Cove [a resort development that destroyed an ancient village and burial site] didn't listen to our traditions. Then a young girl got killed after working there. They've gone through six managers. And Bear Mountain [a large, upscale mountainside housing and golf course development], they didn't listen to our warnings and now they are getting sued" (fieldnotes, 16 September 2009).

Each of these multimillion-dollar development projects notoriously demolished Coast Salish ancestral sites, under very public objections of Coast Salish community members and leadership. Though Coast Salish peoples had taken these serious steps to inform the private landowners and permit-granting governments about the consequences, they didn't listen, or couldn't hear. The elder's assessment was that the consequences of ancestral action were not only bodily (the man who fell ill) but fiscal and legal as well. Non-Indigenous actors were entangled in these outcomes along with others from the Coast Salish community who suffered ill effects.

Such consequences were recently echoed by Penelakut elder Laura Sylvester, who in the summer of 2014 was asked to give advice to a student archaeological field crew before their summer excavations in the Gulf Islands. Working in these places, handling ancestral remains, she said, has the potential to affect everyone, native and non-native alike. She told the crew about one non-native person who had recently been operating a backhoe in the Saanich area. He was moving dirt that contained human remains from one area to another, and to the back of a haul truck. The backhoe operator became so badly affected by disrupting these burials that a local chief had to take him in and "work on him." The chief became particularly concerned for the man's four-year-old daughter, who had also taken ill. This was an important lesson for the students – though they themselves may not be directly impacted, they can take the effects home with them in unanticipated ways. If a student had children at home or a young sibling, not taking care with ancestral remains could put these other people at risk. Wearing a small amount of *tumulh* (a red ochre paint) on the hands or near the eyes can help, and taking care to not yell, holler, or fool around near the dead was also essential to avoiding calamity. Her message highlighted that these relationships must be taken seriously, even if the students, like the backhoe operator, did not share her particular beliefs. She was taking care to point out to them that the experiences they would have as young scientists excavating at an archaeological site are invariably entangled with the possibility of ancestral encounter. The students at this fieldschool respected and practised the advice given, and their summer's work unfolded without mishap. During a previous archaeological fieldschool, however, a student sustained serious injuries in an accident that occurred in the off-hours of the dig. Concerns were expressed by the elders, who told the fieldschool that while this may have been an accident, it was no coincidence, as the off-hours activities of that student failed to embody the spirit of the advice they had given. The student was entangled with ancestral agency whether he believed it or not, and the signs were there for everyone about what respectful, cautious behaviour should and should not be.

This brings me to my final example of the potential consequences of ancestral agency and action. It is a disturbing story in many ways, and one that is necessarily here only a partial retelling. This is the story of when the government built and operated a public toilet in a Coast Salish grave. In 1974, provincial government archaeologists recorded a thick and deep cultural shell deposit on Cabbage Island – one of the smaller Gulf Islands in the Salish Sea – as part of their regional archaeological survey. In 1985, when Cabbage Island was being managed as a Marine Park by the provincial government, plans were made to improve the facilities, building a set of stairs and several outhouses directly into these cultural shell deposits, which by then were registered in the Provincial Archaeology Branch's records as DeRs-25. Significantly, during the excavation of one of the pit toilets, the ancient skeletal remains of a person were found at a depth of two metres by BC Parks staff (Maxwell et al. 1998: 58–9). The remains recovered in the excavated soil (amounting to about half the body) were put into storage at the Royal British Columbia Museum. The other half were left in the wall of the pit toilet, which was then used for its intended function continuously from 1985 until 2004. As repugnant and disrespectful as it is inept, the provincial government allowed the (largely unknowing) public to defecate in a known and documented Coast Salish burial for nearly two decades.

When Parks Canada took over the provincial park lands in the southern Gulf Islands late in 2003, they inherited all of these facilities and related records. When this particular burial record was discovered, Parks Canada staff immediately moved to close the toilet facility and set about a process to find a way to address its complicated legacy. The partial remains in storage at the Royal BC Museum were located, and all neighbouring First Nations community representatives were alerted.

I recall being at a meeting in 2004, shortly after Gulf Islands National Parks Reserve had been established, where a group of about twenty-five elders were reflecting on what to do about the new park. One of the members stated what seemed to be the obvious: "If there are outhouses, they have to be removed from the grave and archaeological site" (fieldnotes, 8 June 2004). The direction they decided to give to Parks Canada was that that it is unacceptable to use burial sites for toilets. "We all need to be on the same page on this," one of the elders at the meeting emphatically said (fieldnotes, 8 June 2004). Though this sentiment, which spoke to basic human dignity and respect, was unanimously approved, exactly how to act upon it was not straightforward.

By early in 2007, what to do about reuniting the ancestral remains in the wall of the decommissioned toilet with those in the museum continued to challenge everyone concerned. While all agreed that dignified reburial was critical, a solution of exactly how, when, and where to do this was elusive. Auggie Sylvester, who had expressed deep concern about these remains since they had been revealed to him three years prior, said:

> Leaving these things undealt with is like having a lit fuse. It is just a question of how long that fuse is before it goes off. If we don't do it right, it is just a matter of time before someone loses a grandchild, a great-grandchild. It is serious ... The bones from the museum have to come out at the same time, same place as the pit toilet bones. (Fieldnotes, 8 January 2007)

This was an urgent matter. Such an undignified disturbance was a desecration that would not be without consequences. People could die, another committee member warned, vulnerable people, children. One elder who had the inherited rights to care for the dead agreed:

> The bones that have been exposed must be attended to as soon as possible. No matter how difficult, those remains must be wrapped and reburied. Then food has to be burned for them. You have to know the words for doing it. When you burn for these remains, burn traditional food; fish clams, wild potatoes. Those old people won't know what modern food is. Don't send clothes, send blankets. (Fieldnotes, 8 January 2007)

Like the burning that had been held at the Somenos Creek site, these ancestors require the care and feeding and attention that ritual specialists know how to perform. The special words – *siwin* in

Hul'q'umi'num' – are not only the privately known ritual power words needed for performing the ritual (Suttles 1984: 69), but also the calming explanations needed to give those ancestors when they come to take the meal that is shared and hear what has happened on the other side.

Another year passed, and the concerns about the consequences of leaving the reburial and ritual action undone became pressing. A younger community member expressed his worries to me: "People are having too many problems. So many people have died. Four and a half years discussing Cabbage Island; it is just too long. We have to settle this soon" (fieldnotes, 7 December 2007). There had been a series of tragic deaths in the community; suicides, fatal house fires, elders lost. His uncle agreed: "Years is too long to wait. It is safer if we don't talk about it unless we are going to do something about it" (fieldnotes, 7 December 2007). By this point, there was a palpable concern about the safety of people in the community, and a few people had explicitly linked the tragic deaths of several children in one nearby community to the inaction by everyone concerned to make things right on Cabbage Island.

Irrespective of the particular issues that caused such a grievous delay, or even the initial act of desecration, my point is to draw attention to a critical understanding of the strength of ancestral power and the urgency of action required to restore respectful relations. Tragic deaths become explainable when people talk repeatedly about the vulgar and dehumanizing events, but take no action. It seems to me that defecating into a grave is widely unacceptable, irrespective of one's understanding of ancestral power or disbelief in spirits or the "ghostly presence" of ancestors (cf. Boyd 2009). While there is a profoundly colonial logic at play in the expedient partial removal of a body for a pit toilet, these events also show a failure of state and institutional action. Such complicated entanglements had consequences proportionate to the level of disrespect; in this case very serious ones, with the death of children being bound up with the prolonged wrangling over what to do and how to do it.

Finally, by the summer of 2008, the logistical, political, legal, and cultural issues which had delayed the needed action were resolved and the reburial was done, with the remains from the museum being reinterred near the other half of the ancestor, who remained two metres below the surface. All concerned felt guarded relief, and a sense that the dignity of this ancestor had been restored. A middle-aged man

from one of the Hul'qumi'num communities who attended the reburial
ceremony reflected to me that he had:

> felt really sombre at that time, but also really good because we were bring-
> ing that ancestor's remains home back to where he belonged. And you
> could feel the appreciation that was taking place because that person was
> finally being whole again. We brought them home, made them whole
> again ... I know that that day we went to Cabbage Island will always be a
> memory in my heart. I remember [the elders] holding candles and pray-
> ing for our ancestor that was going to be reburied back home where he
> belonged. So those are the kind of things we need to work on. We need to
> work on the protection. (Fieldnotes, 19 September 2009)

His message shows the relational logic at play. We cannot simply consider the events closed with the reburial. Rather, attending to ancestral
presence requires continued work and attention, particularly in ongoing colonial settlement and actions. Making the situation right required
not only Coast Salish ritual specialists but also the joint action of provincial, federal, and First Nations governments, archaeologists, curators,
and Parks staff. Everyone who knew about it – everyone entangled –
had some responsibility to deal with it, as a principle, indeed as an
article of Coast Salish law.

Law and Coexistence

Principles of Indigenous law can be understood through these stories,
which in turn can guide and inform governments and the public in
land development decisions, offering an avenue for reconciliation of
colonial settlement. The problem of how to have the principles of this
relational ontology taken up by the general population has become
significant, particularly in places like Coast Salish territories, where private land is extensive, and there is a rapid pace of urban development
(Thom 2014).

In a political meeting held in the fall of 2009 to discuss this problem,
a prominent leader from one of the SENĆOŦEN Coast Salish communities of the Saanich peninsula raised his concerns:

> The same thing is happening all over the Gulf Islands. Our people were
> brought out [to those islands] in canoes, not buried. They were left out
> there, and you weren't allowed to go there anymore ... Now there are no

laws. The policies have no enforcement. Developers tell their workers to hide what they find because they don't want to lose their job. We need to change the way government works so people are forced to deal with it properly. (Fieldnotes, 16 September 2009)

His comment that "now there are no laws" with respect to ancestral grave sites is poignant on several registers. It is first a rebuke to existing provincial heritage legislation – which has the potential to protect such places from disturbance, but which paradoxically works to transform these powerful ancestral sites (*shmukw'elu*) into heritage resources that can be readily altered or destroyed (McLay 2011), subverting Coast Salish law. It is also an ironic lament that while Coast Salish peoples have long pushed for the recognition and respect of their laws, governments have fervently resisted recognizing these, particularly on private lands. As such, as he points out, colonial law creates what appears to be a legal vacuum in these places.

Like the friends and elders who worked to teach me, Coast Salish leaders have frequently taken public positions that governments need to be educated about Coast Salish laws – the responsibilities of a relational ontology – and act in accordance. Echoing the sentiments above, another SENĆOŦEN leader at the same meeting emphasized the importance of Aboriginal and non-Aboriginal peoples working together to achieve this. He said: "Our ancestors are here, they are listening to us. This is about desecration. We have to correct the *Xwulunitum* [non-native people]. There is no private property, our ancestors are our landmarks." Just as others and I have been corrected and guided to incorporate and respect this ancestral ontology, Coast Salish leaders see the potential for the coexistence of settler and Indigenous laws and the positive possibilities of respectful ancestral relations. Indeed, respect for the dead is not a particularly difficult idea to understand in any world. However, the particular modalities of how relationships of respect can be manifest in entangled worlds do not always generate mutual expectations for political action.

Coast Salish political leaders are not willing to walk away from their responsibilities to these ancestors – nor the many other non-human persons and places that also demand relationships of respect and reciprocity. When faced with bounds of "private land" or the title-extinguishing terms of "full and final settlement" agreements in modern-day treaties, Coast Salish peoples continue to care for these ancestors and places, particularly when they demand our attention, brought forth through disturbance, erosion, development, or even merely perambulation through graveyards and cemeteries, which in a land occupied for ten thousand years can be nearly anywhere. This caring is not only for themselves and their communities but also for all peoples living in the Coast Salish world. They don't wish for ancestral agency to impact the children or the vulnerable, to make anyone sick or poor. This care comes from Coast Salish ideologies of living well in this world as persons – human and non-human – together. It embodies the often-heard Hul'q'umi'num' proverb: *Uy' ye' thut ch 'u' suw ts'its'uwatul' ch*. Be kind, and you help each other.

Understanding this can lay the path for better land claims and co-management outcomes, and for reconciliation more generally. As negotiated arrangements provide a seminal point for resetting relations, it is critical in these spaces to take Aboriginal peoples' experiences of ancestral territories seriously and resituate unchallenged notions of personhood, agency, knowledge, power, labour, and exchange (Nadasdy 2007: 26). To be effective, settlement agreements and co-management structures must proceed in a way that acknowledges that these relationships with ancestors (and other non-human persons and places that have agency in the world) matter (Blaser 2012: 3). There is some space for optimism, as respectful ancestral relations have been considered in Maori treaty implementation (Salmond 2012). Even in Coast Salish territories, Hul'qum'num Treaty Group has negotiated a non-treaty provision in their agreement with the Provincial Archaeology Branch (Hul'qum'num Treaty Group 2007) requiring statutory decision makers to listen to and take into account Indigenous principles for assessing the "significance" of a site, beyond the rather narrow set of values provided for by provincial policy. The potential of such a clause is to guide and inform decision making based on the particular modalities of what constitutes respectful relations at these ancestral sites in Indigenous terms, though in practice to date it has remained challenging to implement. However, as such negotiated arrangements unfold, perhaps treaty relations will be reframed, or a fuller scope of Aboriginal title and jurisdictions will be recognized, providing more opportunities for Canadians and Indigenous peoples to engage in this transformation.

Coda: Belief, Metaphor, and Political Action

I want to turn back to the difficult question posed about whether we need to "believe" in order to live respectfully in our shared social worlds, and to complicate my story. Anthropologist Bruce Miller, in his article on the politics of research on ecstatic and extraordinary experience (2007), asked Sonny McHalsie, a cultural advisor for the Stó:lō Nation (a Coast Salish community near Vancouver), what he made of researchers who did not take seriously the Stó:lō view of reality. Miller reported how McHalsie had become

> ... distraught because an anthropologist who formerly worked in his community had unexpectedly announced that he was an atheist and did not believe in spirits or spirit helpers ... [McHalsie] felt betrayed because the anthropologist had not revealed his views earlier and because ... the gift of knowledge given by [McHalsie] appeared to be wasted, unappreciated, and even intentionally slighted ... (Miller 2007: 198)

In an interview with Miller, McHalsie further elaborated on his particular view:

> I can't see how an atheist who doesn't believe in any form of spirituality is able to respect [our beliefs] ... Without an individual's own spirit there is no way to connect to the metaphors, the teachings of others which allows us to relate to others' beliefs ... A Christian can relate to our *shxwelí* [spirit or life force] and the connections to rocks, trees, and fish. A person without that belief can't relate to it and that must affect their understandings and interpretations. (Miller 2007: 190)

Miller goes on to discuss how McHalsie was concerned that being an atheist – which in his view includes not having the capacity for belief – can put the work of a researcher who is hoping to support Aboriginal title and rights claims in jeopardy because such land claims "rest on their own notions of the landscape and epistemology, and human relationships to other entities" (Miller 2007: 190).

McHalsie was, I believe, commenting on an off-hand rebuke I had made in the 1990s when a mutual colleague pressed me on why I wasn't interested in joining him in the Catholic church and Masonic lodge, to which McHalsie had also been invited (McHalsie 2007: 121–2). Recalling my high-school experiences with evangelists, I had closed the door on the colleague's invitation by saying that I didn't believe in God, that I was an atheist. McHalsie, who had crystallized "belief" as an important measure for epistemological congruency, tried "to think of a way to respect that belief [atheism]" (Miller 2007: 190), but could not.

I appreciate the cultural bridging work of McHalsie's explanation to Miller – in drawing a comparison between the Spirit and *shxwelí*, for instance – and how he was working to underscore how mutual understanding can flow from the potential of such metaphorical resonance. However, I think such a view reduces the possibility of engaging and experiencing multiple worlds to the narrower epistemological problem of what we may know to be true. Blaser (2012: 4) has expressed the concern that performing this kind of "saming" of Indigenous and European cultures is, in many ways, simply the flip side of essentialist "othering" discourses and maintains a colonial relationship that dissolves the possibility of radical alterity of personhood, realities, and worlds. Relegating our experiences to "belief" or "metaphor" reinforces the idea that they are cultural constructions, and does little to break down the hierarchies of what is "factual" or "true," debates which are replete with power, colonial and otherwise (Nadasdy 2007; Povinelli 1995).

Rather than attending to our shared experiences and the possibilities of mutually encountered personhood, made through a continued coming into being (Ingold 2004; Bird-David 1999), McHalsie's particular focus on "belief" and "metaphor" forecloses on the possibilities arising from entanglements of shared experience. I would argue that in a massively secular society, requiring "belief" and drawing on "common metaphor" for mutual understanding closes the door to the recognition of entanglement in multiple worlds. Entanglement does not mean that our truths must merge. Such a position sets an impossible standard of *common truths*, which in most cases will fail to meet Indigenous peoples' political expectations, as knowledge and truth claims are laden with social power. All-or-nothing truth claims risk perpetuating intolerance and the rejection of neighbours genuinely working to live together without having to subvert their own respective "truths." Rather, people may stand together entangled at the juncture of multiple worlds, they will have their own truths about those worlds, and they may come into relations of respect and acknowledgment of the responsibilities that living together in those worlds entails.

While there is always tension in relationships – even respectful ones – I want to emphasize here the personal imperative and implications of these relational ontologies and their consequences for political action. While I still am hesitant to make categorical declarations about my beliefs, in my encounters in the Coast Salish world, I have experienced something of what it takes to be human in these territories. In my own movements in and through the Coast Salish ancestral world, I – and many others – have become a relational self, engaging the land, ances-tors, and non-human persons with feelings, recollections, intentions, dreams, and speech. Living in Coast Salish ancestral territories in the twenty-first century allows for emergent personhood (Ingold 2004). Being respectful, circumspect, and maintaining an uncertainty about one's knowledge allow for this emergence. It provides a model of living together without getting into value judgments over what is "truth" or whose "belief about the experience" is more valid than the other. Fol-lowing Coast Salish wisdom, attending to relationships that are respect-ful, reciprocal, and ongoing allows us to open up, making minds and hearts strong – *qwamqwum sqwaluwun*, as it is said in Hul'q'umi'num'. It opens the possibility of shared experience, bringing us together as one: *nuts'a'maat squaluwun*. And upon reflection, it opens up something of the knowledge about ourselves and the others with whom we engage these relationships.

ACKNOWLEDGMENTS

I have been privileged to live and work in Coast Salish territories for many years, and to have had numerous colleagues and friends share their teachings with me. This work was made possible by the leaders, elders' committees, and staff at the Hul'qumi'num Treaty Group (2000–15), Cowichan Tribes (1994), Stó:lō Tribal Council (1993–4), and the Scowlitz and Chehalis First Nations (1993). In addition to those people whose words I share in the chapter, I would also like to acknowledge the provocative and insightful discussions I have been fortunate to have with Joey Caro, Lea Joe, Robert Morales, Mabel Mitch-ell, and the late Peter Seymour, Willie Seymour, Abner Thorne, Angus Smith, and Simon Charlie, all of whom contributed in many ways to my understand-ing of living respectfully in the Coast Salish world.

REFERENCES

Amoss, Pamela. 1978. *Coast Salish Spirit Dancing: The Survival of an Ancestral Religion*. Seattle: University of Washington Press.
Barnett, Homer. 1955. *The Coast Salish of British Columbia*. Eugene: University of Oregon Press.
Bierwert, Crisca. 1996. *Brushed by Cedar, Living by the River: Coast Salish Figures of Power*. Tuscon: University of Arizona Press.

Bird-David, Nurit. 1999. "'Animism' Revisited: Personhood, Environment, and Relational Epistemology." *Current Anthropology* 40 (S1 Supplement): S67–S91. http://dx.doi.org/10.1086/200061.

Blaser, Mario. 2012. "Ontology and Indigeneity: On the Political Ontology of Heterogeneous Assemblages." *Cultural Geographies* 21 (1): 1–10.

Blaser, Mario. 2013. "Ontological Conflicts and the Stories of Peoples in Spite of Europe: Toward a Conversation on Political Ontology." *Current Anthropology* 54 (5): 547–68. http://dx.doi.org/10.1086/672270.

Boyd, Colleen. 2009. "'You See Your Culture Coming Out of the Ground Like a Power': Uncanny Narratives in Time and Space on the Northwest Coast." *Ethnohistory* 56 (4): 699–731. http://dx.doi.org/10.1215/00141801-2009-027.

Brown, Douglas. 1996. Archaeological Investigations at the Somenos Creek Site (DeRw18). BC Investigation Permit 1994-12 2(g). Unpublished Report. BC Archaeology Branch, Victoria.

Cruikshank, Julie. 2005. *Do Glaciers Listen? Local Knowledge, Colonial Encounters and Social Imagination*. Vancouver: University of British Columbia Press.

Feit, Harvey. 1986. "Hunting and the Quest for Power: The James Bay Cree and Whitemen in the Twentieth Century." In *Native Peoples: The Canadian Experience*, ed. Bruce Morrison and Roderick Wilson, 171–207. Toronto: McClelland and Stewart.

Feit, Harvey. 2004. "James Bay Crees' Life Projects and Politics: Histories of Place, Animal Partners and Enduring Relationships." In *In the Way of Development: Indigenous Peoples, Life Projects and Globalization*, ed. Mario Blaser, Harvey Feit, and Glenn McRae, 92–110. London and New York: Zed Books and Ottawa: Canadian International Development Research Centre.

Hul'qumi'num Treaty Group. 2007. Memorandum of Understanding: First Nation Heritage Site Conservation in Hul'qumi'num Tumuhw, between British Columbia and Hul'qumi'num Member First Nations. Accessed 7 December 2015. https://www.for.gov.bc.ca/ftp/archaeology/external/!publish/web/Hul'qumi'num_Treaty_Group_MOU.pdf

Ingold, Tim. 1996. "Hunting and Gathering as Ways of Perceiving the Environment." In *Redefining Nature: Ecology, Culture and Domestication*, ed. Katsuyoshi Fukui and Roy Ellen, 117–55. Oxford: Berg.

Ingold, Tim. 2004. "A Circumpolar Night's Dream." In *Figured Worlds: Ontological Obstacles in Intercultural Relations*, ed. John Clammer, Sylvie Poirier, and Eric Schwimmer, 25–57. Toronto: University of Toronto Press.

Jenness, Diamond. 2016. *The W̱SÁNEĆ and Their Neighbours: Diamond Jenness on the Coast Salish Peoples of Vancouver Island*. Ed. Barnett Richling. Oakville: Rock's Mills Press.

Kew, Michael. 1990. "Central and Southern Coast Salish Ceremonies since 1900." In *Handbook of North American Indians, Volume 7, Northwest Coast*, ed. Wayne Suttles, 476–80. Washington, DC: Smithsonian Institution.

McHalsie, Albert (Sonny). 2007. "We Have to Take Care of Everything That Belongs to Us." In *Be of Good Mind: Essays on the Coast Salish*, ed. Bruce Miller, 82–130. Vancouver: University of British Columbia Press.

Maxwell, John, Tina Christensen, Jim Stafford, and Tal Fisher. 1998. Southern Gulf Islands, B.C. Pacific Marine Heritage Legacy Lands Archaeological Inventory and Assessment. BC Archaeology Branch Permit 1997-344. Unpublished Report. BC Archaeology Branch, Victoria.

McLay, Eric. 2004. "To Preserve and Protect the Archaeological Heritage of the Southern Gulf Islands." *Midden* 36 (3/4): 12–17.

McLay, Eric. 2011. "'Site Alteration': The Demolition of British Columbia's Archaeological Heritage." *Midden* 43 (4): 3–7.

McLay, Eric, Douglas Brown, and Nicole Oakes. 2013. "Archaeological Impact Assessment of Lot Bemb, Somenos Creek (DeRw-018), Timbercrest Estates Ltd., North Cowichan, BC." HCA Permit 2011-225. Unpublished Report. BC Archaeology Branch, Victoria.

McLay, Eric, Douglas Brown, Nicole Oakes, and Lindsay Oliver. 2009. "Archaeological Investigations of Ground Penetrating Radar Mapping at Somenos Creek (DeRw-018), B.C." HCA Permit 2006-393. Unpublished Report. BC Archaeology Branch, Victoria.

McLay, Eric, Kelly Bannister, Lea Joe, Brian Thom, and George Nicholas. 2008. "'A'lhut tu tet Sul'hweentst [Respecting the Ancestors]: Understanding Hul'qumi'num Heritage Laws and Concerns for the Protection of Archaeological Heritage." In *First Nations Cultural Heritage and Law*, ed. Catherine Bell and Val Napoleon, 150–202. Vancouver: University of British Columbia Press.

Miller, Bruce. 2007. "The Politics of Ecstatic Research." In *Extraordinary Anthropology: Transformations in the Field*, ed. Jean-Guy Goulet and Bruce Miller, 186–207. Lincoln: University of Nebraska Press.

Nadasdy, Paul. 2007. "The Gift in the Animal: The Ontology of Hunting and Human-Animal Sociality." *American Ethnologist* 34 (1): 25–43. http://dx.doi.org/10.1525/ae.2007.34.1.25.

Poirier, Sylvie. 2004. "Ontology, Ancestral Order, and Agencies among the Kukatja of the Australian Western Desert." In *Figured Worlds: Ontological Obstacles in Intercultural Relations*, ed. John Clammer, Sylvie Poirier, and Eric Schwimmer, 58–82. Toronto: University of Toronto Press.

Poirier, Sylvie. 2013. "The Dynamic Reproduction of Hunter-Gatherers' Ontologies and Values." In *A Companion to the Anthropology of Religion*, ed.

Janice Boddy and Michael Lambek, 50–68. New York: John Wiley and Sons. http://dx.doi.org/10.1002/9781118605936.ch2.

Povinelli, Elizabeth. 1995. "Do Rocks Listen? The Cultural Politics of Apprehending Australian Aboriginal Labor." *American Anthropologist* 97 (3): 505–18. http://dx.doi.org/10.1525/aa.1995.97.3.02a00090.

Salmond, Anne. 2012. "Ontological Quarrels: Indigeneity, Exclusion and Citizenship in a Relational World." *Anthropological Theory* 12 (2): 115–41. http://dx.doi.org/10.1177/1463499612454119.

Scott, Colin. 2006. "Spirit and Practical Knowledge in the Person of the Bear among Wemindji Cree Hunters." *Ethnos* 71 (1): 51–66. http://dx.doi.org/10.1080/00141840600603178.

Stern, Bernhard. 1934. *The Lummi Indians of Northwest Washington*. New York: Columbia University Press.

Suttles, Wayne. 1984. "Productivity and Its Constraints: A Coast Salish Case." In *Indian Art Traditions of the Northwest Coast*, ed. Roy Carlson, 67–87. Burnaby: Simon Fraser University Archaeology Press.

Thom, Brian. 2014. "Reframing Indigenous Territories: Private Property, Human Rights and Overlapping Claims." *American Indian Culture and Research Journal* 38 (4): 3–28. http://dx.doi.org/10.17953/aicr.38.4.6372163053512w6x.

8 Transmission of Knowledge, Clans, and Lands among the Yolŋu (Northern Territory, Australia)

SACHIKO KUBOTA

Introduction

Knowledge, according to Fredrik Barth, is "what a person employs to interpret and act on the world" (2002: 1). Barth argues that knowledge is distributed unevenly between persons and across social groups. He urges anthropologists to produce "a comparative ethnographic analysis on how bodies of knowledge are produced in persons and populations in the context of the social relations that they sustain" (2002: 1). He points out that a comparative perspective on human knowledge allows us to unravel a number of aspects of the culturally constructed world, and that actions become knowledge to others only after the events (2002: 1).

Barth questions Bertrand Russell's point that one's knowledge is based on one's experience and valid inference based on experiences (Russell 1948), and asks how, then, "a knowledge that must have its wellsprings in individual experiences yet became to a large extent conventional in social circles?" and "whereby these conventional bodies of knowledge assume their locally characteristic shapes?" (Barth 2002: 2). Although Clifford Geertz argues that knowledge is inevitably local (Geertz 1983), Barth tries to separate "knowledge" from "culture" to clarify the inner process of production of a localized body of knowledge. He argues that knowledge always has three faces: a substantive corpus, a range of representation, and a social organization (Barth 2002) He shows how these faces interrelate and generate specific criteria and how the trajectory of tradition of knowledge is determined locally based on the comparative field data. He then concludes that already established thoughts, representations, and social relations of the local area filter as well as reconfigure individual experiences to generate conventional and culturally unique world views.

Since the mid-1980s I have conducted research at Galiwin'ku, a northeastern Arnhem Land town in the Northern Territory and the largest community on Elcho Island, with Yolŋu people. The knowledge most valued by Yolŋu is that of the land. According to their world view, Ancestral Beings constructed, transformed, and produced the various current geographical features of their land. For them, knowledge about this land – its sacred places, songs, stories, paintings, dances, and rituals – is crucial, as is its ownership embedded in complex patterns of social organization and inheritance. Their whole system of such local knowledge is substantial, and encompasses many different ways of representation that are communicated and handed down. Thus, they share the knowledge of the land as a conventional entity (Keen 1994; Morphy 1991).

From the perspective of the Yolŋu, rights to the land are owned by the members of patrilineal clans and are handed down through patrilineal descent. This local knowledge is commonly shared and distributed, among Yolŋu senior members, and is a common discussion topic. The core of this dense body of knowledge includes their understanding of the environment, of animals and plants connected to ancestral stories, and of Ancestral Beings in the area. Since the beginning of the twentieth century, their knowledge of and their relationships to and with the land have been rearticulated as they experienced the stressful entanglements of colonization, forced sedentarization, policies of assimilation, self-determination, Christianization, and the pressures of the market economy. So how have the Yolŋu people continued to maintain their manifold responsibilities to the land through such drastically and rapidly changing times? How are their local knowledge and practices towards the land challenged and modified by encounters with missionaries and non-Yolŋu people and institutions? And how do senior people pass on their knowledge of the land to the younger generations?

As noted by Françoise Dussart and Sylvie Poirier (in this volume), it is useful to apply the notion of "entanglement" in a discussion of how and why the body of knowledge of the land is rearticulated through time.

For the Yolŋu, as for many Aboriginal societies, the location of burial sites has a unique importance (see also Nicolas Peterson in this volume). In Yolŋu society, discussions or disputes over the locations of mortuary rituals provide one important and practical way for young people to learn about the clan relationships to the land. In these discussions, people mainly argue about why it is appropriate to have a funeral or burial at a particular place. They ground their arguments in the ancestral stories of the spiritual Beings associated with the territories that are owned by each clan, which means that the area is occupied not only by Yolŋu clan members but also by their ancestors, natural creatures, and other phenomena associated with the clan. Thus, these discussions function as occasions for sharing the knowledge of each clan's relationships to the land. Just as the land has a direct connection to Ancestral Beings and their stories, the location of mortuary rituals and burials is of great importance to the Yolŋu people in their daily life.

Although the establishment in 1942 of the Christian mission town changed the Aboriginal people's life dramatically, the deaths of kin and their "traditional" mortuary rituals continue to be key public events. Funerals are an occasion for relatives to travel to other communities, and are expected to be attended by many. Leading up to most funerals, there are disagreements over the ritual and burial location, and it usually takes a few weeks of discussions before people can settle on the actual funeral ground and before any funeral preparations can begin in earnest. These discussions function as occasions for the Yolŋu people to confirm and share their knowledge concerning clan rights over the land.

In this chapter, I first describe the historical changes that have transformed the lives of the Aboriginal people in northeastern Arnhem Land, dividing these changes into three periods. I examine more specifically how mourning practices have been rearticulated over the years while at the same time remaining a critical part of everyday Yolŋu life. I end with a discussion of three case studies involving recent disputes over mortuary rituals, to show how – influenced by the policies of external agencies – senior people's knowledge of the land has been, and is being, shared with the younger generations, and how it is rearticulated and reconventionalized. With such a rich body of local knowledge, how has the entanglement occurred? Over time, the Yolŋu idea of land ownership has become entangled with those of outsiders, such as the state and the Christian mission, while also maintaining its specificity. I analyse the complex and dynamic dimensions of the ontological entanglements between the Indigenous and non-Indigenous peoples' relationships with the land. Such issues of ontological entanglement over land, and what is negotiated over the land, have economic and political reverberations in everyday Yolŋu life.

The Studied Area and Its Mortuary Rituals

About three thousand Yolŋu people reside today in Galiwin'ku. The township was originally established by Methodist missionaries in 1942, but Aboriginal people have managed it by themselves since the 1970s, following the implementation of federal policies of self-determination. The area was accordingly designated as Aboriginal Reserve with unalienable freehold title, the course of which is described by Frances Morphy in detail in her chapter in this volume.

I carried out my original research at Galiwin'ku in 1986 and 1987, and have continued to visit it ever since. It has changed considerably since the 1980s in various ways. There are far more commercial products in people's lives, including cars, boats, home electronics, clothes, and daily cooking utensils. In other words, the Yolŋu are far more affluent than they were in the 1980s. Although many of them continue to hunt and gather bush food, some work for different organizations in town, others receive income from their artwork, and most rely on social security income. As Nicolas Peterson has shown, radical changes have taken place in remote Australia since the granting of citizenship to all Aboriginal people in 1968 and the welfare payment in 1977 (Peterson 1998).[1]

Today, many Yolŋu individuals travel to various places in Australia and overseas for conferences, meetings, and exhibition openings, or to visit doctors and friends. They use mobile phones or smart phones, and communicate with outsiders, including European friends. As a result, most have a reasonable understanding of European life and its concepts.

As the town has grown from about two thousand in the 1980s to nearly three thousand today, the population is far younger than ever before. Thus, it has become more difficult for the older generation to insist on traditional ways of thinking. At the end of the 1980s, when I was conducting research for my PhD, few women had babies out of wedlock, and there were various attempts to accommodate such irregular occurrences within the kinship system and marriage rules. Such accommodations showed how senior members changed both the term of address and the term of reference to reintegrate mother and child into a traditional domain of clan relationships. For example, family members, especially the senior members, changed the terms of address. There has always been a strict rule concerning marriage among the Yolŋu people. For a man, a desirable marriage partner is his mother's mother's brother's daughter, whom he calls *galay*. She, in turn, calls him *dhuway*. Today, if someone marries without adhering to this rule, they change the term of reference between the couple to *dhuway-galay*, and also change the terms accordingly for the people directly related to, and around, the couple. In doing so, they intend to readjust people's relationships back into "proper" ones to fit the larger ideal patterns of clan and social organization. At one time, senior members of a few clans even decided to introduce a new ritual to rearrange the clan filiation of children born out of wedlock back to the "proper" clan (Kubota 2005). Thus, social relationships of the close kin members were also rearranged. Although the new ritual itself was discontinued, senior members of some clans continue the practice of reintegrating children born out of wedlock – they actually locate the clan affiliation of the children.

While these examples of renegotiating kin relationships point to how different it is to be a young adult in Aboriginal society in the twenty-first century compared to thirty years ago, it paradoxically also shows how Aboriginal people are negotiating to keep their ideal social organization, which they consider as their tradition. It is quite common for young people to take part seriously in rituals, especially funerals, which are filled with knowledge concerning land ownership of the clans and spiritual knowledge.

Despite the major changes in town life, mortuary rituals (*bapurru*) are still vital to Aboriginal life, as many have pointed out (see also Schwarz 2007; Morphy 1984; Morphy and Morphy 2012). The death of a relative and the associated funeral plans are always the most important news: funerals are regarded as crucially important occasions, closing the life of the person, and should be done properly, based on the knowledge of the clan and land relationship. Any obstacles that may stand in the way of a proper burial are major topics of conversation.[2] Literally all the members of the town are expected to attend all funerals.

As other authors have already pointed out, mortuary rituals in Arnhem Land are quite elaborate, compared to those in other Aboriginal areas (Keen 1994; Morphy 1984; Peterson 1976; Schwarz 2007). A funeral is important to the Yolŋu not only because it is the burial and the last rites for the dead, but also because it is regarded as the occasion to complete the cycle of life. As Carolyn Schwarz notes, for that reason they have to choose the right "individual being buried in that one can only become whole when one is buried in the proper lands"

(Schwarz 2007: 145). Specifically, Howard Morphy writes: "On the death of a person you have to look back to where they came from, tracing the genealogical and social connections that resulted in that particular individual, the lines of descent that coincide in his or her person" (1984: 128). He contends that funerals also provide a major context for the demonstration and affirmation of social relations among clan groups. He describes how the grandmother-grandchild (*maari-gutharra*) relationship between the clans is important to the funeral. A person's *maari* clan is the one his own mother's mother and her brothers are members of. The deceased's *maari* clan is important because it is believed that a person is the product of his *maari* clan and his own clan spiritually (Morphy 1984: 105–6). Thus, mortuary rituals are key events during which people learn about land ownership within and among clan groups. In other words, how the dead are handled and where they are buried play a central role in identity production in relation to land ownership.

Nowadays, the Yolŋu people often die in distant hospitals in Darwin or Melbourne.[3] When the news of the death reaches the town, a "hearing ceremony" (*ngaama ga walu*) is held. People are summoned by a loudspeaker announcement to get together at a certain place, and a group of senior men announce the death with singing (*manikay*). Once the death becomes public knowledge, relatives start to prepare the mortuary rituals. Nowadays, the body is kept at a mortuary in the hospital until the date and the location of the funeral are decided. As many have already noted, the preparation of the funeral always creates great tension and conflict. According to Schwarz (Schwarz 2007: 145–6), there are typically three primary causes for the conflicts: 1) accusations of the death being caused by sorcery, 2) disagreement over the site of the funeral ceremony and the person in charge of it, and 3) arguments about the day and location of burial. Talks, gossip, and accusations concerning black magic always continue until the funeral starts.

Right away, relatives and friends of the deceased try to figure out "why" the person has died. It is an important element in deciding the funeral content and place. There are always at least two opposing disputants who discuss the location of a funeral. There is a commonly agreed standard about the roles close kin have in the management of the funeral. The most important role is expected to be performed by the members of the *maari* clan (mother's mother's clan) of the deceased. As I mentioned earlier, this clan – as the spiritual producer of the deceased person – assumes the crucial role in planning a funeral. Its members have primary ownership of the body of the deceased, and have rights and responsibilities in deciding important issues, including the place of burial.

Another important role is performed by *djungayi*, who are the *waku* (sisters' children) of the deceased person. They act as the managers for the funeral and make major decisions. Among the *djungayi*, the closest male blood relative is appointed as "the number one *djungayi*," responsible for the funeral as a whole.

Although the rules are based on kinship and their rights to land, matters are complicated because people have some choice in tracing their genealogical relationships. The situation can be further muddied because there are now many irregular relationships, or so-called "wrong marriages," which do not conform to the traditional "ideal" rules. Nevertheless, kin try to rearrange and normalize their kin relationship with these spouses and their future children. Moreover, with increased knowledge of, and exposure to, the European way of life, the Yolŋu people have started to sometimes include other kin as important in decision making for the funeral. The wife of the deceased, for example, now often demands that her opinion be considered concerning the place of the funeral and burial.

The Mission and Its Mortuary Rituals

In the early twentieth century, a Methodist mission started to expand its area of work from north Australia to Arnhem Land, and began to set up several settlements. The township of Galiwin'ku was established in 1942. Aboriginal people were quite cooperative with missionaries and helped to build the town (McKenzie 1976). The Christian mission assumed the role of superintendent, managing the town and taking care of the Aboriginal people, who did not then have citizenship status. The mission applied the policy of assimilation, sedentarizing them, educating them in English, and Christianizing them, in order to impart to them the values of "civilized" life.

In consultation with the Yolŋu people, the missionaries chose the specific location of Galiwin'ku. Traditionally, the area where the town was built had been owned by clan G.[4] This clan had only three elderly sisters remaining at that time, which meant that its line would soon end. Its mythological content and rights were handed down to a related clan, clan D. As clan D has a *maari-gutharra* (grandmother-grandchild) relationship to clan G, it was granted the caretaker's role[5] of clan G's mythology and land. It is said that missionaries thereafter always consulted the people of clan D for the use of the land.

The Second World War (1939–45) had a great impact on Aboriginal people's life in Arnhem Land. People in the south started to hear more about the north during the war, with the possibility of attack by the Japanese air force. Following the world movement for human rights after the war, the attitude towards Aboriginal people started to change in Australia. At the same time, war had a more immediate and direct impact on Aboriginal people. For the first time, they experienced "proper" employment in the army base, where they gained experience with modern machinery and had contact with people other than missionaries.

In 1957, Yolŋu people initiated an incident, later named the "Adjustment movement," in Galiwin'ku (Berndt 1962). Groups of Aboriginal clans headed by three Aboriginal leaders publicly exhibited secret and sacred objects permitted only to be shown to the initiated clansmen. The act was meant to show their acceptance of Christianity and its values by their abandoning of sacred rituals, and to show the unification of the clans. The disagreements between the clans on various everyday matters were the main causes of the disputes. However, some clans did not agree with this attempt and did not participate, and thus the incident had limited effect. Still, anthropologists valued the nature of the incident. For example, Ronald Berndt interpreted the movement as a reaction to the social circumstances of rapid changes (Berndt 1962), while Morphy analysed it as a Yolŋu attempt to allow outsiders a better understanding of Aboriginal norms (Morphy 1983).

Mortuary rituals have no doubt changed after the Methodist mission established the town (Morphy 1984). In earlier mortuary procedure, the Yolŋu built a platform with a bark roof, on which they placed the body of the deceased; they then left the place and the body. After a while, the family returned to gather the bones, which they wrapped in the sheet of a paper-bark tree, to be carried by the widows or the mothers of the deceased until the final funeral ritual. In this interval, which sometimes lasted more than a year, women (the widows or the mothers) shaved their heads and continued mourning, making personal sacrifices such as prohibiting themselves from eating particular kinds of food. After the proper mortuary ritual was held for a prolonged time, sometimes for weeks, the bones of the deceased were placed in a hollow log coffin, which was itself placed at the far reaches of the village. For the coffin, they used a log about two metres long and hollowed by termites (Morphy 1984).

According to W, who was in his early fifties at the time I interviewed him (in 1992), the missionaries used to prohibit the Yolŋu's old ways, insisting that funerals should last only three days. By the end of the three days, the body had to be buried in the cemetery, which is located behind the school at the end of the township. The missionaries, in consultation with the elders, selected where the cemetery would be located. People called for a ban of the sacred-secret rituals in the adjustment movement in 1957, announcing the unification of the clans and their acceptance of Christianity. In other words, the mortuary ceremonies during the mission days followed stricter Christian rules and had to be completed within a specific allotted time, and all the bodies were placed in the mission-designated cemetery.

After the 1967 Referendum: Self-Determination Era

As a result of the national referendum in 1967, Aboriginal people were granted the social rights of citizenship in Australia. In the 1960s, they had also started the procedures to claim land rights. In 1972, the Labor Party, after winning the election, made good on its promise to reform Aboriginal land rights. Prime Minister Whitlam of the Labor government changed the national policy on Indigenous peoples, ushering in the self-determination policy, intended to restore Indigenous self-management. Missionaries who had been working for Aboriginal people left Arnhem Land to let them have full autonomy.

This brought a great deal of change in the lives of the Yolŋu people at Galiwin'ku.[6] Abundant cash income from social security started to flow into Aboriginal hands, as they started to receive a full array of social entitlements. Peterson cites this as the start of Aboriginal people's welfare dependency (Peterson 1998) – although he notes that, because of the influence left behind by the missionaries' regime of structured work, and because of the geographical isolation, Aboriginal people did not instantly become dependent. Also, some people used the money to move back to their clan territories to establish small villages, called outstations or homelands. To build the outstations (Kerins 2009), land ownership and social relationships of the clans had to be clarified, and it became a matter of concern for them.

Meanwhile, at the end of the 1960s, an attempt to develop bauxite mining began in the Yirrkala area in Arnhem Land, about two hundred kilometres east of the site of my research. Aboriginal people resisted the mining efforts, leading to the first Aboriginal legal case.

Although the Aboriginal people lost the case, a royal commission was set up to research their idea of Aboriginal land ownership. As a result, the 1976 Northern Territory Aboriginal Land Rights Act was passed. Arnhem Land was registered as an Aboriginal Land Trust. Under the Act, Land Trusts, acting as statutory bodies holding the title to land, handed it back to the traditional owners.

In the course of the negotiations leading to the legal case of land rights, there had been many hearings by outside agents, including a royal commission, about the relationships between clans and the land. The Yolŋu people had to explain over and over again about clan ownership of the places, how they represent it, the stories behind it, the mechanism of succession, and so on. This became another occasion for Aboriginal people to reaffirm their patterns of clan land ownership.

To sum up, in the 1970s in Arnhem Land there were drastic changes for Aboriginal people. Their new legal status of citizenship had a great impact. While they lost the land rights case in Yirrkala to stop mining, the bauxite mining development began immediately and the landowners started to receive royalty money. Not all but at least some clans sharing rights over the mining area have started to get extra cash income. Although they were originally against the development, royalty money became a big interest for some clans, and the cause of many disputes. In Galiwin'ku, only a handful of clans were entitled to royalty money. However, another handful of clans could make a claim to such money on the basis of kin relationships. Clan relationships with the land became rearticulated, not just in a traditional sense but also in an economic and political sense.

There have been many changes and much confusion since the end of the 1960s, with the missionaries leaving and the beginning of a new era of self-determination. Aboriginal initiatives flourished, social welfare income in cash was received, the outstation movement had begun, and compensation money was coming in after the mining dispute. Nevertheless, the people's strong spiritual connection to their ancestral lands still endures. One example of it was found in the so-called Christian Revival. By 1979, this climate of social change and confusion helped to usher in a Christian Revival in Galiwin'ku. The Revival was a large evangelical and charismatic Christian movement. Yolŋu revivalists talked about miracles and the power of Jesus and spoke in tongues. Yolŋu people got together regularly in Galiwin'ku, as well as other towns, to perform charismatic healing ceremonies. As Robert Bos has pointed out, the Revival can be understood as a reaction to the new social conditions (Bos 1988). However, it served also as an occasion for Aboriginal people to realize that they needed to reaffirm their identity, which of course was based on the knowledge of relationships among clans and the land and its spirituality.

With regard to mortuary rituals during this period, more variations started to emerge. The rituals now lasted longer than three days, sometimes over a week. Alongside traditional Yolŋu dances and songs, they included newly composed Western-style songs and dances, some of these directly borrowed from the Revival movement. In other words, there was greater variety in each funeral. More people also started to bury their deceased next to their houses, outside of the mission-designated cemetery, as well as in outstations.

As noted in Morphy and Morphy (2012), the greater affluence that followed the granting of citizenship rights allowed the Yolŋu people to devote more time and money to their mortuary rituals. Furthermore, as they can also keep the deceased relative's body in a morgue in Darwin or Gove hospitals, they are in a position to prolong the discussion over burial rituals and sites. They now have the body transported by plane into the town at the start of the funeral, creating more time for discussing possible locations to hold the funeral, as well as the burial. But all this also means more disputes over the location of funerals and burials among the related clans.

The Current Situation in Arnhem Land

In 1996, after the general election, John Howard became prime minister and the Liberal government took power, again changing the situation of Aboriginal people. The government started to minimize the effects of Native Title, cutting the financial support for various endeavours, including bilingual education; it also dismantled the ATSIC (Aboriginal and Torres Strait Islanders Commission) in 2005, which had functioned as the representative body for Aboriginal people in the federal government since 1990. Prime Minister Howard at that time cut off funding for many specialized Aboriginal sections and policies in the name of "mainstreaming" Aboriginal issues.

In 2007, the Northern Territory National Emergency Response Act, often called "The Intervention," was declared.[7] On 21 June of that year, the prime minister and the minister in charge of Indigenous affairs announced a national emergency in Aboriginal communities, calling for public measures (Altman 2012). The action was in response to allegations in the media of the sexual abuse of children in remote Aboriginal communities. There had been several reports of frequent such abuse in these communities in the previous year, and the emotionally heated cries of "something has to be done for the poor people in our country" began to grow. The Northern Territory National Emergency Response Act 2007 was passed, based on a report by the Northern Territory government entitled "Little Children Are Sacred" (Wild and Anderson 2007). The report brought to national attention what the researchers saw as an alarming number of abused children in Aboriginal communities. The government used the report to set in place a number of initiatives to protect children, but mostly to further restrict Aboriginal agency and self-determination.

Many new policies, initiatives, and surveillance mechanisms – implemented and controlled by outside agencies – were introduced to "normalize" Aboriginal communities and make Aboriginal people more accountable for their "deficiencies." Since 2007, many new visitors have been travelling to Galiwin'ku, and it is now common to see an unfamiliar Euro-Australian person visiting just for the day. Faced with new policies and patchwork initiatives, many Aboriginal people have been disempowered and have expressed confusion and frustration. Kept at bay from running their town affairs, people at Galiwin'ku have turned their frustrations inward, and there are more clan disputes today than in the past thirty years. They talk a lot more about clan ownership and its violations, and about jealousy between clans. The discussion about the ownership of the town still continues. There is gossip about *galka* – a source of black magic – which many people feel is real, and responsible for the many deaths plaguing their community. Many suggest that some clans are better off because of the compensation money they receive from the mining company, and that this is unfair. People talk about "jealousy" and the possible use of black magic. The tendencies to engage in disputes and accusations of black magic have been continuous from the 1970s on, but people are more suspicious about black magic today, and anxiety in the town has grown compared to the 1980s. It is probably at least partly because of the development of communication and transportation technology. People have more information concerning deaths and attend more funerals in distant areas, travelling by air and sea. As a result, the most discussed topic in their conversation is black magic.

With regard to mortuary rituals, more disputes over the locations of rituals and burials have emerged. After more than fifty years of sedentarized living in the town, it looks as if people are striving for a new understanding of the ownership, or at least "the priority rights," of the clans over the area on which their houses stood. People know that the now extinct clan G originally owned the land on which the town was built and that clan D acts now as a caretaker, and members of the latter tend to be diplomatic and have never claimed "ownership" strongly. Rather, they say that although they have the caretaker's role, it is all right for everyone to share the land on which the township was created during colonization. And now many people belonging to other clans have started to claim that the area around where they live in the town is the proper place for their clan people as an area of burial.

Many people have also started to bury relatives' bodies in their out-stations and places near their houses in the town. Most of the outsta-tions are situated on the island, which is about an hour's drive from the town. But some are located on the mainland, which they have to travel to by air or by boat. Today, when people talk about closing the life cycle at the "proper" clan's place, they may mean that their idea of land own-ership has shifted to take in a new pattern of "residency," especially when they have their relatives and family members buried at the site.

In the following section, I present three case studies of disputes that have taken place during and around the mortuary rituals in the town since the 1990s. These cases highlight how people actually negotiate land ownership of the clans and how such negotiations have changed over time. I highlight in this discussion, as well, how the Yolŋu people acquire and share knowledge of the land in everyday life.

Case Study 1: An Accusation of Sorcery, *Galka*

In 1998 and 1999, three women of the same patrilineal clan D, in their thirties, died in succession. Although the medical reasons for their deaths were clear – G died of heart disease, J of high blood pressure, and B of terminal breast cancer – these consecutive deaths were a great shock to their clan members. In Aboriginal society, most deaths are not regarded as "normal" or "natural," and the possibility of black magic, or *galka*, precipitating such events is always suspected (Morphy 1984). *Galka* is believed to be a supernatural person with the knowledge and power to secretly conduct the special ritual procedures of black magic, in order to cause serious illness and death. According to L, who was in her forties at the time of the interview, there are a few ways *galka* are believed to practise black magic. Such *galka* collect the blood or excretions of the targeted person, let them decay, and then dash them between burnt stones to complete the magic. Another method involves the use of a special bone to target the victim.

Faced with such seemingly unnatural and untimely serial deaths, people became very emotional, including the younger generation, and they spent a long time discussing the possibility of *galka*'s responsibility for the deaths. Although it is common to evoke *galka*, there were additional reasons in this particular case, having to do with the long-standing tension between clans over the ownership of the township's location. As previously mentioned, the extinct clan G had been the original owner of the area. Clan D was now entitled to take care of the area, because clan G is the mother's mother's clan for clan D – they are in a *maari-gutharra* (grandmother-grandchild) relationship. The unusual serial deaths in clan D prompted suspicions of *galka*'s involvement. It is a common assumption among members of clan D that other clan members are "jealous" because clan D has the caretaker's position and priority rights over the township, even though they do not claim them strongly. A few specific names of clans were mentioned in the discussion. Although these claims were little more than gossip, people took them seriously and were frightened by them.

One afternoon after a particularly heated discussion, a senior man belonging to clan D made a move. He suddenly grabbed a bundle of spears from his house and walked out angrily. He started to walk around the town, shaking the bundle over his head. This act signalled that he was extremely upset and angry. Adults and children both rushed back to their houses, locked doors and windows, and stayed inside holding their breath. Everyone was peeping out from narrowly opened windows to see what would happen next. After a while, the old man started to shout out to *galka*:

> Listen *galka*, stop killing young women of my clan. Stop killing men of my clan. All of them were my dear beloved children and grandchildren. Do not kill anyone of my clan members! Stop the evil acts! This land is our clan's land. This land is that we have been handed down and we are the proper caretakers. If you continue this evil act I won't permit you. If you keep doing it, you will be punished. If you keep doing it, you will be diagnosed with AIDS and will surely be dying!

The old man's relatives and other members of his clan, including young ones, found the act satisfying and said that the old man had done the right thing. People of clan D were always feeling targeted because of the "irrational" jealousy of other clans, especially accused clans. In this case, the fear and possibility of black magic, and the talk about relationships concerning *galka*, dominated many discussions about these three deaths. Many young people of clan D were eager to hear why the *galka* was targeting people of their clan. It served as an occasion for them to gain knowledge about their clan's relationship to the land.

Case Study 2: A Dispute over the Location of a Burial

Carolyn Schwarz provided the details of a case of conflict over funeral and burial locations in Galiwin'ku (Schwarz 2007). Her in-depth analysis focused on the disputants' assertion of their Christian identity. But at the same time, the case can also be seen as an occasion for some in the community to renegotiate their clan identity. During Schwarz's fieldwork, there were fourteen mortuary rituals held, and many disputes. One of the cases she reports on was the funeral for a senior man, D. First, the dispute was over the place of the funeral. There were three disputants, 1) G (wife of D), 2) Y (nephew of D), and 3) B (classificatory daughter of D). G wanted the funeral to be held at her house, Y argued for his place, and B wanted the ceremony held at a clan estate of D. Y was the main *djungayi* for the funeral, and in the public meeting, he made it clear that he wanted to control the ceremony. With group B's support, Y got the approval in the end, making G very unhappy.

After the funeral started, another dispute arose, over the place of burial. This time, the disputants divided themselves into two groups: site 1 was proposed by G and some clansmen of D, and site 2 was proposed by Y and another clansman of D. G wanted a location close to her home in town, while Y asked that it be at a clan estate, a short distance from the town. In the end, members of the *maari* clan (mother's mother's clan of D) made the decision that the body should be buried at site 1. This prompted Y to leave and visit another town, in order to express his discontent.

Whenever these kinds of disputes happen, everyone in the town commits to the discussion. Conversations at households are dominated by the topic. People examine the details of each disputant's claims, and take sides, usually based on kinship relations. Thus, through these disputes, the younger generation gains knowledge about the ties of clans and the land.

Case Study 3: A Demand for Respect after the
Tragic Death of a Young Man

In February 2012, a tragic accident occurred in one of the outstations not far from the main town. The outstation faces the sea and it is the usual place for family members and visitors to fish and gather shellfish, and for children to play. It was Sunday, and many of the members of more than one clan were at the beach. Jim, a young man aged twenty-three, son of the eldest brother of the family, was fishing there with one of his cousins. Children were running and having fun at the beach, and a few men and boys were around too. All of a sudden, the sea became very rough and big waves crashed to the shore. Three teenage girls, who had been playing on the shore, were swallowed by the wave. Jim and his cousin jumped into the sea to rescue them. One of the girls made her way back by herself, another was rescued by Jim's cousin, and Jim grabbed the last girl, held her in the air, and made an effort to send her back towards the shore. The girl was rescued, but Jim did not return and was lost. All of the family members prayed all night. The next morning, Jim's body washed up on shore, next to the family outstation.

When I visited the family the following year, I found that they had closed the beach since the accident. They said that after the accident they decided to block the road to the beach and announced to people in the town that the beach was not going to be accessible for a while. At first, family members explained that, since everyone loved Jim, keeping the place undisturbed was an act of respect for the deceased. But in reality there was another more complicated reason for the long closure. This outstation had originally been the land of clan G, which was now extinct. A senior man, Jim's grandfather, had been a leader of clan D (the clan Jim was also from), and Jim's grandmother was one of the last three sisters of clan G. Clan D, in its stories, is caretaker of clan G's land. This is the reason that clan D or a senior man of clan D acts as owner of this outstation and surrounding seashore. The area encompasses important sites, including rocky stretches, water holes, and a big tree on the seashore. Besides clan D, through a kinship connection to clan G, there are a few other clans – mainly two – who sing and dance the stories concerning this place. Some members and people related to clan D had criticized those other clans for singing and dancing the songs without "proper" measures taken, thus not showing enough respect to clan D. In addition to this complicated situation, there had been a series of deaths of clan D members in recent years, which culminated in Jim's drowning: Jim's grandfather, the senior man and leader of clan D, died in March 2010, and Jim's first baby died in the middle of 2010, followed by Jim himself in 2012.

So, for his family members, Jim's death was not seen purely as an accident. Jim had drowned in the part of the sea claimed by clan G. The two clans who have kin relationship to clan G had been singing and dancing the stories of clan G in the rituals – singing about this seashore without showing respect to clan D for a long time. So, according to the logic of the family members of clan D, the members of these two clans should make financial amends. The members of clan D demanded that the two clans pay AUS$2,000 and said that they would not open the seashore until the people of the two clans showed respect and paid the compensation. Within the family, this discussion has continued on various occasions for nearly two years. The problem was resolved when the members of the two clans showed enough respect by performing dancing for the deceased, especially when one of the senior men said how their predecessors were diplomatic and not demanding, and the current generation must follow in their footsteps. The seashore was reopened in the end.

One critical aspect of this story is that not only senior members of the family but also family members in their twenties were quite involved in the discussions and in relating the story to others. As young girls were the central figures of this accident, young people who were relatives and friends of the rescued girls felt they had an emotional stake in the discussion over the complicated relationship between clans and clan D's demand for compensation. Also, as Jim was beloved by his peers, an intense interest was shared by many of the young people. Jim's male relatives and friends were very concerned about how the whole incident would be resolved. They eagerly listened to stories about the kin relationship between two clans and clan G, and wanted to understand why they had a right to sing about the place. They are also quite interested in the amount of the compensation and insist that it should be paid directly to Jim's family.

Conclusion

Senior Yolŋu members in Galiwin'ku often say that their cultural tradition is weakening in the face of a monetary economy and the influx of merchandise, and that it is necessary for children and the younger generation to be taught traditional knowledge. In fact, as I have shown in this chapter, social changes have not led the younger generation to become detached from the bulk of rich local knowledge. On the contrary, they are actively taking part in everyday conversations on negotiations and disputes surrounding mortuary rituals. The cases I described show the presence of the traditional knowledge of the clan and land in everyday occurrences in the town.

In this chapter I divided the local history since the colonization in North Australia into three separate periods to demonstrate how the historical situation in the area has changed, and how the mortuary rituals have been altered accordingly. The mission era was a time of control. During this period, the Yolŋu basically held the mortuary rituals according to the given missionary rules and buried the bodies in the mission's cemetery. Compared to earlier and subsequent periods, there were fewer disputes over land ownership or over the intrusion of *galka*. After the referendum of 1967, people started to have more freedom and initiative under the self-determination policy. They could manage their income without the control of missionaries. Their mortuary rituals grew longer and more varied with the modern technology and affluence that the Yolŋu have obtained (Morphy and Morphy 2012). Accordingly, the sites of burials began to change. Since 2000, with the pressure of normalization and commercialization, there have been more disputes between the clans concerning mortuary rituals. These disputes show that the idea of "priority rights" is emerging and contesting the original idea of land ownership.

The three case studies I described illustrate specific current causes of disputes over mortuary rituals and burials. The first case showed how the belief concerning *galka*, practitioners of black magic, is shared among people in daily life, and how extremely afraid of *galka* and their acts people are. Through their discussions about *galka*, people repeatedly talk about the ownership of the land and the jealousy of the other clans. This case shows that discussions of *galka* and mortuary rituals take place against a background of discomfort over the unequal status and unfair economic rewards brought about by land ownership, and jealousy over the supposed economic benefits reaped by some. In discussions concerning *galka*, people talk a lot about a clan's kinship relationship to land and why the jealousy of that ownership emerges to make black magic.

The second case describes the dispute over the location of a funeral and subsequent burial. It shows that there is a changing notion concerning ownership of or priority rights to places in the township. After the self-determination era, people more freely express their preferences about burial location, creating more disputes. These disputes become the main concern of everyone in the town, including younger people. They discuss the validity of the disputants' opinions, again creating an occasion for younger ones to acquire knowledge about clan and land. The second case study highlights how the notion of place ownership has changed under the influences of Euro-Australian notions of occupancy. The continuing disputes show that the notion of "priority rights" based on the continuous occupancy of the house is emerging and contesting the original idea of land ownership by the clans.

The third case study, of the tragic death of the young man, Jim, and of people's reactions to it, shows another instance of cultural transmission. The claim for compensation by the clan of the deceased was made according to the traditional discourse. The sea of the area owned by clan G which is taken care of by clan D swallowed Jim, so the clans who have been singing and dancing about the seashore area must pay the compensation; they are responsible for the incident because they have been using the songs and dances without paying enough respect to clan D. This discourse itself is a quite familiar one as a traditional claim concerning ritual and myth. Again, young people were as consumed by the discussions and disputes as older members of the town.

It is clear that the "cache of knowledge" concerning land among Aboriginal people has been constructed, negotiated, and altered since sedentarization. Although the knowledge has been handed down from the previous generation, drastic changes in policies from outside – ranging from assimilation by the colonial mission to self-determination and neoliberalism – have inevitably influenced the Yolŋu state of knowledge. As shown in the second case study, a new notion of "priority rights" emerging into their discourse may be a good example. The idea of ownership and priority over the area is gradually changing after a long sedentary life in the town, and especially since its self-management, which began in the 1970s. No one states it directly, but many feel and share the notion of priority ownership of the clan regarding homes and surrounding areas. These notions have then influenced opinions about proper mortuary rituals and burials.

Looking into the reactions to the tragedies and deaths of both older and younger people, one realizes how the Yolŋu value cultural knowledge concerning the place and its ancestral spiritual connection that is deeply entrenched in the various aspects of everyday life today.

As these case studies show, this complex and entrenched knowledge itself is the result of entanglement. And this entangled knowledge is transmitted and shared with the younger generation through everyday conversation concerning "ownership." To at least some extent, it occurs through the application of material culture, a cash economy, and communication technology.

People's understanding of the "ownership" of the place is the result of their negotiation and adaptation, and is dependent on their notion of spirituality and ancestral spirits strongly connected to the entangled understanding of the land. And through the everyday discussion of clan ownership of land, clan story, and black magic, and through the negotiations of social relationships between clans, the experienced and entangled reality of life by individuals as inner reflection is shared between the generations and becomes conventional in modern Yolŋu society. Through everyday discussions, including those about mortuary rituals and burial, Yolŋu people have formed and conventionally shared the always updated and renewed knowledge concerning land and clan.

ACKNOWLEDGMENTS

My research in Arnhem Land was made possible by the financial support of Grants for Scientific Research in Japan. I am also grateful for the friendship of the Yolŋu in Arnhem Land, who have been supportive of my researches for a long time. I want to thank Françoise Dussart and Sylvie Poirier for their useful comments.

NOTES

1 These towns were originally run by missionaries, and then became self-governing secular places with no structures for employment and greater access to cash (Peterson 1998: 107).
2 In my own personal experience, the very first thing an Aboriginal family informs me of upon my arrival is who has passed away during my absence. Then they tell me where and how the funerals were, and where the cemeteries are.
3 Darwin is the nearest city, with its medical facilities about a two-hour flight from the town, and Melbourne is about three thousand kilometres south, a four-hour flight.

4 According to the Yolŋu concept, each area of land is separately owned by patrilineal clans. There are about sixty clans, and each has its own ancestral stories, which connect it to a particular land.

5 The area of land where Galiwin'ku is built was originally owned by clan G, which lost all it members and went extinct. In these cases, the clan in a particular kin relationship to the extinct clan will become caretaker. As clan G was the mother's mother's clan (*maari* clan) of clan D, clan D had the role of caretaker. It takes care of the stories, songs, dances, and land of clan G.

6 Under the self-determination policy, one of the major changes was the move for Aboriginalization. Since the 1980s, many institutions in town have tried to Aboriginalize their structure and employ Aboriginals as heads of the institutions. Schools and clinics started similar initiatives. In 1990 in Galiwin'ku, a woman became the first Aboriginal school principal.

7 The Northern Territory National Emergency Response Act, issued in 2007, introduced the following measures to "aid" the people in the remote communities of the Northern Territory: 1) Alcohol was banned from communities; 2) "Welfare reforms" were introduced; welfare money is given as a plastic card, not cash, so that the usage of money is controlled (i.e., alcohol or drugs cannot be bought with welfare money); 3) School attendance was enforced and strong pressure was placed on parents to send their children to school; 4) Compulsory health checks for children were declared; 5) Seventy-three townships were prescribed; 6) A police officer was sent to each town to increase policing; 7) The leasing system of housing and tenancy was changed to a normal renting system; 8) Pornographic films were banned and computers in public offices were censored; 9) The permit system for Aboriginal communities was scrapped; and 10) Governance was reformed and all managers of government business in prescribed communities were appointed (Altman and Hinkson 2007).

REFERENCES

Altman, Jon 2012. "Too Much 'Dreaming': Evaluations of the Northern Territory National Emergency Response Intervention 2007–2012." *Evidence Base* no. 3: 1–21.

Altman, Jon, and Melinda Hinkson, eds. 2007. *Coercive Reconciliation: Stabilise, Normalise, Exit Aboriginal Australia.* Carlton North: Arena Publications Association.

Barth, Fredrik. 2002. "An Anthropology of Knowledge." *Current Anthropology* 43 (1): 1–18. http://dx.doi.org/10.1086/324131.

Berndt, Ronald. 1962. "An Adjustment Movement in Arnhem Land." *Cahiers de L'Homme* 2.

Bos, Robert. 1988. "The Dreaming and Social Change in Arnhem Land." In *Aboriginal Australians and Christian Missions: Ethnographic and Historical Studies*, ed. Tony Swain and Deborah Bird-Rose, 422–37. Bedford Park: Australian Association for the Study of Religions.

Geertz, Clifford. 1983. *Local Knowledge: Further Essays in Interpretive Anthropology*. New York: Basic Books.

Keen, Ian. 1994. *Knowledge and Secrecy in Aboriginal Religion*. New York: Oxford University Press.

Kerins, Seán. 2009. *First-Ever Northern Territory Homelands/Outstation Policy*. *Indigenous Law Bulletin* 7 (14): 7–10.

Kubota, Sachiko. 2005. *Aborigini Syakaino Bunka Jinruigaku* [Gender Anthropology in Aboriginal Society]. Kyoto: Sekaishiso-sha.

McKenzie, Maisie. 1976. *Mission to Arnhem Land*. Adelaide: Rigby.

Morphy, Frances, and Howard Morphy. 2012. "'Soon We Will Be Spending All Our Time at Funerals': Yolngu Mortuary Rituals in an Epoch of Constant Change." In *Returns to the Field: Multitemporal Research and Contemporary Antholopology*, ed. Signe Howell and Aud Talle, 49–72. Bloomington: Indiana University Press.

Morphy, Howard. 1983. "Now You Understand: An Analysis of the Way Yolŋu Have Used Sacred Knowledge to Retain Their Autonomy." In *Aborigines, Land and Land Rights*, ed. Nicolas Peterson and Marcia Langton, 110–33. Canberra: Australian Institute of Aboriginal Studies Press.

Morphy, Howard. 1984. *Journey to the Crocodile Nest*. Canberra: Australian Institute of Aboriginal Studies Press.

Morphy, Howard. 1991. *Ancestral Connections: Art and an Aboriginal System of Knowledge*. Chicago: University of Chicago Press.

Peterson, Nicolas. 1976. "Mortuary Customs of Northeast Arnhem Land: An Account Compiled from Donald Thomson's Fieldnotes." *Memoirs of the National Museum of Victoria* 37: 97–108.

Peterson, Nicolas. 1998. "Welfare Colonialism and Citizenship: Politics, Economics and Agency." In *Citizenship and Indigenous Australians: Changing Conceptions and Possibilities*, ed. Nicolas Peterson and William Sanders, 101–17. Cambridge: Cambridge University Press. http://dx.doi.org/10.1017/CBO9780511552243.006.

Russell, Bertrand. 1948. *Human Knowledge: Its Scope and Limits*. New York: Simon and Schuster.

Schwarz, Carolyn. 2007. "Aboriginal Identities at Galiwin'ku and the Conundrum of Christian Practices." Unpublished PhD thesis, Department of Anthropology, University of Connecticut.

Wild, Rex, and Patricia Anderson. 2007. "Ampe Akelyernemane Meke Meke Mekarile 'Little Children Are Sacred.'" Northern Territory Board of Inquiry into the Protection of Aboriginal Children from Sexual Abuse. http://www.inquirysaac.nt.gov.au.

9 Alien Relations: Ecological and Ontological Dilemmas Posed for Indigenous Australians in the Management of "Feral" Camels on Their Lands

PETRONELLA VAARZON-MOREL

Introduction

The colonization of Indigenous people and their lands typically involved the introduction of domesticated species integral to the development of settler economies. These animals were bound up with European social and ontological understandings that were profoundly different from those of the peoples being colonized – in particular, notions of the human-animal divide. In central Australia, Indigenous people have responded to introduced animals variously with fear, resistance, openness, creativity, and resilience. In doing so, they have had to negotiate incommensurable differences and disjunctions, involving the nature of the animals themselves and the "pastoral" relations Europeans have with these animals compared to Indigenous people's totemically based relations with native animals.[1] Now, irrevocably entangled, they have to re-negotiate their relations with domesticated animals such as camels, which have become free-ranging and are increasing in number on their land. The management of these animals creates tensions and dilemmas for people who want to maintain proper relationships with their country and the other-than-human constituents who inhabit it. This chapter addresses the situation with regard to camels in central Australia, focusing on Aboriginal people who adopted camels for use as transport. It considers the conflicts and challenges people face in reconciling their responsibilities towards beings to whom they are ancestrally related with their responsibilities towards camels, with whom they have a shared history and whose cosmological significance has shifted with the adoption of Christianity. I argue that the choices people make have implications not only for other entities in their environment but also for the people themselves and for their relational ontologies.

Although addressing a local case, the argument is relevant to questions of "whether and how ontologies can change" (Naveh and Bird-David 2014: 74) and how transformations in people's relations with animals figure in such change – if at all (see, for example, Ingold 2000; Descola 2014a; Naveh and Bird-David 2014). To date, debates have largely centred on Indigenous peoples with an animist ontology.[2] However, in his recent work Philippe Descola (2014a) extends the discussion, and, as it is of particular importance in thinking about relations between humans and animals and ontological change, I quote it at length here. In analysing how different societies model nature-culture, Descola has delineated four practical and cognitive "modes of identification" that constitute different ontologies as follows: the naturalism of the Western tradition, the totemism of Aboriginal societies, the animism of Amazonian societies, and the analogism associated with certain Chinese and African societies. Descola couples these with dominant "modes of relation" such as predation, reciprocity, and protection to arrive at "schemas of practice." According to his matrix, the naturalism of Australian settler society objectifies nature in that it recognizes physical continuities between humans and animals but posits a "discontinuity of interiorities" (Descola 2014a: 172). In contrast to naturalism, Descola characterizes the animistic form as one in which human and other-than-human animals have different physicalities but similar interiorities such that both "mutually... [apprehend] each other as subjects engaged in a social relationship" (2014a: 165, 201). He describes the Aboriginal totemic mode as a symmetrical one in which people and animals of the same "totemic collective" share physical and interior (selfhood – temperament – intentionality) characteristics that are realized in Dreaming beings (2014a: 165, 172). According to Descola (Kohn 2009: 145), because Aboriginal Australians do not personalize relationships with totemic animals in the way that animists do, they have "downplayed" or "inhibited" the "consequences" of recognizing animals as animate, intentional beings whom they communicate with and respect. While Aboriginal people do not personalize their relations with animals in the same ways that animistic hunter-gatherers do (see, for example, Bird-David 1999; Ingold 2000; Scott 2006 and in this volume; Nadasdy 2007; cf. Knight 2012), my chapter shows that the Aboriginal situation is more complex than Descola's characterizations indicate. I discuss contexts in which people recognize animals as subjective beings whom they must respect, and how people's concern about consequences articulates with their evolving relations with camels. In doing so, I attend to the changing social and biopolitical contexts in which people's relations with camels are constituted, and their subjectivities are "provoked" (Ortner 2005). The chapter contributes to scholarship on introduced and "invasive" animals (see Fortwangler 2013), showing that Aboriginal people's responses to the exotic animals cannot be characterized simply in static, dichotomous terms of resistance–acceptance and belonging–not belonging (see, for example, Rose 2002; Franklin 2006: 192; but see also Bowman and Robinson 2002; Trigger 2008). To do so elides the complex, contextual nature of people's engagement with the animals and their unfolding ontological and ecological significance through time.

As well as being informed by long-term research with Anangu (Pitjantjatjara and Yankunytjatjara) and Warlpiri, the chapter draws on historical material, a study of Aboriginal perceptions of camels that I conducted in central Australia, and more recent work (Vaarzon-Morel 2008, 2010, 2012; Vaarzon-Morel and Edwards 2012). The chapter is structured in three main sections. To contextualize contemporary issues, the first section indicates how people's relations with camels have transformed over time and how this history has shaped their perceptions of camels today. I consider the nature of people's early encounters with certain domesticated animals and then discuss people's adoption of camels as a form of transport. In the second section I explore people's changing relations with camels in the context of their relational ontology and mode of relating to totemic animals.

The third section focuses on the contemporary situation in which people confront increased numbers of free-ranging camels and their associated negative environmental impacts. Reflecting on findings from my earlier study on people's perceptions of camels, I consider implications of the conjunction of people's involvement in bioconservation programs with the implementation of a government-funded "feral" camel management program in which camels have been killed or removed from Aboriginal lands. In doing so, I suggest how camels figure in the redefinition of people's relational ontologies and the re-articulation of their relationships to the land.

Encountering European Domestic Animals

The centre of the Australian continent, in which Aboriginal people lived for millennia as hunters and gatherers, comprises desert and semi-desert regions with low and unpredictable rainfall. Although Europeans first settled the eastern coast of the continent in 1788, it was another century before they explored the arid interior, using horses, camels, and donkeys to do so. For local Aboriginal peoples, the concept of an animal being used for transport was alien because no autochthonous species could be so employed. While first encounters with Europeans have attracted considerable anthropological attention (e.g., Veth et al. 2008), encounters between Aboriginal people and the animals that accompanied the strangers have not (but see Altman 1982; Vaarzon-Morel 2012). With accounts of such events being within living memory and revealing pertinent dimensions of Aboriginal ontology, they warrant greater scrutiny.

Most such accounts bear witness to the shock people felt on first coming across the alien beings. Drawing on early settler accounts, the historian Robert Kenny (2007) has discussed the reactions of Wotjobaluk people to the arrival of Europeans on horses in the early 1800s in Victoria. Employing the metaphor of the "centaur dismounting" and contrasting the huge size and bizarre forms and behaviours of animals such as horses and cattle to native animals, Kenny argues that it was not Europeans but their animals that had the most impact upon Aboriginal people's consciousness and world view at first contact (Kenny 2007: 168–9). Yet, he maintains, it was not a complete rupture because the Wotjobaluk were able to assimilate Europeans and their animals within their totemic framework of understanding. Kenny suggests that for Wotjobaluk, domestic animals such as horses, sheep, and cattle were perceived as totems of the settlers. Noting the "mutuality of relations" (2007: 172) that existed between animals and humans because of the animals' totemic link to ancestral beings, he argues that apparently senseless killings of European animals by Wotjobaluk should be read as an attack on Europeans. Conversely, citing a historical account in which the lives of settlers were threatened after they offered a bull for slaughter to the Wotjobaluk, Kenny interprets the attack not as treachery (as the settlers did) but as an attempt by Wotjobaluk to rid their environment of animals that were devastating it. Extending his argument, Kenny speculates that the incident was "an attempt to re-define and re-establish a relationship with the environment that had been disrupted" (2007: 173). If indeed Wotjobaluk did assimilate Europeans and their totemic animals to their "relational schemas" (Descola 2014a), then their attacks demonstrate the significance of the material to the symbolic and also the centrality of transgressive behaviour to the limits of coexistence. In effect, introduced animals were treated as invading strangers.

In contrast to the Wotjobaluk situation, colonization of central Australia occurred relatively late, and historical accounts survive of people's reactions to the animals. Most accounts indicate that, at first, Aboriginal people regarded the creatures as kinds of monsters. Individuals fled before them, while larger groups attempted to kill them (see, for example, Strehlow 1960; Reynolds 1986). As I have noted elsewhere (Vaarzon-Morel 2012), after their initial shock people made sense of the animals by mimicking them, by comparing their distinctive corporeal forms and behavioural attributes with those of familiar beings, and by naming them. Many accounts also indicate that at first people attempted to interact with the animals using spoken language.[3] Intriguingly, according to the late Arrernte man Kwementyaye Johnson, when his people first saw a horse, they interpreted the flick of the horse's tail as it swished upward as the Arrernte hand sign for "What's happening?" (Jennifer Green, personal communication with author, 12 July 2012). What is remarkable in these accounts is the ontological openness that Aborigines exhibited when confronting alterity – that, although the animals had different corporeal forms from their own, people at first assumed they shared their personhood. In the event, the creatures' incapacity to interact *mutually* using language proved a distinguishing feature of personhood. Today, elders laughingly tell self-deprecating stories about their former ignorance of now-familiar horses and camels.

Encounters similar to those just described occurred across central Australia over several decades as Europeans ventured away from the Overland Telegraph Line. Once it became clear that the foreigners intended to stay, and as the impacts of their animals on the environment increased along with their numbers, Aboriginal people's tolerance lessened. The introduction of herd animals such as sheep and cattle in their thousands resulted in the despoliation of plants on which people subsisted and the defilement of sacred waterholes and other entities. Aboriginal people often retaliated, spearing and maiming the animals and defending themselves against the invaders (Reynolds 1986). In central Australia, competition between settlers, their animals, and local people over access to waterholes contributed to intercultural conflict, displacing many people and having a negative impact upon their subsistence economy. Attracted by the possibility of obtaining tobacco and flour, numerous Aboriginal groups took up work on cattle stations established on their land. As I now outline, over time many people adopted camels for their own use, thus developing a new form of relationship with the animals.

Developing Engagements with Camels

From the late 1880s to the 1920s, dromedary camels were the settlers' choice of animal transport across the arid interior because, unlike horses and donkeys, they could survive for long periods without water. Aborigines assisted "Afghan"[4] cameleers, who were responsible for transporting goods on "camel trains" from the railhead in South Australia to settlements such as Alice Springs and Hermannsburg Mission in central Australia, and they learnt camel-handling techniques during this process (see Strehlow 1960; Vaarzon-Morel 2012).

In the late 1920s and 1930s, settler use of motorized transport increased and their reliance on camel transport diminished. No longer of value to them, hundreds of camels were shot, while others were released to range free in the bush. Suffice to say, such treatment demonstrates the ontological significance of camels for Europeans as objects and chattels. Subsequently, Aboriginal people obtained them from settlers in exchange for work or by capturing free-roaming camels (Rose 1965). By 1960 Aboriginal people near cattle stations and missions owned more than 250 camels (McKnight 1969: 100). However, in more remote places such as the Ngaanyatjarra region, people only hunted camels (Gould et al. 1972: 265, 278).

Anangu, in particular, used camels to ride and carry belongings as they moved between missions and sheep and cattle stations, where they obtained seasonal work and traded dingo scalps with bounty collectors in return for European rations (see Rose 1965; Hamilton 1987; Vaarzon-Morel 2012). In addition, as Robert Layton (1986: 80) observed, Anangu from the Uluru region learnt "camel husbandry" techniques (see also Sandall 1969) and acted as cameleers for white people. Camels facilitated extended mobility, enabling people to visit kin and attend ceremonies in distant places. People used camels for transport until the early 1970s when, as a result of changed government policy, they obtained cash in place of rations and could purchase motorcars (Peterson 2009). In the process I have sketched, Aboriginal people developed a different kind of human-animal relationship from what had existed previously. Initially regarding camels as monsters, then forced to accommodate their invading presence, individuals nevertheless showed a remarkable open-mindedness towards them, and many people incorporated them in their lives.[5]

Indigenous Identifications and Relations with Animals

Superficially, Aboriginal people's interactions with camels resembled those of settlers. Yet, there were significant differences arising from the nature of Aboriginal people's relations with autochthonous animals and their mode of engagement with camels. Furthermore, while settler and Aboriginal worlds overlapped, they remained substantially different. Descola notes that "domestication does not necessarily imply a radical change of perspective, provided the society remains a mobile one" (2014a: 36). This was the case in central Australia; that is to say, Aboriginal ontologies were not radically transformed by the use of domesticated camels. I now consider this matter.

As is well known, Aboriginal people's relationship with native animals is totemic. People associated with particular tracts of country regard themselves as spiritually descended from Dreaming beings who gave form to their country. These beings, many of whom are themselves held to have taken animal form, further endowed country with all natural (including faunal) species, by travelling across the landscape, depositing their spiritual essence in the ground, and becoming metamorphosed as features in the landscape. Stories, ceremonies, and "doctrines" about such theriomorphic beings form the basis of Aboriginal cosmology (Keen 2004: 133), and are commonly referred to in English as "Dreaming" (*Jukurrpa* in Warlpiri, *Tjukurrpa* in Pitjantjatjara, and *Altyerre* in Arrernte). The Dreaming is not confined to a past period but continues in the present; in waking life people are constantly alert to the presence of Dreaming beings and signs of their activity, and people may receive new stories and interact with the beings while they dream (Poirier 2004).

A characteristic feature of totemism is that it differentiates landed groups of people from each other; patrilineal clans in the case of Warlpiri and "person-sets" (constituted through various means including birthplace) in the case of Pitjantjatjara (Sutton and Vaarzon-Morel 2003). At the same time, Dreaming tracks link individuals and groups belonging to the same totem. People directly identify with Dreaming

beings from whom they are descended.[6] For example, they may identify as goanna, kangaroo, or other animal people. The relationship is
not merely symbolic but consubstantial: people share substances and
attributes with ancestral Dreaming beings and may bear marks on their
body that visibly identify them with their ancestor. Furthermore, people employ their knowledge of social and physical characteristics of
animals in constituting human social relations that differentiate according to gender and social status.[7]

However, for Aboriginal people, animals are not merely totemic
entities with which it is "good to think" (Lévi-Strauss 1963: 89). They
are also sentient beings, with whom people may interact. While people perceive differences in the nature of animals in terms of physical and behavioural attributes, they also recognize certain qualities
of personhood among them. For example, as Anangu elder Peipai
explained to me: "All the little animals hold their own Tjukurrpa
along with emu, kangaroo and dingo. They all have living bodies.
Animals all have living animal bodies, in the same way that people
do. People live in community groups and animals are exactly the
same. You know, witchetty grubs, spiders, dingoes and people live
in various different communities – well, they have the same existence. Human communities live the same kind of existence as animals.
Animals have the same feelings inside towards their children as us"
(cf. Meggitt 1962: 252). However, while people perceive certain shared
qualities among humans and animals based on practices of communal living and affect, other social practices serve to distinguish human
personhood.

While all entities in the Aboriginal world are subject to Dreaming
Law, the human social order is unique in symbolically and practically
elaborating links with other beings. As Fred Myers noted, Aboriginal
social practices involve distinctive cultural understandings that are
"objectified and transmitted through a range of activities of kinship
and social relations" (2002: 104), especially in ritual. Human existence
is regarded as the "same but different" to animal beings because of
this fact. For example, one basis on which Warlpiri contrast themselves
with dogs is that the latter mate indiscriminately and not according to
human social rules instituted by Jukurrpa Law. Yet, as illustrated here,
the differences that distinguish humans from animals are not understood as a radical separation of nature and culture.

Recently, Marshall Sahlins (2014: 281) has critiqued Descola's ontological scheme, suggesting that totemism is but a form of "segmentary

animism." In response, Descola stated that he was "adamant that the kind of relations that Australian Aborigines maintain with nonhumans of *every denomination* is very different" (2014b: 298, emphasis added) from those of animist societies. In my view, however, Descola overlooks the fact that the nature of Aboriginal people's relations with animals differs according to whether they cohabit with them and form intimate bonds with them (as, for example, domestic dogs), or whether they co-dwell in country but live apart from the animals (as, for example, kangaroos). Reflecting this distinction, many Aboriginal people use the English terms "tame" and "wild," respectively, to refer to them. In doing so, the distinction made is between animals who tend to run away on encountering humans and those who have a trusting relationship, albeit one that may involve elements of domination, companionship, or protection.[8] The distinction does not involve a correlation with wilderness as place, because people regard their entire country as home (see Myers 1986). Significantly, animals such as dogs that live with humans are not killed for consumption.

In that camels lived in close proximity to humans, they occupied a conceptual and physical space similar to dogs. People formed strong bonds with them, attributing human qualities such as emotion to them (see also Elodie Fache in this volume). As with dogs, they gave personal names to them. Although people no longer use camels for transport, they sometimes adopt baby camels and raise them until they reach adolescence, when they become cantankerous and are taken out bush. People who have had close relationships with camels do not like them killed for meat and feel sympathy for them. As one man told me: "I feel sorry … when I see its face. I remember when I was riding, sitting on that camel." And as another man commented: "I don't like the idea of eating camels for meat because I grew up with them. They are [like] part of the family … They carted everything" (Vaarzon-Morel 2008: 8). The following examples also demonstrate that people treated their camels not as objects but as subjective beings: "Camels really understand people, like a dog. Camel and human being understand one another. Camel knows its owner" (Vaarzon-Morel 2008: 107). "Camels have a memory like a human being. If you get cheeky he'll remember you and go for you" (Vaarzon-Morel 2008: 55). Similar to dogs, some owners viewed their camels as protectors, in that they warned them of strangers. As one man commented: "They are really good when you are travelling. They see things miles away and they tell you … like *kurdaitcha* [malevolent being] following you" (Vaarzon-Morel 2008: 20).

As the examples indicate, affective ties with camels were based on shared experiences, co-dwelling, labour, and concern – qualities that Myers notes for Pintupi ground human social relationships (1986: 110). Furthermore, today, many people regard camels as "belonging" to country (see also Rose 1995), because the animals were born and grew up on the land. This sentiment was particularly notable among Anangu, who had close relationships with camels in the past and for whom being born on country is a pathway to gaining rights in the country.

Yet camels are not regarded as part of the Dreaming and people do not have consubstantial relations with them. Nor, with one reported exception, have camels been incorporated into traditional ceremonies, as happened with buffalo in parts of Arnhem Land and elsewhere (see Altman 1982; Trigger 2008).[9] While maintaining traditional beliefs and practices, many people also identify as Christian. As I have described elsewhere (Vaarzon-Morel 2012), older people were introduced to Christianity by missionaries who taught Bible stories, including that of the Three Wise Men, who followed the star to Bethlehem on camels.[10] At Ernabella Mission, Anangu performed Christmas pageants in which they dressed as the Three Wise Men and rode camels, thus reinforcing this link between camels and Christianity (Vaarzon-Morel 2012). As a result of this history, many people symbolically associate camels with Christianity, and the cosmological significance of camels has shifted for them.[11] As Peipai explained, "Camels were the number one, it was they who followed the star. It is because of this that we hold camels in such high regard." Furthermore, because some people conceptualize the relationship between Christianity and Aboriginal religion in hierarchical terms, stating that God made the Dreaming beings and other animals such as camels and donkeys, they feel that these animals are equally worthy and should not be treated as Other. The positing of certain introduced and totemic species as level – at least in relational terms – serves to foster coexistence. This resonates with the way that totemic species "that are forced to enter into contact are all positioned at the same ontological level" (Descola 2014a: 399).

This leads me to consider attitudes towards the hunting and killing of native animals as they influence attitudes towards camels. Today, Warlpiri and Anangu no longer live by hunting and gathering, but they hunt animals to eat when the opportunity arises. Although they objectify game animals to the extent that they classify them as "meat" and do not have personal, social relations with them, Anangu may nevertheless approach animals as responsive beings. To take some examples: Children are told not to tease sleepy lizards (*kalta*) lest they become ill. According to Eileen Wingfield and Emily Austin (2008: 20), Anangu coax echidnas to unroll themselves by promising to kill their head lice if they poke their heads out. Similarly they note that carpet snakes and goannas "lie still for you to knock him in the head too. [Because] he knows he's been caught by people that eat him ... Poor thing!" (Wingfield and Austin 2008: 18). As I observed with Anangu who had cornered a perentie (*Varanus giganteus*), which assumed an upright pose, they called out a ritual invocation to get him to lie down. The same invocation is used by Anangu to alert people to the passage of a novice en route to initiation so that they bow their heads. According to Wingfield and Austin (2008: 26), when the goanna hears this call "he shows respect and gets down, lies down flat and you walk up and kill him there." Although the latter examples involve deception, as Aram Yengoyan observed, deception is based "in the moral givens of myth [and] is tolerable and socially accepted" (1993: 243).[12]

Although Warlpiri do not respond to animals in the way previously described for Anangu, both Warlpiri and Anangu emphasize that game animals must be respected and that there are serious consequences for not doing so (cf. Descola 2014b). The killing, distribution, and cooking of native animals is circumscribed by prohibitions and protocols, which derive from Aboriginal Law.[13] While these do not apply to introduced animals such as camels, moral assumptions derived from them inform "proper" practices of killing animals, regardless of whether the animals are autochthonous or not. Thus, animals should not be killed wantonly;[14] to do so is to transgress Aboriginal Law. While successful hunters are admired, and people take pride in being plentiful providers of meat, the numbers of animals killed should not be more than people can utilize. To illustrate, the late Japangardi Poulson, an admired hunter, told me about an occasion when he chastised a younger man who shot several kangaroos and took only the tails, leaving the "skinny ones" to rot. Japangardi admonished him: "You can't do that. You are wasting for the future ... That's against the Law ... we respect animals; that's Jukurrpa" (Vaarzon-Morel 2008: 61). Furthermore, Japangardi stressed that hunters should be selective in the animals they chose, leaving thin animals, "breeders,"[15] and old animals.

Here it is important to recall that people share the spirits of Dreaming ancestors with the native animals they hunt,[16] and that they are compelled by Aboriginal Law to respect the animals (see also Thomsen, Muir, and Davies 2006). Thus, for example, Peipai explained how the ill treatment of certain animals might result in repercussions for their ancestral country and vice versa. Pointing out that animals have bodies and spirits just as humans do, she stated: "Any damage done to land affects their children and causes them to become sick and to die, because they hold the spirit of the land inside of them." Furthermore, she observed, the wanton killing of animals could result in the deaths of people who share the Dreaming spirit of the animal. Peipai's observations illustrate the relational nature of Aboriginal ontology and the importance placed on respectful social relations among humans and non-human entities for environmental well-being. Debbie Rose (1999) has described this phenomenon as an "ethic of connection" and emphasizes that it involves both *respect* and *restraint* with regard to animals. As I show later, this ethic extends to the treatment of camels.

The Contemporary Situation

Since the 1970s, when Aborigines ceased using camels for transport, dramatic changes have occurred in people's lives with the shift in government policy from assimilation to self-determination, and the recognition of Aboriginal land rights. The outstation movements in the 1970s and 1980s saw many people return to their homelands from government settlements. Although the process of decentralization has reversed somewhat, some homelands expanded to become large villages. Since the introduction of the Native Title Act 1993, Aboriginal people's rights and interests in land have been recognized over substantial areas.

In the past few decades, the camel situation has also changed – as has the nature of people's engagements with camels. Although most people no longer closely associate with camels, encounters with free-ranging camels have increased in concert with an increase in the population and distribution of the animals. Now distributed over 3.3 million square kilometres of the continent, camels are highest in density in central Australia, with twice as many on Aboriginal land as on non-Indigenous pastoral and conservation reserve land (McGregor et al. 2013). However, camels range across different land tenure boundaries and, in so doing, they entangle groups with differing nature-culture relations and concerns about the animals (Vaarzon-Morel and Edwards 2012).

In 2007 I was engaged by Desert Knowledge Cooperative Research Centre (DKCRC) to conduct stakeholder research in central Australia on Aboriginal perceptions of free-ranging camels for a multidisciplinary "feral" camel research project (Edwards et al. 2008). At the time, the camel population was estimated to be one million, and expected to double in nine years (Edwards et al. 2008). This figure was subsequently revised to six hundred thousand (McGregor et al. 2013: 1–2, 58). Elsewhere I have described the methodology, aims, and findings of my research (Vaarzon-Morel 2008, 2010), which involved a qualitative survey in twenty-five Aboriginal settlements in the Northern Territory, Western Australia, and South Australia and two in-depth case studies. In addition to people who had used camels for transport, I interviewed people with no such history and people who had hunted camels for meat. The research focused on people's awareness of the presence and impacts of free-ranging camels and attitudes towards their management. Here I summarize some key points, briefly noting contrasting perspectives of non-Indigenous stakeholders, whose views were presented in findings reported by other researchers in the project.

Unlike Aboriginal people (and reflecting a naturalist ontology), non-Indigenous pastoralists and conservation land managers categorized free-ranging camels as a feral, pest animal. While recognizing positive and negative impacts associated with the animals – pastoralists emphasized economic considerations, whereas conservation land managers emphasized natural and cultural considerations – both groups thought that they needed to be managed, preferably by culling (shooting-to-waste) and through commercial use (Zeng and Edwards 2010).

In contrast to the other stakeholders, Aboriginal people held views on free-ranging camels and their management that revealed intertwined socio-cultural and environmental dimensions, reflecting their nature-culture relations and historical associations with camels. At the same time, people's perspectives on free-ranging camels were not homogeneous. While they recognized negative and positive environmental impacts associated with the animals, people's views differed depending on factors such as the density of camels in a particular place, their own long-term familiarity with the place, and their historical relationship with camels. Many people in areas where the density of feral camels was high expressed concern that camels were causing significant harm to their country, whereas such concerns were limited in areas with few camels. As my interest in this chapter is to explore the dilemmas facing people in the former situation, I now provide examples of perceived harms.

Camels were said to be "killing country" by depleting, fouling, and degrading water places on which other beings depend, many of which are of sacred significance. People expressed concern that the desecration of these sites could cause the traditional owners to fall ill. Camels were said to be driving away kangaroos, reducing the availability of bush medicine and food plants, and stripping and displacing trees, many of which have sacred significance and provide shade for animals (Edwards et al. 2010). People were fearful of bull camels and avoided areas with camels when hunting and visiting country (Vaarzon-Morel 2008). Elders, especially, expressed concern about the effects of camels on country for future generations (Vaarzon-Morel and Edwards 2012). In some places, camels had damaged material infrastructure including taps, air conditioners, and fences and were involved in vehicle accidents. Worried about the increasing numbers of camels and associated harms caused to the environment, many people expressed a need to manage the animals. Such views contrasted with earlier findings from studies Robert Nugent (1988) and Bruce Rose (1995) undertook in the southern part of the Northern Territory that, in general, Aboriginal people were not concerned about the effects of free-ranging camels on their land and that many people regarded camels as "belonging to country." Rose, a scientist, argued that "people see the contemporary ecosystem as an integrated whole so they don't see some species as belonging while others do not" (1995: xx). In framing people's views in terms of "ecosystem" thinking, he imputes a naturalism that was alien to Aboriginal ontology (see Descola 2014a: 197–8). Nonetheless, the implication is that, at one level at least, introduced animals were incorporated into people's relational schema. Significantly, camel numbers were low in most areas that Nugent and Rose studied during the 1980s and 1990s respectively (see Vaarzon-Morel 2010). Clearly, the recent shift in people's perspectives is associated with the growth of the camel population. In reflecting on harms caused by camels, some people reasoned that camels behaved transgressively because, unlike totemic animals, they have no Dreaming and hence no law, or are outsiders, like orphans, wandering around creating trouble (Vaarzon-Morel 2012: 68).

Nevertheless, despite some people positioning camels as outsiders, their relational ontology influenced their views as to how the camel situation should be managed. For the most part, people wanted camels to be reduced in number but not eradicated from their country, and live removal was the preferred option. Many people identified potential opportunities associated with the capture and sale of live animals, tourism activities, and also hunting of the animals for pet and human consumption. Importantly, there was substantial opposition to culling on

Aboriginal land, which many people perceived as "cruel" and wasteful (Vaarzon-Morel 2008; see also Fache in this volume).

The logic underlying this position relates to a cultural ethic against mass killing and the wasting of animals, which as discussed earlier derives from Aboriginal morality and Law. Furthermore, in Aboriginal cosmology, mass death is associated with morally transgressive behaviour and a lack of compassion and respect for others.[17] In Warlpiri mythology, acts of mass slaughter are commonly committed by monsters who were once human persons but transformed as a result of ill treatment by relatives, on whom they subsequently seek revenge. As mentioned, Aboriginal people do not posit a radical division between nature and culture, and in their world of enmeshed relationships, mass death implicates human as well as other-than-human beings. According to the logic of Aboriginal relational ontology, killing for waste will attract cosmic retribution, with possible punishments including ill health, death, and environmental repercussions such as drought. Although the primary focus of this chapter is on people who used camels for transport, these sentiments concerning mass killing and wasting of animals are widely shared by people with little experience of camels (see also Fache in this volume).

Camel Management

Since my research, different strategies to manage camel impacts have been implemented in central Australia, including on Aboriginal lands. I have had no involvement in these developments, on which I now reflect. The DKCRC study (see Edwards et al. 2008), of which my research constituted a small but significant part, resulted in increased recognition of the negative impacts of camels in central Australia. In 2010 the Australian government provided funds to implement the "cross-jurisdictional camel management framework to manage the impacts of camels across Australia" (see McGregor et al. 2013) under the "Caring for Our Country" program.[18] The Australian Feral Camel Management Project (AFCMP) was contracted to reduce camel numbers according to a suggested "feral" camel target density (see McGregor et al. 2013). The AFCMP was a collaborative partnership involving the national, state, and territory governments, representatives from regional Natural Resource Management agencies, commercial and animal welfare interests, local pastoralists and Aboriginal Land Councils, ranger groups, and communities.

It is beyond the scope of this chapter to consider the negotiations that took place between Aboriginal landholders and the AFCMP. Suffice to say that Aboriginal landholders were invited to participate and that their informed consent was required (after lengthy consultations) before any activities were undertaken on their land (see McGregor et al. 2013). Nevertheless, despite people's preferred options, strategies for managing camel impacts were necessarily influenced by practical, economic, and livelihood considerations. For example, in responding to the "invasion" of camels in their communities on the Anangu Pitjantjatjara Yankunytjatjara lands of South Australia, Anangu adopted a "no-shoot-to-leave" policy. For a time they were able to manage the situation by mustering the camels to watering points provided outside the communities (McGregor et al. 2013: 19). However, as the camel numbers increased, this strategy proved ineffective. The transportation of camels to an abattoir for slaughter was then arranged as part of a commercial operation, which provided local people with employment and income. Approximately fifteen thousand camels were removed from the lands in this way (McGregor et al. 2013: 19–20). As this example illustrates, due to the vast numbers of camels on Aboriginal land, managing impacts inevitably meant removing camels from the land. However, in some regions the preferred option of live removal was not economically feasible and culling was implemented. This was the predicament that Aboriginal people at Kaltukatjara faced in 2009, when, during a drought, camels entered their community in search of water. At one stage there were approximately fifteen thousand camels circulating within one hundred square kilometres of the settlement and thousands more beyond that range. Worried by this event, and tired of the damage the camels were doing to their country and settlement infrastructure, local traditional owners agreed to the camels being herded away from the community by helicopter and culled. These cases highlight people's responses when camels are experienced as highly invasive.

What I want to focus on now is the wider biopolitical context surrounding the implementation of the camel management project in less extreme situations. As Richard Baker, Jocelyn Davies, and Elspeth Young have noted (2001), the development of a sustainable development paradigm in Australia has seen increasing recognition of the value of Indigenous ecological knowledge and the development of natural resource management projects involving Aborigines. In central Australia these projects are administered through representative

Aboriginal bodies, such as the Central Land Council (CLC),[19] whose role has increasingly focused on environmental land management as large areas of land have come under Aboriginal ownership. At the same time, with the consent of traditional owners, thousands of square kilometres of inalienable Aboriginal Freehold land have become incorporated as Indigenous Protected Areas (IPAs), with associated Indigenous Ranger programs (Altman and Kerins 2012; see also Frances Morphy in this volume). The convergence of these events means that Aboriginal people in central Australia are increasingly engaging with the land in the context of Western bioconservation models (see also Fache in this volume).

In many cases, environmental management plans have been developed for the IPAs that adopt a "two-way" approach, which seeks to combine Indigenous and non-Indigenous knowledge (see, for example, Preuss and Dixon 2012; Fache in this volume). Thus, in addition to local understandings regarding free-ranging camels, people are introduced to Western scientific methods and considerations derived from broadscale scientific modelling, which focuses on population aggregates (Strang 2008; cf. Scott in this volume). Let me be clear here that people have asked for such information to assist them in looking after country (Vaarzon-Morel 2012: 69). Yet, the fact remains that the language and practices of biodiversity conservation reflect ontological understandings of nature-culture relations that are radically different from those of Aboriginal people.[20] The following example from a research report on an IPA project illustrates the situation that results when economic constraints governing management options are added to the mix.

The report was co-authored by a Warlpiri ranger and a non-Indigenous land management officer. In it they describe an occasion when non-Indigenous staff familiar with "national biodiversity concerns regarding feral camels, shared their knowledge with *yapa* [Warlpiri] while they were cleaning camel bones out of rockholes together, visiting trampled soakages ... or noticing camel impacts on bush foods and other vegetation" (Preuss and Dixon 2012: 12). They then note that two years later the Warlpiri participants in the activities were identifying camels as a threat to "natural and cultural resources." Moreover, the authors note, these Warlpiri assisted with "negotiations and discrepancies" between conservation and "more traditional approaches to leave camels as they belonged to country" (Preuss and Dixon 2012: 12). Although the preferred method for managing camels was live removal, it was uneconomical, so ground-based culling was implemented.

Conclusion

In his chapter "Histories of Structures," Descola (2014a) describes how ontologies may transform through time by the replacement of one "relational schema" with another. He identifies changes in modes of treating others as one possible factor that can contribute to such transformation. Thus he notes "a mode of treating 'others' is superseded and another, previously marginal, acquires a dominant position; what has been considered normal now seems impossible and what has seemed unimaginable eventually becomes common sense" (Descola 2014a: 365). In this chapter I have sketched how Aboriginal people's relations with camels changed over time as they became increasingly entangled with them. Initially treated as invading strangers, camels then became a familiar animal in the landscape. Some people hunted camels for meat, thus continuing a traditional form of interaction with game animals. However, others adopted camels for use as transport and, in doing so, they developed yet another mode of relating to animals. But as I have shown, there were overlaps between the kind of relationship that people developed with camels and the kind of relationship that they have with dogs. Importantly, the use of domesticated camels did not radically transform people's ontological relations with their world. More recently, many people's views on camels have changed due to increasing numbers of free-ranging camels and associated environmental harms. That camels are familiar beings and not invading strangers, however, creates moral dilemmas for people who, in wanting to manage perceived transgressive behaviour, must choose which beings should live and which should die.

This moral dilemma involves questions of identity and cosmology. Much Aboriginal ritual is concerned with the life cycle and the reproduction of the world, both human and non-human. In the past, and to a much lesser extent in the present, ceremonies drawing on ancestral powers in the land were performed to increase the different kinds of plants, animals, and other entities on which Aborigines depended. As with Indigenous peoples elsewhere (see Harvey Feit in this volume), traditionally Aboriginal economy and cosmology were inextricably linked to vital concerns. And while death is accepted as part of the normal course of things, the power to take human life (to punish transgressions, for example) was bound up with social considerations structured by Jukurrpa or the "Law." Similarly, the taking of animal life whilst hunting was governed by prohibitions connected to Jukurrpa Law. Although the subsistence economy has changed, Aboriginal cosmological beliefs and teachings continue to frame their relations with the various non-humans inhabiting their world.

In maintaining proper relationships with the land today, however, Aboriginal people are faced with quandaries involving questions of life, death, and identity, as shifts occur in their relations with camels and as they increasingly engage with radically different "forms of knowledge, regimes of authority and practices of intervention" (Rabinow and Rose 2006: 197). The case of camels demonstrates that the inclusiveness that characterized Aboriginal relations with other beings in the past is now contingent, and increasingly being governed by a politics of exclusion, which involves a different way of treating others. This new biopolitical order is premised on the control and mass death of one kind of animal in order for others to live. What once seemed unimaginable is now accepted. At stake in this process are not only material and symbolic matters but also the nature of people's subjectivities and their relational ontology.

To conclude, the camel case illustrates the ongoing, complex, and dialectical nature of Indigenous entanglements with Australian settler society, the land, and introduced animals who inhabit it. In this chapter I have shown how differing facets of people's "ontological schemas" are highlighted, articulated, and potentially transformed in this process.

ACKNOWLEDGMENTS

I presented an initial version of this chapter at the 10th Conference on Hunting and Gathering Societies (CHAGS) held at the University of Liverpool. I thank Françoise Dussart and Sylvie Poirier for their invitation to participate in their panel "Relationships to the Land: Ontological Resistance and Entanglement in the 21st Century." The chapter has benefited greatly from discussions with them. I also thank Nicolas Peterson, Jim Wafer, Geoff Bagshaw, and the anonymous reviewers for providing feedback. The chapter draws, in part, on Vaarzon-Morel 2008 and 2010 and Edwards et al. 2008. Work reported in these publications was supported by funding from the Australian government Natural Heritage Trust through the Desert Knowledge

Cooperative Research Centre. The views expressed herein do not necessarily represent the views of the Australian government or the Desert Knowledge CRC or its participants.

NOTES

1 Furthermore, they had to confront colonial practices and representations of themselves that were linked with European attitudes toward domesticated animals and the perceived capacity to transform the land (see Reynolds 1986; Povinelli 1995; Ingold 2000: 64; Franklin 2006: 48).

2 In particular "whether either evolving animal husbandry or hierarchical inter-human social relations co-occur with either ceasing or beginning to perceive animals as co-persons" (Naveh and Bird-David 2014: 75).

3 For example, Reynolds 1986; Kenny 2007: 170; Tjilari 2009.

4 The term was used to refer to camel handlers from north India and surrounding regions who worked with camels (see Jones and Kenny 2007).

5 Considering such "intellectual openness" towards introduced animals, David Trigger develops the idea of "'emergent autochthony' in Aboriginal cultures, whereby new species become 'naturalized,' in cultural terms" (2008: 630).

6 Personal identity is also determined by people's conception Dreaming, in the case of Warlpiri, and place of birth, in the case of Anangu.

7 For example, John Morton (1997: 154, 170) describes how Arrernte "sociobiological" knowledge of native cats is employed in the *ingkura* fire ceremony, in which male novices attain seniority.

8 Wild dingoes were hunted for food, and while people adopted dingo pups to raise, they did not selectively breed them (Meggitt 1965). Although people now also keep "European" domestic dogs, their relations with them differ from those that Europeans have with their dogs. For example, among Warlpiri, dogs roam freely and may be given subsection names, such as that of a parent, which denotes their role as guardians who protect people by warning them of strange beings.

9 They arrived a century before camels were introduced to central Australia. The exception I refer to was noted by Glowczewski (1991: 14), who, in 1984, was told about an earlier event in which Warlpiri performed a camel "danse des bosses et des os" ("bump and bones" dance).

10 See Schwarz and Dussart 2010 for an overview of Christianity among Aborigines.

11 Similarly, as Fache also notes in this volume, donkeys are associated with Christianity. In central Australia people interpret the cross on their back as signifying this connection.

12 Tim Ingold argued that the capacity for reciprocal exchanges between humans and animals is a feature that distinguishes animist hunter-gatherers from pastoral herders, whose relationship with animals is "founded on a principle not of trust but of domination" (2000: 72). However, Paul Nadasdy points out that reciprocity can also involve deception, as occurs with northern American animists who conceptualize animals as "persons who give themselves to hunters" (2007: 25). While my example concerning carpet snakes and goannas is suggestive of the latter, the relationship is on a species, not individual, level and, hence, very different.

13 As is well known, there are taboos on people eating animals associated with their personal totem, although this varies among groups and according to context.

14 As Ingold (2000: 67) notes, an aversion to wasting animals is common among hunter-gatherers.

15 Michael Pickering described a similar selection process at work among Aborigines in northern Australia when hunting cattle and buffalo, and notes that "a degree of respect was given to older animals which were left unmolested" (1995: 18).

16 Contra John Knight (2012), the animals are not thought of as strangers.

17 See Scott in this volume for a discussion of the Cree ethic of respect for living beings that inhabit their world.

18 See Morphy in this volume for background to the program.

19 The CLC was set up to give effect to the Aboriginal Land Rights (Northern Territory) Act 1976 by organizing land claims and helping manage Aboriginal land.

20 Knight suggests (2012: 52) that hunting and modern forms of bioconservation control such as culling are not that different. However, as my analysis shows, people consider them very different.

REFERENCES

Altman, Jon C. 1982. "Hunting Buffalo in North-Central Arnhem Land: A Case of Rapid Adaptation among Aborigines." *Oceania* 52 (4): 274–85. http://dx.doi.org/10.1002/j.1834-4461.1982.tb01503.x.

Altman, Jon, and Seán Kerins, eds. 2012. *People on Country: Vital Landscapes/Indigenous Futures*. Sydney: Federation Press.

Baker, Richard, Jocelyn Davies, and Elspeth Young. 2001. "Managing Country: An Overview of the Prime Issues." In *Working on Country: Contemporary Indigenous Management of Australia's Lands and Coastal Regions*, ed. R. Baker, J. Davies, and E. Young, 1–23. Melbourne: Oxford University Press.

Bird-David, Nurit. 1999. "'Animism' Revisited: Personhood, Environment, and Relational Epistemology." *Current Anthropology* 40 (S1): S67–S91. http://dx.doi.org/10.1086/200061.

Bowman, David M.J.S., and and Cathy J. Robinson. 2002. "The Getting of the Nganabbarru: Observations and Reflections on Aboriginal Buffalo Hunting in Northern Australia." *Australian Geographer* 33 (2): 191–206. http://dx.doi.org/10.1080/00049180220151007.

Descola, Philippe. 2014a (2005). *Beyond Nature and Culture*. Trans. J. Lloyd. Chicago: University of Chicago Press.

Descola, Philippe. 2014b. "The Grid and the Tree: Reply to Marshall Sahlins' Comment." *HAU* 4 (1): 295–300. http://dx.doi.org/10.14318/hau4.1.015.

Edwards, Glen P., Ben Zeng, W. Keith Saalfeld, and Petronella Vaarzon-Morel. 2010. "Evaluation of the Impacts of Feral Camels." *Rangeland Journal* 32 (1): 43–54. http://dx.doi.org/10.1071/RJ09037.

Edwards, Glen P., Ben Zeng, W. Keith Saalfeld, Petronella Vaarzon-Morel, and Murray McGregor, eds. 2008. "Managing the Impacts of Feral Camels in Australia: A New Way of Doing Business." DKCRC Report 47, Desert Knowledge Cooperative Research Centre, Alice Springs, NT. http://www.nintione.com.au/resource/DKCRC-Report-47-Managing-the-impacts-of-feral-camels-in-Australia-A-new-way-of-doing-business.pdf.

Fortwangler, Crystal. 2013. "Untangling Introduced and Invasive Animals." *Environment and Society: Advances in Research* 4 (1): 41–59. http://dx.doi.org/10.3167/ares.2013.040104.

Franklin, Adrian. 2006. *Animal Nation: The True Story of Animals and Australia*. Sydney: UNSW Press.

Glowczewski, Barbara. 1991. *Du rêve à la loi chez les Aborigènes: Mythes, rites et organisation sociale en Australie* [From Dreaming to the Law among the Aborigines: Myths, Rituals, and Social Organization in Australia]. Paris: PUF.

Gould, Richard A., Don D. Fowler, and Catherine S. Fowler. 1972. "Diggers and Doggers: Parallel Failures in Economic Acculturation." *Southwestern Journal of Anthropology* 28 (3): 265–81. http://dx.doi.org/10.1086/soutjanth.28.3.3629223.

Hamilton, Annette. 1987. "Coming and Going: Aboriginal Mobility in North-West South Australia. 1970–1971." *Records of the South Australian Museum* 20: 47–57.

Ingold, Tim. 2000. *The Perception of the Environment: Essays in Livelihood, Dwelling and Skill.* London: Routledge. http://dx.doi.org/10.4324/9780203466025.

Jones, Phillip, and Anna Kenny. 2007. *Australia's Muslim Cameleers: Pioneers of the Inland 1860s–1930s.* Kent Town: Wakefield Press, in association with South Australian Museum.

Keen, Ian. 2004. *Aboriginal Economy and Society: Australia at the Threshold of Colonisation.* Melbourne: Oxford University Press.

Kenny, Robert. 2007. *The Lamb Enters the Dreaming: Nathanael Pepper and the Ruptured World.* Carlton North, Vic.: Scribe Publications.

Knight, John. 2012. "The Anonymity of the Hunt: A Critique of Hunting as Sharing." *Current Anthropology* 53 (3): 334–55. http://dx.doi.org/10.1086/665535.

Kohn, Eduardo. 2009. "A Conversation with Philippe Descola." *Tipití, Journal of the Society for the Anthropology of Lowland South America* 7 (2): 133–7. Electronic document. http://digitalcommons.trinity.edu/tipiti/vol7/iss2/1, accessed 14 August 2012.

Layton, Robert. 1986. *Uluru: An Aboriginal History of Ayers Rock.* Canberra: Aboriginal Studies Press.

Lévi-Strauss, Claude. 1963. *Totemism.* Boston: Beacon Press.

McGregor, M., Q. Hart, A. Bubb, and R. Davies, eds. 2013. "Managing the Impacts of Feral Camels across Remote Australia: Final Report of the Australian Feral Camel Management Project." Ninti One Limited. Electronic document, http://www.nintione.com.au/resource/ManagingImpactsFeralCamels_FinalReportAFCMP.pdf, accessed 5 January 2015.

McKnight, Tom L. 1969. *The Camel in Australia.* Melbourne: Melbourne University Press.

Meggitt, Mervyn. 1962. *Desert People: A Study of Warlbiri Aborigines of Central Australia.* Sydney: Angus and Robertson.

Meggitt, Mervyn. 1965. "The Association between Australian Aborigines and Dingoes." In *Man, Culture, and Animals: The Role of Animals in Human Ecological Adjustments*, ed. A. Leeds and A. Vayda, 7–26. Washington, DC: American Association for the Advancement of Science.

Morton, John. 1997. "Totemism Now and Then: A Natural Science of Society?" In *Scholar and Sceptic: Australian Aboriginal Studies in Honour of L.R. Hiatt*, ed. Francesca Merlan, John Morton, and Alan Rumsey, 151–70. Canberra: Aboriginal Studies Press.

Myers, Fred R. 1986. *Pintupi Country, Pintupi Self.* Washington, DC, and Canberra : Smithsonian Institution Press and Australian Institute of Aboriginal Studies.

Myers, Fred R. 2002. "Ways of Place-Making." In *Culture, Landscape, and the Environment*, ed. H. Morphy and K. Flynt, 72–110. Oxford: Oxford University Press.

Nadasdy, Paul. 2007. "The Gift in the Animal: The Ontology of Hunting and Human-Animal Sociality." *American Ethnologist* 34 (1): 25–43. http://dx.doi.org/10.1525/ae.2007.34.1.25.

Naveh, David, and Nurit Bird-David. 2014. "How Persons Become Things: Economic and Epistemological Changes among Nayaka Hunter-Gatherers." *Journal of the Royal Anthropological Institute* 20 (1): 74–92. http://dx.doi.org/10.1111/1467-9655.12080.

Nugent, Robert. 1988. "Some Aboriginal Attitudes to Feral Animals and Land Degradation." Unpublished. Land Management Section, Central Land Council, Alice Springs.

Ortner, Sherry B. 2005. "Subjectivity and Cultural Critique." *Anthropological Theory* 5 (1): 31–52. http://dx.doi.org/10.1177/1463499605050867.

Peterson, Nicolas. 2009. "Camels and the Pitjantjara: Filming the End of an Era." Abstract. Indigenous Participation in Australian Economies Conference. Canberra: National Museum of Australia.

Pickering, Michael. 1995. "Notes on the Aboriginal Hunting and Butchering of Cattle and Buffalo." *Australian Archaeology* 40: 17–21.

Poirier, Sylvie. 2004. "Ontology, Ancestral Order and Agencies among the Kukatja (Australian Western Desert)." In *Figured Worlds: Ontological Obstacles in Intercultural Relations*, ed. John Clammer, Sylvie Poirier, and Eric Schwimmer, 58–82. Toronto: University of Toronto Press.

Povinelli, Elizabeth A. 1995. "Do Rocks Listen? The Cultural Politics of Apprehending Australian Aboriginal Labor." *American Anthropologist* 97 (3): 505–18. http://dx.doi.org/10.1525/aa.1995.97.3.02a00090.

Preuss, Karissa, and Madeline Dixon. 2012. "Looking After Country Two-Ways: Insights into Indigenous Community-Based Conservation from the Southern Tanami." *Ecological Management and Restoration* 13 (1): 2–15. http://dx.doi.org/10.1111/j.1442-8903.2011.00631.x.

Rabinow, Paul, and Nikolas Rose. 2006. "Biopower Today." *Biosocieties* 1 (2): 195–217. http://dx.doi.org/10.1017/S1745855206040014.

Reynolds, Henry. 1986. *The Other Side of the Frontier*. Sydney: NewSouth Books.

Rose, Bruce. 1995. *Land Management Issues: Attitudes and Perceptions amongst Aboriginal People of Central Australia. Report*. Alice Springs: Central Land Council.

Rose, Deborah B. 1999. "Indigenous Ecologies and an Ethic of Connection." In *Global Ethics for the 21st Century*, ed. N. Low, 175–86. London: Routledge.

Rose, Deborah B. 2002. *Country of the Heart: An Indigenous Australian Homeland.* Canberra: Aboriginal Studies Press.

Rose, Frederick G.G. 1965. *The Wind of Change in Central Australia: The Aborigines at Angas Downs, 1962.* Berlin: Akadamie-Verlag.

Sahlins, Marshall. 2014. "On the Ontological Scheme of *Beyond Nature and Culture.*" *HAU* 4 (1): 281–90. http://dx.doi.org/10.14318/hau4.1.013.

Sandall, Roger. dir. 1969. *Camels and the Pitjantjara.* 45 min. Australian Institute of Aboriginal Studies Film Unit.

Schwarz, Carolyn, and Françoise Dussart, eds. 2010. "Engaging Christianity in Aboriginal Australia." Theme issue. *Australian Journal of Anthropology* 21.

Scott, Colin. 2006. "Spirit and Practical Knowledge in the Person of the Bear among Wemindji Cree Hunters." *Ethnos* 71 (1): 51–66. http://dx.doi.org/10.1080/00141840600603178.

Strang, Veronica. 2008. "Cosmopolitan Natures: Paradigms and Politics in Australian Environmental Management." *Nature and Culture* 3 (1): 41–62. http://dx.doi.org/10.3167/nc.2008.030104.

Strehlow, Theodor G.H. 1960. "Journey Northwards: Comment on Camel Transport by T.G.H. Strehlow." Archived material. Alice Springs: Strehlow Research Centre.

Sutton, Peter, and Petronella Vaarzon-Morel. 2003. *Yulara Anthropology Report.* Alice Springs: Central Land Council.

Thomsen, Dana, Kado Muir, and Jocelyn Davies. 2006. "Aboriginal Perspectives on Kangaroo Management in South Australia." *Rangeland Journal* 28 (2): 127–37.

Tjilari, Andy. 2009. "Seeing Camels." Oral history text recorded and translated by W. Edwards. Made available to Petronella Vaarzon-Morel, 30 October 2009.

Trigger, David S. 2008. "Indigeneity, Ferality, and What 'Belongs' in the Australian Bush: Aboriginal Responses to Introduced Animals and Plants in a Settler-Descendant Society." *Journal of the Royal Anthropological Institute* 14 (3): 628–46. http://dx.doi.org/10.1111/j.1467-9655.2008.00521.x.

Vaarzon-Morel, Petronella. 2008. *Key Stakeholder Perceptions of Feral Camels: Aboriginal Community Survey. DKCRC Report 49.* Alice Springs: Desert Knowledge Cooperative Research Centre. http://www.nintione.com.au/resource/DKCRC-Report-49-Key-stakeholder-perceptions-of-feral-camels-Aboriginal-community-survey.pdf.

Vaarzon-Morel, Petronella. 2010. "Changes in Aboriginal Perceptions of Feral Camels and of Their Impacts and Management." *Rangeland Journal* 32 (1): 73–85. http://dx.doi.org/10.1071/RJ09055.

Vaarzon-Morel, Petronella. 2012. "Camels and the Transformation of Indigenous Economic Landscapes." In *Indigenous Participation in Australian Economies 11: Historical Engagements and Current Enterprises*, ed. Ian Keen, 73–95. Canberra: ANU ePress; Available at http://press.anu.edu.au//wp-content/uploads/2012/07/prelims1.pdf.

Vaarzon-Morel, Petronella, and Glenn Edwards. 2012. "Incorporating Aboriginal People's Perceptions of Introduced Animals in Resource Management: Insights from the Feral Camel Project." *Ecological Management and Restoration* 13 (1): 65–71. http://dx.doi.org/10.1111/j.1442-8903.2011.00619.x.

Veth, Peter, Peter Sutton, and Margo Neale. 2008. *Strangers on the Shore: Early Coastal Contacts in Australia*. Canberra: National Museum of Australia.

Wingfield, Eileen W., and Emily M. Austin. 2008. *Living alongside the Animals – Anangu Way*. Alice Springs: IAD Press.

Yengoyan, Aram A. 1993. "Religion, Morality, and Prophetic Traditions: Conversion among the Pitjantjatjara of Central Australia." In *Conversion to Christianity: Historical and Anthropological Perspectives on a Great Transformation*, ed. Robert W. Hefner, 233–57. Berkeley: University of California Press.

Zeng, Ben, and Glen. P. Edwards. 2010. "Perceptions of Pastoralists and Conservation Reserve Managers on Managing Feral Camels and Their Impacts." *Rangeland Journal* 32 (1): 63–72. http://dx.doi.org/10.1071/RJ09036.

10 Nehirowisiw Territoriality: Negotiating and Managing Entanglement and Coexistence

SYLVIE POIRIER

We are not Canadians, we are not Québécois, we are Atikamekw Nehirowisiw and we belong to Nitaskinan.

Excerpt from the Atikamekw Nehirowisiw
Declaration of Sovereignty, 8 September 2014

Introduction

In Canada, the issues around the definition and recognition of Indigenous land rights and titles, and ultimately sovereignty, at the political and legal levels, remain largely unresolved and of profound concern for the great majority of First Nations. A formal recognition would contribute to better clarify the terms for a fairer coexistence between Indigenous and non-Indigenous interests, presence, and practices within the territories claimed. Even those First Nations who have signed "modern treaties"[1] are aware that they must constantly remain vigilant to ensure that the treaties are respected by the federal and provincial states and non-Indigenous interest groups from, among others, the forestry, hydroelectric, mining, sport hunting, and recreational sectors. Ever since they have been "sharing" their lands with non-Indigenous settlers, Indigenous people have learned to remain suspicious of the Whiteman's words, spoken or written. Indigenous people have always been willing to "share" customary lands with the newcomers – it is part of their value system – as long as their own presence, practices, and rights are respected, and as long as the presence, needs, and movements of non-human others are respected. That is their understanding of a fair coexistence.

While First Nations find themselves confronted with unequal power relations, they have demonstrated, over the last 150 years, a strong and

ongoing resistance to their dispossession, if not to say to their disappearance, as well as a tremendous capacity to evolve new ways in order
to adapt to new contexts, means, and constraints. Over the different
periods in Canadian (colonial) history and with the political and legal
means available to them, they have never ceased to claim ancestral, historic, and distinct collective land rights. Their dispossession and marginalization did not result in the dissolution of their political action.
Furthermore, the pitfalls and slowness of the negotiation processes
concerning land rights recognition, alongside their marginalized position within Canadian society, have not stopped the First Nations from
reproducing and transforming their ancestral engagement with their
lands. Such an evolving reproduction has meant exploring and putting
into practice new strategies of dialogue and negotiation in the hope of
eventually being recognized as valuable partners, on an equitable basis,
on all issues pertaining to their lands. It has also meant exploring novel
ways for the intergenerational transmission of their knowledge, values,
and ethos in relation to their lands.

It is these kinds of issues that I am addressing in this chapter, by taking the example of the Nehirowisiwok, officially and commonly known
as the Atikamekw Nation.[2] Formerly semi-nomadic hunters and gatherers, the Nehirowisiwok, who number around seven thousand people,
live for the most part in three communities, Wemotaci, Manawan, and
Opitciwan, in the midst of the boreal forest and the rich watersheds of
Tapiskwan Sipi (St-Maurice River), in north-central Quebec. The Council of the Atikamekw Nation (Atikamekw Sipi) is a representative body
for the three communities that was founded in 1982.

Like most Indigenous peoples in nation-states like Canada, the
Nehirowisiwok have been "invited," since the early 1900s, to exclude
themselves from their territory – socially, politically, economically,
ritually, ecologically, and aesthetically. For nearly two hundred years
prior to that time, the Nehirowisiwok had been most useful and faithful fur trade partners. However, they became a "problem" as soon as
the *Emitcikociwicak* (Whitemen) turned their interests to other "natural resources" and industries. Through their flexibility and ability[3] as
hunters to adapt to new contexts and circumstances, through their
creative resistance and political action, and through their sense of who
they are (in spite of a colonial history of marginalization, dispposses-
sion, humiliation, and suffering), they keep to this day reproducing
and irrevocably adapting their relationships with their family territories. They thus maintain towards the latter a sense of responsibility and

respectful stewardship. Their territory, *Nitaskinan*, and the forestlands, *Notcimik*, which they inherited from their forebears, remain an intrinsic part of their identity, historicity, and sociality, despite obvious differences between the generations as to how the land is known, experienced, and related to.

The Nehirowisiwok have never ceased to be concerned with the dynamic reproduction of their customary tenure system, based on extended family territories. They have constantly adapted it to new constraints and presences, namely Quebec's administrative delimitations and resource management legislation, and other non-Indigenous interests and activities in *Nitaskinan*. These include, among others, logging and resort leases, controlled harvesting zones, and outfitting camps (having exclusive or non-exclusive rights) (Poirier 2001). The Nehirowisiw family territories, as post- and neo-colonial spaces, have thus become the grounds of a complex coexistence, negotiations, and entanglement between Indigenous and non-Indigenous regimes of values, land tenure systems, forms of governance, and conceptions of the forestland and its non-human inhabitants.

In view of these growing constraints and in order to regain and affirm their "relative autonomy" (see Frances Morphy in this volume) and thus a form of sovereignty, the Nehirowisiwok are engaged at three interrelated levels: 1) at the national political level in arduous land claims negotiations with the federal and provincial governments as part of the Comprehensive Land Claims policy; 2) at the regional level with municipal governments, but also in their attempts to conclude joint ventures or co-management agreements with third parties and non-Indigenous interest groups such as the forestry and recreational industries; and 3) at the level of the communities as regards their manifold social and cultural efforts and initiatives to transmit Nehirowisiw knowledge (hunting practices, language, oral tradition, etc.), values, and ethos and to adapt their customary tenure system to current constraints.

An element I also wish to stress in this chapter is the amount of work and human resources, but also the various competencies, that the Nehirowisiwok, men and women, must mobilize in order to be present and active on all these fronts simultaneously. And while all this is done with limited human, economic, and logistical resources, it is supported by a strong commitment to the land and the life projects (Blaser 2004) of the Nation. I will first consider the conceptual avenues that orient my understanding of such "entangled territorialities."

Entangled Territorialities

In my attempt to better understand the challenges faced by the Nehi-rowisiwok in reproducing their close, knowledgeable, and long-lasting relationships with *Notcimik*, the forestlands, I am drawing from a range of interrelated conceptual avenues, which have been evolving over the last few decades in anthropology and other social sciences. These avenues pertain to the field of Indigenous studies, with a focus on the issues of land and resources, to the anthropology of place, and to the ontological turn. Taken together, these conceptual avenues give us a better understanding of the complex encounters and negotiations that take place between Indigenous life projects and non-Indigenous inter-ests in relation to the land. The following notions are thus called upon: entangled territorialities and relative autonomy, coloniality (Escobar 2008), ontological obstacles (Clammer, Poirier, and Schwimmer 2004) and political ontology (Blaser 2013), senses of place (Feld and Basso 1996), and the multilocality and multivocality of place (Rodman 1992). As far as ontology is concerned, I have already expounded on the concept of "relational ontologies" (Poirier 2008, 2013) as it pertains to Indigenous and hunters' worlds like the Nehirowisiwok.[4] In relational ontologies, and unlike a naturalist ontology (Descola 2005), the onto-logical boundaries between the human and the non-human (animals, plants, places, "natural" elements, the spirits of ancestors and others, etc.) are permeable, and the relations between them are negotiable. Relational ontologies place relatedness/"relationality" as a paramount embodied value, perception, and experience, such that relations take on a reality of their own. Relational ontologies consider that the voli-tion and agency of non-human others are facts of life (largely docu-mented in ethnographies of hunter-gatherers), and that sociality and historicity are indisputably inclusive of non-human others (Poirier 2013: 54).

With regard to Indigenous peoples like the Nehirowisiwok, the concept of entanglement allows us to inquire into the dialectical and the dialogical dimensions of the encounters and coexistence between Indigenous and non-Indigenous worlds, ontologies, and actors (see Thomas 1991). As regards the local Indigenous people's point of view and their aim of securing a relative autonomy, this concept also encom-passes their responses to state policies and ideologies and to dominant modernity and "global coloniality" (Escobar 2008), responses which are not necessarily those expected by the state and the majority society.

The concept of entanglement – rather than hybridity – allows a better understanding of the tensions, conflicts, readjustments, compromises, and negotiations going on between Indigenous and non-Indigenous actors within the territories, and between their respective ontologies, life-worlds, and practices (see Françoise Dussart and Sylvie Poirier in this volume). The concept of hybridity tends somehow to underestimate, and even negate, differences (Poirier 2004; Friedman 2004), whereas entanglement stresses the politics of coexistence and difference and provides a window into social change. Encounters and coexistence between Indigenous and non-Indigenous worlds and actors, on and in the land, are always a matter of politics, in the widest sense of the term, but also of ontological obstacles (Clammer, Poirier, and Schwimmer 2004; Blaser 2013). From the Nehirowisiwok's perspective, the forestland and its non-human inhabitants, as sentient and interacting agencies (Poirier 2014), also have their part to play in these entangled territorialities and participate in their own interactive way and with relative autonomy. The moose (*mos*), the beaver (*amiskw*), the bear (*masko*), the fir tree (*cikopi*), the north wind (*kiwetinorowew*), to name but a few, all have their own sensitivities and thus their own voices in the unfolding and the potentialities of the entanglement.

As for the term *territoriality*, I take it to be an all-encompassing concept that is the forestland as conceived, experienced, and acted upon by different groups of actors and agencies, and, in the case that interests us here, as a space of conflicting interests, unequal power relations, and ontological gaps. While previous approaches to the concept of territoriality have focused almost solely on land tenure systems and resource management practices, I consider that these latter are undoubtedly informed by knowledge and value systems as well as by epistemological and ontological principles. Indigenous territorialities are further informed by memories and oral tradition, by a rich and detailed toponymy, as well as by the cosmological and aesthetic potentialities of the land, including the voices and intentionalities of its non-human inhabitants – the animals, trees, plants, water, wind, fire, and various kinds of spirits, including those of deceased relatives. An elderly Nehirowisiw man explained how, after the construction of a small dam by Hydro-Quebec in 2009, the waterfall near the community of Wemotaci became silent, its voice and reverberation no longer heard. From his perspective, the absence of this voice/sound was the main cause of the deterioration of the local flora and fauna that followed the construction of the dam. This example admirably portrays how, from a hunter's perspective, the phenomenological/sensorial, aesthetic, and ecological dimensions are intertwined.

In nation-states like Canada, the contemporary forms of such entangled territorialities are best understood by taking into account the colonial context, Canadian policies towards Indigenous peoples,[5] and provincial legislation for land and resource management. This raises the question of how to qualify the current context: as post-colonial or neo-colonial? I would answer both. Post-colonial in the sense that, unlike the colonial period, there now exist, within Quebec and Canadian institutions, explicit forms of recognition of Indigenous voices and rights, and spaces for negotiation. However, such spaces and the political and legal means through which Indigenous peoples like the Nehirowisiwok can voice their claims are still profoundly grounded in modernist institutions, ideology, and ontology. Considering the dominant modernity and the "global coloniality of knowledge, power, and nature" (Escobar 2008: 4), the current era could just as well be considered as neo-colonial. Considering entangled territorialities or "territories of difference," the notion of "coloniality" brings forward the unequal relations of power with which Indigenous peoples have to deal, while acknowledging their creative and strategic attempts to make their voices heard, to play an active part in the destiny of their territories, to forge new alliances, and to confront systems of knowledge (on this last issue, see Elodie Fache and Frances Morphy in this volume for Australian examples).

Entangled Territorialities and Their Settings

My field research since the early 1990s with the Nehirowisiwok has taught me to consider the various settings within which such encounters and negotiations, specifically with regard to the destiny of *Nitaskinan* ("our land"), are taking place. First of all, there is the institutional/ bureaucratic world of numerous meetings held in city offices situated far away from the territories in question. In such meetings with governmental and other non-Indigenous representatives, within the setting of the dominant modernist constitution, the Nehirowisiw representatives, while a minority, are still in a position to voice their own perspectives and concerns. In such settings, the French language and the language of secular political modernity are dominant. In the course of time, the Nehirowisiwok have not only learned both of these languages, they have also learned that, in such settings, some dimensions of their own world, like the volition of animals or the voices of the ancestors, have to be concealed. In this way, if they show their non-Indigenous vis-à-vis that they partake – at least in such settings – in the non-Indigenous naturalist ontology and conception of a disenchanted world, they have more of a chance of being taken seriously. Such ontological compromise, while a form of ontological violence (Poirier 2013: 61), also undoubtedly demonstrates the limits of the so-called politics of recognition and reconciliation.

A second type of setting is the offices of the Council of the Atikamekw Nation, in the small town of La Tuque, and the offices of the three Band Councils of Wemotaci, Manawan, and Opitciwan, in all of which there is a majority of Nehirowisiw employees.[6] And despite the bureaucratic environment,[7] the Atikamekw language is still dominant. As for the third setting, the forestlands, they also bear witness to the multiple encounters between the Nehirowisiwok and non-Indigenous actors, such as sport hunters or foresters (see below for more details). It must be stressed here that many Nehirowisiwok of working age are involved, to varying degrees, in all of these settings, moving back and forth from the settlements to the cities, and, whenever possible, to their hunting territories and their family camps (permanent or temporary).

We could add that the forestlands, as experienced and acted upon, are definitively plural. The polysemy of *Nitaskinan* and the plurivocality and plurilocality of the myriad of named places are expressed in the coexistence and the entanglement of the two systems, Indigenous and non-Indigenous, for mapping and naming the land and the places. One such example in *Nitaskinan* is the entanglement between Quebec administrative delimitations (e.g., logging and resort leases, controlled harvesting zones, outfitting camps) and Nehirowisiw extended family territories (Poirier 2001). That is to say that, from a more phenomenological perspective, the forestlands are conceived, experienced, and related to differently depending on whether you are a Nehirowisiw hunter, a forester, an engineer, a sport hunter, a Hydro-Quebec representative, or a tourist. These perspectives are not incommensurable; they encounter and coexist with each other, and they enter at times into a fair and intelligent dialogue (and not always a dialogue of the deaf); they are entangled while maintaining their distinctiveness. However, among all the groups of actors who interact with the forestlands, only the Nehirowisiwok are in a position to relate to these places as "home," as living spaces that they have inherited from their forebears and towards which they feel a deep sense of responsibility. A reality that only a handful of *Emitcikociwicak* are willing to recognize.

Entangled Territorialities and Governments

The Atikamekw Nation has been engaged for over thirty years now (following the Comprehensive Land Claims policy of 1976) with the federal and provincial governments in a land claim negotiation for the recognition of some form of Aboriginal title and rights. There have as yet been no tangible results. It is noteworthy that *Nitaskinan* – the territory under claim – has never been subjected to any form of treaty, and, as César Newashish (1903–1994) proclaimed in 1994: "Tell them we have never given up our territory. Tell them we have never sold or traded it. Tell them that we have never reached any other sort of agreement concerning our territory."

In this negotiation saga,[8] the aim of the Atikamekw Nation is the following: to produce a "modern treaty" that would provide them with legal and political recognition to exercise their relative autonomy, as a form of sovereignty; to be considered as valuable partners on all matters and in decision-making instances pertaining to their land and its resources; to have access to economic development resources, and to thus gain respect as a people, as a self-determined Nation. From their perspective, the spirit of such a treaty would allow them to restore the relationships with the states and the settler's society on a fairer, more equitable, and honourable basis.[9] But the road to a final agreement is arduous and full of large obstacles, one of these being the extinguishment policy put forward by the Canadian state as an obligation for any comprehensive land claim agreement (see Asch and Zlotkin 1997). The extinguishment policy means that, while a modern treaty would recognize modern rights, it would extinguish ancestral title. The Nehirowisiwok, for their part, firmly refuse such an extinguishment clause pertaining to their ancestral relationships with and responsibilities towards the land. They see the extinguishment clause as a betrayal of their ancestors and future generations of Nehirowisiwok, as a betrayal of their historical and social distinctiveness as a Nation. The extinguishment policy is a form of neo-colonial violence.

The slowness of the negotiating process (over thirty years), which could be read as a lack of political will on the part of the governments when it comes to Aboriginal land rights and titles, but also as a negotiation strategy, has had mixed effects. For the last thirty years, it has necessitated tremendous human and financial resources from the Atikamekw Nation as a whole, and more specifically from the Council of the Atikamekw Nation.[10] The overall situation has, at times, tested the patience of some Nehirowisiwok and created friction and disagreement, either between older and younger political representatives or between the three communities, as to the best way to go about the negotiations. Various examples of this would include which negotiating strategies to put forward, which attitude to adopt vis-à-vis the contesting states, and how to secure revenue from the land. Every few years, such disagreements bring about a political crisis within the Nation. These crises and disagreements alternate, however, with strong moments of solidarity. Two recent examples of the latter follow.

In May 2012, the three communities joined forces and decided to erect road blockades in order to momentarily stop forestry activities on their land and thus attract the attention of the prime minister of Quebec to excessive forestry activities, but also to their rights and the slowness of the negotiation process. Another strong moment of solidarity is the Atikamekw Nehirowisiw Declaration of Sovereignty. On 8 September 2014, the Atikamekw Nation, through their Grand Chief and the chiefs of the three communities, publicly presented, through the media, a Declaration of Sovereignty. Here is an excerpt from the text: "The protection of *Nitaskinan*, the defence of its lifestyle and its aspirations will guide, at all times, the actions of the Atikamekw Nehirowisiwok and of their current and future institutions. In this regard, the Atikamekw Nehirowisiwok will use whatever means they judge appropriate to defend their rights and interests [our translation]." These kinds of political action, along with disagreements and the occasional political crisis, also help to increase the younger generations' awareness of political issues that concern them and thus the Nehirowisiwok's empowerment, if not as a Nation with "modern rights," at least as a people that has never surrendered its territory.

And even though the Quebec government's representatives have been sitting at the negotiation table for over thirty years – somehow recognizing by their sole presence there the legitimacy of the Atikamekw Nation's claims – the government continues to grant land use permits and other licences to third parties, like the forestry and recreational industries, without necessarily consulting or acquiring the consent of the Atikamekw Nation. Such hypocrisy and double standards are not unrelated to the decision of the Atikamekw Nation to go forward with their Declaration of Sovereignty.

Entangled Territorialities and Third Parties

In their continuing aim to secure a form of relative autonomy on and recognition for *Nitaskinan*, the Council of the Atikamekw Nation and the three Band Councils have been engaged in the last few decades in ongoing dialogues at the provincial and regional levels with different groups of non-Indigenous actors who have interests in their territories, for the most part the forestry and recreational (hunting and fishing) industries.

The forestry industry has been operating in *Nitaskinan* since the end of the nineteenth century, with a notable increase in its logging activities since the 1970s. Since the 1980s, the Nation's Council and each of the three Band Councils, either together or separately, have been quite active in their attempts to negotiate with forestry companies operating in *Nitaskinan* in order to protect the family territories and to propose novel models of logging, but also to participate actively in forestry activities, hopefully in joint ventures or on a co-management basis. In that respect, different initiatives have been put forward over the last decades. Since the mid-1980s, Wemotaci has been operating the Services forestiers Atikamekw Aski, a subcontracting company for logging services (Wyatt 2004). Opitciwan has been, for its part, operating a sawmill for the last fifteen years, as a joint venture between the Council of Opitciwan and one forestry company.

While the forestry companies cannot continue to ignore the presence and claims of the Atikamekw Nation and communities, they are under no real obligation to consider them, given that this First Nation has not signed a "modern treaty." The extent to which these companies demonstrate an interest in taking Atikamekw concerns into consideration in their logging plans (and thus protecting some areas) varies from one company to the other and according to market fluctuations. It is yet to be seen whether the new Quebec forestry legislation, implemented in 2012, will actually provide more space for Indigenous concerns, voices, consultation, and participation in the planning of logging activities (see Fortier and Wyatt 2014).

Furthermore and in order to secure for themselves a voice within the decision-making processes of the industries operating in *Nitaskinan*, the Nehirowisiwok, since the mid-1980s, have put a tremendous amount of work into documenting their hunting knowledge, conducting GPS mapping of the claimed territory, indicating places of historical, cultural, and spiritual significance, identifying hundreds of place names, and surveying hunting and gathering resources. Aside from some occasional monies and funding received from Hydro-Quebec[11] and varying government sources (federal and provincial), all this work is usually accomplished with limited human and financial resources.

It is worth noting that such funding is a form of recognition, however limited, of Nehirowisiw knowledge, presence, and rights.

The Nehirowisiwok continue to invest themselves in such endeavours in order to demonstrate their knowledge of the land and to participate actively in the implementation of what the Quebec government calls the "measures of harmonization" between the different "users" of the forestlands. The term "users" found in official Quebec documents and legislation refers to the different interest groups over a given territory. The Nehirowisiwok are much troubled by such terminology. They do not consider themselves to be "users" of the land but rather dwellers, inhabitants, and the guardians of *Nitaskinan*. Furthermore, on an irregular basis and according to availability and funds, some Nehirowisiwok representatives do participate in a variety of regional consultation tables, alongside representatives of other interest groups. However, their hopes for any significant changes lie for them not so much in such regional tables as at the negotiation table with the provincial and federal states, that is, in a dialogue between Nations (see Fortier and Wyatt 2014).

In all these endeavours, and considering the unequal relations of power, the Nehirowisiwok have come to understand that they are probably the ones who have the most to lose. Nevertheless, they continue to be confident, and on that basis, their motivations and objectives in such investments are many: to be prepared to engage in a fair dialogue with the third parties present on their lands; to be considered valuable partners in all decisions pertaining to their land and its future; to protect, as much as possible, their family territories, and to transmit their traditional knowledge of the forestland to the younger generations.

Entangled Territorialities with Neighbouring First Nations

Talking of coexistence and entangled territorialities, we should not downplay, particularly as regards overlapping territories, the relationships between the Nehirowisiw Nation and neighbouring First Nations, namely the Anishinaabe to the west, the James Bay Cree to the north, and the Innu to the northeast. Traditionally, as semi-nomadic hunters and gatherers, they would have resolved all matters pertaining to lands and land use on the basis of a common language based on flexibility, reciprocity, and consensus. In today's context, each of these groups is trying to secure its own "relative autonomy," is engaged in arduous negotiations with the federal and provincial governments, and is deeply concerned about the shrinking and depletion of its lands by forestry and mining activities. While alliances between extended families and intermarriages between members of these First Nations are still very common – as they have always been – territorial conflicts have now become a complex political issue. This is also a part of Indigenous post-colonial territorialities. As researchers, I think that we have not given sufficient attention to the nature and forms of such relationships between neighbouring First Nations who still share the same hunting territories. I will discuss one particular example in more detail.

The Nehirowisiwok's closest northern neighbours, the James Bay Cree, are, for their part, benefiting from two modern treaties, namely the James Bay and Northern Quebec Agreement signed in 1975, which extinguished their ancestral title, and the Paix des Braves signed in 2002. These treaties give the Cree political and economic means and more opportunities for self-determination over Eeyou Istchee, their territory. It is also worth noting that, on the basis of these treaties, the Grand Council of the Crees and the Cree communities benefit from income, royalties, and other economic resources that are not available to the Nehirowisiwok, a Nation without a treaty. As we have seen, however, this lack of economic resources and political autonomy has not undermined the Nehirowisiwok's strong bond and commitment to their land and family territories. Nor has it affected their commitment to transmitting their traditional knowledge, language, and oral tradition to the younger generations.

Some northern portions of the *Nitaskinan*, neighbouring as they do Cree family territories, offer a potent example of contemporary forms of entangled territorialities. As neighbours, some Nehirowisiw families of Opitciwan and Cree families of Mistissini and Waswanipi used to (and still do) share hunting territories, or at least some of their hunting territories that overlapped. On signing the James Bay and Northern Quebec Agreement in 1975, the Cree Nation agreed to the extinguishment of its ancestral title over the Agreement territories, including those northern portions of *Nitaskinan*. At the time of the Agreement, the Nehirowisiwok were not consulted, nor were they invited to the negotiation table or informed of its outcome. The Cree now claim exclusive "modern" rights over territories which they once shared with Nehirowisiw families, while the Council of the Atikamekw Nation continues to claim an ancestral title over the same territories. It goes without saying that this situation has since given rise to contention between the Council of the Atikamekw Nation and the Grand Council of the Crees.

This dispute will be resolved not within the customary land tenure systems of these two Nations, in which case they would have clearly affirmed their political autonomy and self-determination, but in the settlers' legal system and courtrooms. On the other hand, this bone of contention represents, for the Council of the Atikamekw Nation and the families concerned, an opportunity to document family histories over this part of the territory, and to list and document hunting itineraries and hundreds of place names that will be presented in the courtroom as a testimony of their ancestral and continuous occupation of the contested territory. The forestlands and places concerned are thus plural: Nehirowisiw and Cree family hunting territories and living places; territories under Agreement; claimed territories; and permits for forestry exploitation.

Entangled Territorialities with Sport Hunters

It must be said at this point that sport hunting and fishing are major activities for Quebec people, a significant dimension of their tradition and their identity. Their associations represent a strong lobby that, unsurprisingly, is usually against Indigenous land rights. Under Quebec legislation, the hunting and fishing seasons for the Québécois are limited to certain periods of the year in specific delimited zones for which there are quotas. Members of First Nations are permitted, for their part, to hunt and fish all year long, but only in certain parts of the territory. This situation prompts resentment among the Québécois hunters and fishermen, who feel that the "Indians" get favourable treatment.

At the regional level, the municipal government also delivers permits through a lottery system for resort leases that go exclusively to non-Indigenous people – with no consideration of Nehirowisiw presence and claims on these same territories. This creates all sorts of recurring conflicting situations. For example, a Nehirowisiw hunter who regularly visits his customary territory, inherited from his father and grandfather, and who is recognized within his community as the "guardian" of this territory, may learn one morning that a non-Indigenous person has been randomly granted a resort lease to his territory. The newcomer is entitled to build a cabin and restrict access to his newly acquired lot. In such situations, the Nehirowisiw hunters rarely comply, even if that means being arrested and having their hunting gear confiscated by a provincial gamekeeper. One alternative to these conflicting situations is to rely on good communication with the newcomers. The outcome and the nature of such coexistence is thus a matter of developing interpersonal relationships (see also Colin Scott in this volume). Following an oral arrangement, one Québécois may allow the Nehirowisiw hunter to continue to trap and gather plants on his lot, while another one may strictly forbid it. The relationships thus vary from peaceful coexistence to ongoing confrontation.

Understandably, the Nehirowisiw hunters are deeply insulted and affected by such situations, which remind them that their land title and customary rights are not recognized and are constantly impinged upon. On the basis of their own regime of values based on reciprocity, a relational ontology, and a traditional inclusive ethos (Poirier 2013, 2014), the Nehirowisiwok are more than willing to share their territories and engage in relations of reciprocity with the non-Indigenous "users." The latter tend, however, to privilege private property and exclusive borders.

Coming from an oral tradition, the Nehirowisiwok still value person-to-person negotiations. They still tend to trust the spoken word much more than the written one. In contrast to meetings in offices where bureaucratic language and ways make them at times feel uneasy and out of their element, they are at home in *Notcimik* (the forestlands). The Nehirowisiwok consider that a viable coexistence within the territory – and by extension a sustainable management of the land and its resources – is based primarily on good communication between the different groups of actors. The oral engagements (non-formal contracts) they make every now and then in *Notcimik* with sport hunters, resort managers, or representatives of forestry companies are probably of greater worth for them than any written agreement. That is, as long as they know they can trust their vis-à-vis. By way of example, some verbal mutual arrangements between Nehirowisiw hunters and resort managers, which were agreed upon years ago, are still respected today.

Between themselves, a major dimension of the Nehirowisiw customary tenure system and resource managing strategy is the practice of asking for permission to use someone's territory, for a short period of time or for the hunting season. Permission will usually be granted by the head of the family territory concerned, though it is imperative that the request be expressed. The Nehirowisiwok do not at all like the idea that some *Emitcikociwicak* (Whitemen) may travel through their lands in an anonymous manner, without making themselves known, without informing the heads of the family territories or the Band

Council of their presence and intentions as a gesture of respect. Seeing themselves as the guardians of the land, they expect that anybody
travelling through their land or using it in one way or another should
let them know – this is part of the rules of their customary rights. In the
late 1990s, the Nehirowisiwok were very upset by a group of marijuana
growers who clandestinely grew their merchandise on parts of Nehirowisiw forestlands. What was upsetting to them was not so much the
illegality of the activities as the fact that "They didn't talk to anybody,"
they did not ask for permission, did not acknowledge the presence and
customary rights of the Nehirowisiwok. The latter still value and put
into practice these forms of reciprocal sociality in *Notcimik*.

Entangled Territorialities across Generations
and the Transmission of Hunting Knowledge

Contemporary Nehirowisiw forms of engagement with *Notcimik* are
manifold, and may vary according to the generations and intergenerational relationships. As I mentioned earlier, among the various groups
of actors who interact with the forestlands, only the Nehirowisiwok are
in a position to relate to these places as "home," as living spaces that
they have inherited from their forebears, and to which they feel a deep
and long-lasting sense of attachment, stewardship, and responsibility.
The elders refer to themselves as the *notcimi iriniwok*, "the inhabitants
of the forest." The vernacular language, to this day the mother tongue
of the majority of the Nehirowisiwok, stems from and is inspired by
the forestland and, according to the elders, is the only language able to
render the ecological, aesthetic, and sensorial dimensions of the forestlands and their seasonal variations. In a 2003 documentary prepared
by the Nation's Council and entitled *Kirano*, a group of elders present a
vibrant testimony about *notcimi arimowewin*, which is translated as "the
language/the voice of the forest." Another expression, *notcimi iriniw
otarimwewin*, is translated as "the language of the inhabitant of the forest." While the younger generations of Nehirowisiwok do not have the
same deep and intimate knowledge of the forestlands as their elders
do, many of them are in a position to appreciate and, to some extent,
embody the nature of the relationship inherited from their forebears.
Place names are a potent example of *notcimi iriniw otarimwewin*, con-
veying ecological, geographical, hydrological, historical, anecdotal, or
aesthetic aspects of any given place over the extent of *Nitaskinan*. The
myriad of Nehirowisiw place names thus coexist with Quebec's French

toponyms, one such example being the names of the numerous lakes throughout *Nitaskinan*. In such entangled naming systems, only the Nehirowisiwok are in a position to know and make use of both.

I have explained elsewhere (Poirier 2014) how hunting, trapping, fishing, and gathering activities are still very much a part of contemporary Nehirowisiw lives.[12] Temporary and permanent camps are established on family territories that are still suitable for hunting, and people visit them whenever possible, outside of working hours (on weekends, at night, during holidays or cultural weeks in the spring and autumn). As some family hunting territories are becoming less and less accessible or unsuitable for hunting for different reasons (logging activities and clear cutting; resort leases; or because they are situated too far from the settlements), members of the families concerned will usually find an arrangement with other families to use their territory. The Council of Manawan, in order to ensure that everyone has access to a hunting territory, has, for its part, delineated "community lands" situated near the settlement and accessible to all.

As hunting, fishing, trapping, and gathering are still a part of the Nehirowisiw way of life, it is understandable that the extended family territories, the foundation of their customary tenure system, maintain to this day their importance, and this in spite of the major constraints and annoyances the Nation has had to face in the last fifty years. The guardianship and transmission of such territories are the responsibility of the *ka nikaniwitc*, the head of the territory, "the one who is in front." The roles of the *ka nikaniwitc* are many: to respect and to compel respect for the custom governing the modes of resource management that he himself was taught; to ensure that all members of his extended family have an area of land that is sufficient for conducting their hunting, trapping, and other activities; and to settle internal disputes concerning the said territory (Poirier 2001: 108). In the last ten years or so, the Council of the Atikamekw Nation and the three Band Councils have been looking at ways to reaffirm, within the structures of negotiations with the federal and provincial states and the forestry industry, the political authority of the *ka nikaniwitc* (see Houde 2014). It must be stressed here that the decision-making and political powers of the Band Council, implemented under the Indian Act, are limited to the confines of the reserve land (the "community"). It is thus with the aim of expanding and strengthening their political and decision-making powers over the extent of their ancestral territory that the Atikamekw Nation is gradually reaffirming the value of its own political and decision-making structures, namely the role of the *ka nikaniwitc*, which were discredited during the colonial era and since the imposition of the Band Councils.

In today's context, there are notable differences between the families regarding the extent to which they still practise the traditional activities; some have a strong commitment while others show little interest. Whatever the case, all kinds of game, fish, and medicinal plants are still widely available and shared within and between families; most households have freezers filled with wild meat and fish, which they have caught or received as gifts. It is also quite frequent to hear adults and elders deplore the lack of hunting knowledge and interest among the younger generations. Such a reality cannot be denied. On the other hand, whenever a young adult, man or woman, does express an interest in traditional activities or in visiting *Notcimik*, there will always be an experienced person, usually kin, willing to teach him or her. The older generations also deplore the fact that the hunting ethos and the gestures of respect towards the animals have fallen into disuse among the younger generations. Whenever possible and appropriate, knowledgeable persons will remind the ones at fault of the right practices.

An experienced hunter told me about the following event. He went one day to collect his beaver traps with his son, a young adult. The son took the beavers they had caught and threw them negligently into the back of the pick-up. At once, his father told him to gather some fir branches; then, the father laid these down into the back of the pick-up and gently deposited the beavers on the branches. Another example of knowledge transmission and practices of respect was recalled to me by a woman in her sixties. Her eldest son, now an accomplished hunter, was teaching his own sons and his younger brother hunting skills and the right ways to treat the hunted animals. One day, after he had killed a moose, he performed in front of his sons and young brother a hunting ritual called *nakotiso*. This rite of passage is addressed to the animal just killed in a gesture of respect, but also to allow his passage from one state to another, from animal to game. In today's context, while this rite is seldom performed, the term *nakotiso* is still in used and refers to the action of taking the animal out of the forest and to the camp (or the settlement). I give these two examples to demonstrate that knowledge transmission is still occurring, though on an irregular and uneven basis and generally in the intimacy of *Notcimik* and of family camp life, and that, if they so wish, younger people can have access to such knowledge.

Aside from these more traditional family settings, and at the local/community level, the creative resistance of the Nehirowisiwok and their cultural and political imagination are also expressed in the numerous initiatives they have elaborated over the last decades in order not only to document but also to promote their traditional knowledge, language, and history, and to encourage their transmission to the younger generations. Here are some examples. Every few years, the Nation's Council organizes major collective intergenerational gatherings of two to three days in *Notcimik* in order to meet and exchange views on various issues of concern for the Nation; more than one hundred people may attend. Furthermore, aware that some families, for various reasons, are no longer taking on their responsibilities for the transmission of knowledge, and that many young people, even though living and attending schools on the settlements, grow up without much relationship to *Notcimik*, the schools and the Councils of the three communities have established, in the last fifteen years, various initiatives and programs for outings on the land. Each of the three communities has thus established a permanent camp in *Notcimik*, with the consent and active participation of members of a local family, these camps being used specifically for school outings that take place a few times a year and may last from a few days to a week. Elders and knowledgeable persons are present to guide and accompany the youths, both girls and boys.

This overall presentation of Nehirowisiw engagement with *Notcimik* would not be complete without the mention of a new relationship that some have recently evolved towards it. Since the early 2000s, *Notcimik* is indeed acquiring a new meaning for a growing number of Nehirowisiwok. It has become a place of healing for those, men and women, in search of a sense of well-being, *Miromatisiwin*. For the elders, *Notcimik* has always been "home," a place of autonomy and well-being despite the hardship; for the younger generations, namely the boarding-school generation and their children, and now grandchildren, their life on the settlements has often been synonymous with the ruptures and sufferings of their ongoing treatment as colonial subjects. Many of them now feel that they have to renew acquaintance, if not with the ways of their ancestors, at least with their forestlands, in order to regain a sense of completeness and well-being (see also Jérôme and Veilleux 2014).

It should be added that since the mid-1980s, Nehirowisiw members of the boarding-school generation, men and women, as a part of their healing processes but also in a gesture of cultural and political affirmation, have revived, within the settlements' grounds, some traditional hunting rituals, like the First Step Ceremony and the sweat lodge, which had fallen into disuse after the evangelization and sedentarization of their parents and grandparents. One of the objectives of such a renewal of rituals was to strengthen new forms of sociality within the settlement in a spirit of healing, as well as to somehow rethread intergenerational relations that had been profoundly damaged in the era of assimilation policies. In keeping with this healing process, which had started in the 1980s and gained impetus in the 1990s in the three communities (see Jérôme 2010), the Aboriginal Healing Foundation (1998–2012), at the national level, provided significant funds to the Atikamekw Council and to each of the three communities. Some of these funds were used to reconnect with *Notcimik*. Camps were erected in *Notcimik* in order to receive Nehirowisiw men and women engaged in a healing process; during their two-week stay, they were under the guidance of a local "healer," man or woman. For some Nehirowisiwok, *Notcimik* has thus become not so much a hunting place as a healing place, if not the healer itself.

Concluding Remarks

The overall picture of Atikamekw post- and neo-colonial territoriality that I have just outlined here brings me to reflect on the difficult relationships between First Nations and mainstream society. As a general rule, mainstream society has very little understanding of Indigenous history and life-worlds, struggle for autonomy, and life projects. In Quebec, as elsewhere, there are many prejudices towards Indigenous people, who are approached at times as passive victims who need to be helped, at times as dishonest adversaries who claim rights that they do not deserve, and at still other times as romanticized, ecologically and spiritually minded peoples. They are very seldom approached as neighbours and as equal partners who share the same lands, and as people with deep knowledge of those lands. I consider that every Québécois is indebted to these First Nations, like the Nehirowisiwok, the Cree, and the Innu, who for the last decades have struggled hard to protect their territories from hydroelectric projects, forestry, and mining. Had it not been for their struggle, the northern lands of Quebec would probably have been destroyed and depleted long ago.

ACKNOWLEDGMENTS

My research with the Nehirowisiwok was made possible through grants from the Social Sciences and Humanities Research Council of Canada (SSHRCC).

I am most grateful for their support. I also wish to thank the Council of the Atikamekw Nation, as well as Gilles Ottawa (deceased January 2013), Christian Coocoo, Charles Coocoo, and Nicole Petiquay for their friendship and for serving as my guides in their world.

NOTES

1 Since the implementation of the Comprehensive Land Claims policy in 1976, sixty claims have been lodged. Among these, twenty-five have been resolved to this day in the form of "modern treaties."

2 The first written occurrence of the appellation "Attikamègues" is found in the Jesuit Relations of 1636 by Father Le Jeune (Gélinas 2000: 32). It has to be said here that the appellation "Atikamekw," meaning "whitefish," which are abundant in the area, has never been an ethnonym, but rather the name given to the people by neighbouring Anishinaabe groups and used since then by the settlers. As a people, those we call the Atikamekw have always used the name Nehirowisiw to talk of themselves. Nehirowisiw means "the autonomous person." In 2006, the Council of the Atikamekw Nation officially adopted the ethnonym Nehirowisiw. The plural form is Nehirowisiwok.

3 On the question of flexibility with respect to the worlds of hunters, see, among others, Bird-David (1992) and Ingold (1996)

4 On relational ontologies, see also Brian Thom, Colin Scott, and Petronella Vaarzon-Morel in this volume.

5 Since Confederation (1867), we can identify three phases or orientations in state policies towards Indigenous peoples: 1) the policies of "protection" implemented with the Indian Act and the reserve lands. From the Indigenous perspective, however, these policies and accompanying legislation were the equivalent of control and dispossession mechanisms; 2) the policies of assimilation, of which the most potent example is the system of residential schools (Niezen 2013); and, 3) the policies of self-determination, implemented since the 1970s, with, for example, Section 35 of the Constitution "patriated" in 1982 and the Comprehensive Land Claims policy.

6 In each settlement, the Band Council is by far the main employer.

7 Working among the Innu, Colin Samson argues that First Nations in Canada had "to adopt institutions that would become miniature images of the state itself" (2001: 239).

8 Such a saga did not start with the implementation of the Comprehensive Land Claims policy. Since the end of the nineteenth century, in the face

of increased settler activities in *Nitaskinan*, the Nehirowisiwok and their representatives have been active in claiming their rights and the recognition of a fair sharing of the land with the newcomers.

9   See Asch (2014) for a sound analysis and understanding of the concept of "treaty" between the Canadian state and First Nations.

10 The monies that support the Atikamekw Nation negotiation process come from a loan by the federal government. These monies will be subtracted from the total amount negotiated in the final Agreement.

11 Prior to a hydroelectric project, Hydro-Quebec has to pay for environmental and social impact studies, which give the Nehirowisiwok the opportunity to conduct anthropological and archaeological surveys of the territory concerned. The community also receives monetary compensations for the construction of a dam on its territory.

12 See also Wyatt and Chilton (2014) for a detailed description of traditional Nehirowisiw activities over a seasonal cycle.

REFERENCES

Asch, Michael. 2014. *On Being Here to Stay: Treaties and Aboriginal Rights in Canada*. Toronto: University of Toronto Press.

Asch, Michael, and Norman Zlotkin. 1997. "Affirming Aboriginal Title: A New Basis for Comprehensive Claims Negotiations." In *Aboriginal and Treaty Rights in Canada: Essays on Law, Equality, and Respect for Difference*, ed. Michael Asch, 208–29. Vancouver: University of British Columbia Press.

Bird-David, Nurit. 1992. "Beyond the Hunting and Gathering Mode of Subsistence: Culture-Sensitive Observations on the Nayaka and Other Modern Hunter-Gatherers." *Man* 27 (1): 19–44. http://dx.doi.org/10.2307/2803593.

Blaser, Mario. 2004. "Life Projects: Indigenous Peoples' Agency and Development." In *In the Way of Development: Indigenous Peoples, Life Projects and Globalization*, ed. Mario Blaser, Harvey A. Feit, and Glen McRae, 26–44. London and New York: Zed Books and Ottawa: Canadian International Development Research Centre.

Blaser, Mario. 2013. "Ontological Conflicts and the Stories of Peoples in Spite of Europe: Toward a Conversation on Political Ontology." *Current Anthropology* 54 (5): 547–68. http://dx.doi.org/10.1086/672270.

Clammer, John, Sylvie Poirier, and Eric Schwimmer, eds. 2004. *Figured Worlds: Ontological Obstacles in Intercultural Relations*. Toronto: University of Toronto Press.

Descola, Philippe. 2005. *Par-delà nature et culture* [Beyond Nature and Culture]. Paris: Gallimard.

Escobar, Arturo. 2008. *Territories of Difference: Place, Movements, Life, Redes.* Durham, NC: Duke University Press. http://dx.doi.org/10.1215/9780822389439.

Feld, Stephen, and Keith H. Basso, eds. 1996. *Senses of Place.* Santa Fe: School of American Research Press.

Fortier, Jean-François, and Stephen Wyatt. 2014. "Cooptation et résistance dans la planification forestière concertée au Québec" [Cooptation and Resistance in Collaborative Forest Planning in Quebec]. *Recherches Amerindiennes au Québec* 44 (1): 35–48. http://dx.doi.org/10.7202/1027878ar.

Friedman, Jonathan. 2004. "Culture et politique de la culture: Une dynamique durkheimienne" [Culture and Cultural Politics: A Durkheimian Dynamic]. *Anthropologie et Sociétés* 28 (1): 23–44. http://dx.doi.org/10.7202/008569ar.

Gélinas, Claude. 2000. *La gestion de l'étranger. Les Atikamekw et la présence eurocanadienne en Haute-Mauricie, 1760–1870* [Managing the Stranger. The Atikamekw and the Eurocanadian Presence in Haute-Mauricie, 1760–1870]. Sillery: Septentrion.

Houde, Nicolas. 2014. "La gouvernance territoriale contemporaine du Nitaskinan: tradition, adaptation et flexibilité" [The Contemporary Territorial Governance of Nitaskinan: Tradition, Adaptation and Flexibility]. *Recherches Amerindiennes au Québec* 44 (1): 23–33. http://dx.doi.org/10.7202/1027877ar.

Ingold, Tim. 1996. "Hunting and Gathering as Ways of Perceiving the Environment." In *Redefining Nature: Ecology, Culture and Domestication*, ed. Roy Ellen and Katsuyoshi Fukui, 117–55. Oxford: Berg.

Jérôme, Laurent. 2010. "Jeunesse, musique et rituels chez les Atikamekw (Haute-Mauricie, Québec): ethnographie d'un processus d'affirmation identitaire et culturelle en milieu autochtone" [Youth, Music and Rituals among the Atikamekw (Haute-Mauricie, Quebec): Ethnography of a Process of Cultural and Identity Affirmation in Indigenous Context]. Unpublished PhD dissertation, Department of Anthropology, Université Laval.

Jérôme, Laurent, and Vicky Veilleux. 2014. "Witamowikok, 'dire' le territoire atikamekw nehirowisiw aujourd'hui: territoires de l'oralité et nouveaux médias autochtones" [Witamowikok, 'Saying' the Atikamekw Nehirowisiw Territory Today: Territories of Orality and New Indigenous Medias]. *Recherches Amerindiennes au Québec* 44 (1): 11–22. http://dx.doi.org/10.7202/1027876ar.

Niezen, Ronald. 2013. *Truth and Indignation: Canada's Truth and Reconciliation Commission on Indian Residential Schools.* Toronto: University of Toronto Press.

Poirier, Sylvie. 2001. "Territories, Identity, and Modernity among the Atikamekw (Haut St-Maurice, Quebec)." In *Aboriginal Autonomy and Development in Northern Quebec and Labrador*, ed. Colin H. Scott, 98–116. Vancouver: University of British Columbia Press.

Poirier, Sylvie. 2004. "La (dé)politisation de la culture? Réflexions sur un concept pluriel" [(De)politicization of Culture? Reflections on a Plural Concept]. *Anthropologie et Sociétés* 28 (1): 7–21. http://dx.doi.org/10.7202/008568ar.

Poirier, Sylvie. 2008. "Reflections on Indigenous Cosmopolitics/Poetics." *Anthropologica* 50 (1): 75–86.

Poirier, Sylvie. 2013. "The Dynamic Reproduction of Hunter-Gatherers' Ontologies and Values." In *A Companion to the Anthropology of Religion*, ed. Janice Boddy and Michael Lambek, 50–68. Oxford: Wiley Blackwell. http://dx.doi.org/10.1002/9781118605936.ch2.

Poirier, Sylvie. 2014 "The Atikamekw: Reflections on Their Changing World." In *Native Peoples: The Canadian Experience*, 4th edition, ed. C. Roderick Wilson and Christopher Fletcher, 129–49. Oxford: Oxford University Press.

Rodman, Margaret. 1992. "Empowering Place: Multilocality and Multivocality." *American Anthropologist* 94 (3): 640–56. http://dx.doi.org/10.1525/aa.1992.94.3.02a00060.

Samson, Colin. 2001. "Rights as the Reward for Simulated Cultural Sameness: The Innu in the Canadian Colonial Context." In *Culture and Rights: Anthropological Perspectives*, ed. Jane W. Cowan, Marie-Bénédicte Dembour, and Richard W. Wilson, 226–48. Cambridge: Cambridge University Press. http://dx.doi.org/10.1017/CBO9780511804687.013.

Thomas, Nicholas. 1991. *Entangled Objects: Exchange, Material Culture and Colonialism in the Pacific*. Cambridge, MA: Harvard University Press.

Wyatt, Stephen. 2004. "Co-existence of Atikamekw and Industrial Forestry Paradigms: Occupation and Management of Forestlands in the St-Maurice River Basin, Quebec." Unpublished PhD dissertation, Université Laval.

Wyatt, Stephen, and Yvon Chilton. 2014. "L'occupation contemporaine du Nitaskinan par les Nehirowisiwok de Wemotaci" [The Contemporary Occupation of *Nitaskinan* by the Nehirowisiwok of Wemotaci]. *Recherches Amerindiennes au Québec* 44 (1): 61–72. http://dx.doi.org/10.7202/1027880ar.

11 Is There a Role for Anthropology in Cultural Reproduction? Maps, Mining, and the "Cultural Future" in Central Australia

NICOLAS PETERSON

Introduction

If any particular group of people are not reproducing an aspect of their culture that they themselves are concerned about, should we anthropologists, or the state, be trying to assist them to do so? Indeed, does it even make sense anthropologically to suggest that we might be in a position to help where we have relevant information especially in a context of changing ontologies?

Anthropologists' notebooks are crammed with details about other people's ways of life. We often have extensive photographic, audio, and film recordings of ceremonies and everyday activities as well as accounts of a wide range of practices and beliefs. I have worked with Warlpiri Aboriginal people in central Australia since the late 1960s, and most of the older generation I knew well, and with whom I mapped their country, are now dead. Increasingly I find that younger Warlpiri assume that I am a repository of these older people's knowledge about the country. However, my knowledge and records are patchy, and I can rarely answer the questions asked of me, which not only makes me feel I could have done a whole lot better job, but is also problematic among a people for whom the politics of knowledge around ceremony, mythology, and the related places is so significant (see Dussart 2000; Anderson 1995). Secrecy and economizing with information is central to the relations between the generations, and everybody, young and old, assumes there is always more to know than what they know or have just been told. So my replies that I do not have the information they are seeking are not always taken at face value.

In 1989 Eric Michaels, writing about the Warlpiri, coined the phrase "for a cultural future." By this phrase, which he used as the title of a short monograph reflecting on the impact of the introduction of television to the Warlpiri, he meant:

> ... an agenda for cultural maintenance which not only assumes some privileged authority for traditional modes of cultural production, but argues also that the political survival of Indigenous people is dependent upon their capacity to continue reproducing these forms. (1989: 72)

In "For a Cultural Future" he speculates that a film of a ceremony held fifteen years earlier at Yuendumu, the remote Warlpiri township three hundred kilometres northwest of Alice Springs, could be used to revive it. But, he asked, is such a film "a fire that has to be fought with fire: a two edged sword that can prove to be an instrument of destruction or salvation" (1989: 74)? He was concerned about secrets being made public, but equally that the public circulation of the film of the ceremony could also be the beginning of its disenchantment.

The idea that a film compressing into twenty-five minutes a ceremony celebrated in late afternoon gatherings over several weeks before two full days at the climax could be the basis of revival seems implausible, not to say unanthropological. Ceremonies are held to achieve specific purposes and as an integral part of social processes that depend on the effectiveness of shared symbols, beliefs, and motivations to achieve socially valued ends. They are the embodiment of emotions, dispositions, and contingent circumstances in a specific historical context, which cannot be reconstituted by mere mimicry. They may appear as dramatic spectacle but they are not dramas.

If using an ethnographic film to revive a ceremony is highly unlikely, it might seem more plausible to argue that recording song cycles, ecological knowledge, mythology, or other aspects of Aboriginal people's culture may help maintain it. However, doing so turns knowledge and belief into information, inevitably distanced from the contexts in which such knowledge and belief were a part of lived experience, and literally disembodies them. Nevertheless, research projects, often partly funded by Aboriginal peoples' own organizations, are sometimes justified on the grounds that they will preserve the knowledge and help people maintain their culture. Maintaining Aboriginal culture is a key element of Australian government policy, strongly endorsed by Aboriginal people and their organizations, all of which believe it is vital for Aboriginal people to do so. Thus such arguments may assist with access to communities, but it needs to be asked whether they are misleading.

The word "culture" was unknown to virtually all Aboriginal people in the 1960s but is now frequently heard even in the remotest parts of the continent. Phrases like "That's my culture," "I've got my culture," "That's the culture way" can be heard anywhere. But as has been observed (e.g., Merlan 1989), the term is now associated with a completely objectified and thing-like understanding that bears little resemblance to any nuanced anthropological view in which much culture is implicit, taken for granted, and embedded in sedimented dispositions.

So the question of what role, if any, my objectified and codified account of some small part of Warlpiri knowledge about their country and its ontological significance can play in helping to ensure a cultural future is quite problematic. It is probably the case, however, that some of the younger generation consider that those of us in whom their older relatives have invested time in teaching us about their culture have some kind of undefined responsibility to help transmit what we know. All the more so because the maps produced are an intercultural product that, in recognizing and codifying their system of land tenure, inevitably transforms it in a number of ways, entangling Warlpiri people with us as both anthropologists and individuals, but also with the state, in an ongoing social contract.

Here I want to explore the issue of the contribution this mapping of the Warlpiri cultural landscape that I and others have been involved with can make to a Warlpiri cultural future. Warlpiri people today are very keen for the information to be returned, but their own Aboriginally controlled organizations deem that it is not in their best interest for that to happen at this time.[1]

It is a case study in which local desires are entangled with changing ontologies, lawyer culture, anthropological obligations, and demography, raising questions about the nature of the Warlpiri cultural future. I will begin with a brief account of Warlpiri people leaving a hunting and gathering existence, and then look at the mapping process, before turning to a consideration of the politics of knowledge and the cultural future.

Moving Away from Country

Although the last Aboriginal people in Australia to leave a completely independent life "beyond the frontier" were only met up with in 1984, in the Western Desert (see Myers and Clarke 1985), by the end of the Second World War, most Aboriginal people had moved to cattle or mission stations or government settlements. In Arnhem Land, a few hundred people remained in the bush, all with knowledge of and contact with Europeans, until the late 1950s, and likewise in central Australia a few score people were living west of the Western Australian–Northern Territory border until the late 1960s.

Among the Warlpiri people, whose country is in the Tanami desert some four hundred kilometres northwest of Alice Springs, everybody had settled down by the end of the Second World War. Before the war, a cattle station, Mt Doreen, had been established on the heartland of the Ngaliya or southern Warlpiri. By the end of the war, this station had the major settled population of Warlpiri, until a government settlement was established in 1946 immediately to the east of Mt Doreen Station at Yuendumu, just beyond Ngaliya Warlpiri country. By the mid-1960s, most Warlpiri had shifted from Mt Doreen to Yuendumu. On the eastern side of the Tanami desert, Warlpiri people were also living on the fringe of their country or had moved off it. The whole northern part of Warlpiri country became, and remains, unoccupied spinifex desert, part of an Indigenous Protected Area declared under the International Union for the Conservation of Nature's category 6, which allows the sustainable harvesting of wildlife.[2]

Those men employed as stockmen kept up knowledge of the country covered by the stations, whether it was their own area or that of other Warlpiri, as they mustered cattle and looked after bores and dams. The older people who had grown up leading a self-sufficient life before the war could also find their way across the spinifex desert, moving from the Aboriginal settlement of Lajamanu in the north of the Tanami to Yuendumu in the south, a distance of five hundred kilometres, using only traditional water sources.

In total, the area occupied by Warlpiri speakers pre-contact was over ninety thousand square kilometres, with the present-day cattle stations of Mt Doreen, Mt Denison, and Willowra covering no more than one-sixth of this area.

Warlpiri people have a range of ties to land (Peterson 1992: 374; Dussart 2000: 28–35). They inherit rights to country through their father, which allows them to live on the land and use its resources without seeking the permission of others, and they also have responsibilities to look after the important religious places in their mother's patrilineal country. The basis of other claims to place is in relation to the locality in which they were conceived, and possibly where their mother and father are buried. There are also links between countries where a common ancestral being travelled across or between them, leading to the patrilineal members collaborating with each other in the holding of ceremonies that celebrate the common ancestral being(s). The patrilineal and matrilateral ties to country remain very important aspects of personal identity. With settling down, the significance of conception links to country has virtually disappeared as a basis for a claim of connection to a place, while burial has recently resurfaced as significant, as some people are now being buried near important places in the country with which they were identified.

Beliefs around conception have undergone considerable change. In the past, they underwrote an individual's consubstantial relationship with place, making Warlpiri country "the fundamental object system external to the conscious subject with which ... consciousness and identity ... [were] anchored" (Munn 1970: 143). Place was thus a fundamental aspect not only of Warlpiri ontology but also of ceremonial life, and it has also played a central part in non-Indigenous understandings of the nature of the spiritual relationship of Aboriginal people with the land. While ties to the country inherited from the father remain central to people's identity, they are less important today than being embedded in a dense network of sociality, living out the sedimented dispositions of a relational ontology (Austin-Broos 2009: 5; Peterson 2015).

With extremely limited cash incomes until 1969, when social security monies started to be paid directly to individuals instead of to some non-Aboriginal person on their behalf, people were unable to buy cars, which only started to become common in the 1970s. By the time people had quite easy access to cars in the 1980s, a major demographic shift was starting to take place among the Warlpiri. Lifestyle diseases were beginning to take their toll, and the ratio of active old people to young was changing. Unlike the older generation, the younger generations were not oriented towards the Tanami desert but towards the regional centre of Alice Springs, some three hundred kilometres away in the opposite direction. While cars have extended the lines of travel, they have also narrowed the knowledge of the country away from the roads. Further, a change in national gun laws in the aftermath of a massacre of tourists by an Anglo-Australian at Port Arthur in Tasmania in 1996 has meant that very few Aboriginal people now have easy access to guns with which to hunt kangaroos and emus, further reducing interaction with the bush.

Thus the result of the grandparental generation having left a hunting and gathering life and the current generations having grown up in the large settled community of Yuendumu has been a modification of the relationship to country and aspects of the ontology associated with it. Now most Warlpiri are living a minimum of 50–100 kilometres from their own paternal country and some as much as 250 kilometres away, and many people under forty may only have made one or two brief visits to these remote places.[3]

Mapping the Warlpiri Cultural Landscape

Since 1977, anthropologists in the Northern Territory have been intensively mapping remote areas of Aboriginal land, collecting associated stories and recording family trees of people related to their particular areas of country, initially as part of the statutory land claims process under the Aboriginal Land Rights (Northern Territory) Act 1976 (Australia 1976), and more recently under the Native Title Act 1993 (Australia 1993) as well. Prior to the 1976 Act, there was no recognition by Australian law of Aboriginal rights in land. Indeed, the Yolŋu (Murngin) people of northeast Arnhem Land lost the first Australian test case for recognition of their property rights in land in 1971 on the basis that their system of laws in relation to land could not be recognized under Australian law (Australia 1971).

Following this judgment, a Labor government was elected at the federal level for the first time in twenty-three years. Part of their platform was the statutory recognition of Aboriginal land rights, and to that end a Royal Commission into Aboriginal Land Rights was established in 1973. The outcome of this was the Northern Territory Act mentioned above, actually passed by the subsequent Conservative government. The architecture of the Act included the establishment of regional land councils, controlled by Aboriginal people, to help them make claims for the return of unalienated crown land and to manage and develop their land.[4] One feature of the land rights legislation is that it gives the traditional owners of a particular area the right to veto prospecting on the land, and hence mining on it. This right to veto, unique to Northern Territory Aboriginal land holders with land held under the Aboriginal Land Rights (Northern Territory) Act 1976, means that they can negotiate royalty payments from the mining companies.[5]

The first thirty years of the land councils' existence was focused on preparing and making claims to the available land. This has been highly successful, with approximately 30 per cent of the Territory being returned to Aboriginal ownership through this process.[6] The claims required mapping the relevant areas, documenting the attachment to them, providing genealogical and other information about the people who had rights and interests in each area, and looking at the connection of the Aboriginal people to these areas post European arrival. Most of this work was done by anthropologists contracted by the land councils to work on specific claims, particularly in areas where they already knew people. These consultants were ably supported by the in-house anthropologists, and other staff of the land councils. It was in this context that I, in collaboration with other anthropologists, mapped some extensive areas of Warlpiri country between the 1970s and 1990s.[7]

The mapping process has involved finding a few elderly people, usually but by no means always men, and taking them off for up to a week visiting areas that they knew in their youth, trying to relocate rock holes, soakages, quarries, burial sites, and other named places. Much of the time is spent off road with the ever-present likelihood of getting punctures. This is relevant because, without robust four-wheel-drive vehicles in good condition, most of this mapping would not be possible, and it is beyond the means of most individual Warlpiri families. Once the basic mapping is completed, associated mythology recorded, and family trees worked out, there often follows a major visit, taking the women, younger men, and children related to the area back to it. These were often huge logistical challenges, and for some remote claims such a visit was the only time that most people were ever likely to get to their land.

As a result, the maps, stories, photographs, and recordings collected by anthropologists on their own research projects or working as consultants for the Central Land Council are now an irreplaceable record of many Indigenous cultural landscapes that incorporate a great deal of information, unknown to most people under forty. Nevertheless, the patrilineal countries in particular, whether known or unknown, have renewed significance, with the advent of widespread prospecting and mining, particularly for gold, but also uranium on Warlpiri lands. In recent times three major gold mines have been active in the Tanami desert – the Granites Mine, the Tanami Mine, and the Dead Bullock Soak Mine – with a new one likely to come on stream in the near future. If the traditional owners approve exploration, mining companies have to pay "look round" monies and then royalties if they move on to actual mining. While the sums involved in "look round" are relatively small, the sums involved if a mine is established run into millions of dollars each year. With three major gold mines in the Tanami and a lot of exploration underway, there is a considerable amount of income. The Act defines how the "statutory" royalties are to be distributed, with 30 per cent going to the affected communities, 30 per cent to a fund that all Northern Territory Aboriginal communities can apply to, and 40 per cent towards funding the land councils. In addition there will be negotiated royalties (see endnote 5).

As a result of the large amounts of money available and the need for legally binding agreements about whether prospecting is to be allowed or denied and who should receive money, the maps and genealogies collected, often twenty or more years ago, have become very important.

For the older generations that have been supplying the information to compile the maps, their knowledge of country was embodied through years of walking and riding over it, making camps on it, collecting food from it, and singing about it. Although they were interested in and indeed often enthusiastic about the maps anthropologists compile and the process of mapping as a chance to visit remote and infrequently visited localities, members of this older generation, almost all of whom are now dead, emphasized that they did not need maps, they knew the country and all the information was in their heads, it is only white people that need maps. Of course today the rest of the Aboriginal people also need maps to know where many places are. But no amount of map reading or occasional visiting of places by the younger generations on so-called country visits, organized by the School and other local agencies, can match the embodied knowledge that the older generations have of the country. Their embodied knowledge has become transformed into information in anthropologists' notebooks, on tape and video recordings.

Derek Elias, as an employee of the Central Land Council, was the principal person to map sites in the remote spinifex portions of Warlpiri country, spending time over seven years in the 1990s doing this (Elias 2001: 4). He estimates that he was only able to locate about a quarter of the totality of places known to Warlpiri people at the beginning of the twentieth century. Many of those unlocatable places were soakages that can quite quickly disappear if not kept open, as blown or water-borne sand fills them in (Elias 2001: 100, 102). This meant that, on average, there was one place for every 331 square kilometres or, in relation to the estimated original number of places, 82 square kilometres (Elias 2001: 99). Of course, this is highly artificial, given that sites vary greatly in the insignificance and the extent of their importance, which can be thought of as a gravitational field, but it gives some idea of the overall density of sites in the spinifex desert area. In the Ngaliya Warlpiri area of Mt Doreen Station, which covers the heartland of their much better watered country, 210 places were identified in approximately 7400 square kilometres, giving an average area per place of around 35 square kilometres. Through working as stockmen right up to the early 1960s, people continued to know this area much better, so Elias's estimate of only a quarter of the places originally known being located would have to be wrong for the station area. With another 100 unlocated names recorded for the station area, it appears that two-thirds of the original place names have been located, which gives an average area per place there at around 23 square kilometres.

The Politics of Knowledge

Older people are keen for young people to know of these places, and obviously the maps are a key way to impart information about the spatial location and to secure it for the future. While their concern is largely with cultural transmission, most adults are also vitally interested in the maps as they relate to the possibility of benefiting from mining exploration. Thus many younger people are involved in a complex remapping of themselves back onto land which is often conflicted because of past marriage and alliance patterns. However, paradoxically, such maps are not freely available; indeed, they are kept under lock and key by the people's own Indigenously controlled organizations, like the land councils, that have financed the map making.

The reasons for this are historical. In the late 1960s, in lieu of granting land rights, the Conservative federal government, responding to great Aboriginal concern at the increased destruction of sacred sites in remote Australia as the mining boom of the time made exploration in the remotest places worthwhile, initiated a scheme to map all "sacred sites" by state and territory across the nation. Mining companies would then be able to consult the relevant map, see where the sites were, and avoid them. The thinking behind this program was quite limited and grew out of the understandings behind the existing protection of "Aboriginal antiquities" and relics legislation (see Ward 2013: 670).

The understanding of site was derived from archaeological interests, which focused on major sites such as rock art sites, caves that had archaeological deposits, stone arrangements, and the more dramatic living sites like the shell mounds of western Cape York, with little awareness that most of these sites were also named places of importance to living Aboriginal people, or of the absolutely huge number of unrecorded named Aboriginal places across the continent that were not spectacular at all. This was before either anthropologists or archaeologists in Australia had developed an interest in or concern for cultural landscapes, despite two exemplary published examples by Ronald Berndt (1964, 1969), one from the Gove peninsula in the Northern Territory, prepared in response to the bauxite mining there and in support of the Aboriginal people's land claim, and the other from Croker Island. Thus the scope of the national site-mapping undertaking and the struggle that was to take place over the definition of sites was not foreseen at the start of this process, although it quickly became evident to those involved.

In 1974, the federal government began funding a program of site recorders to work in all the states. Not only was there not enough money to locate all the sites, but many Aboriginal people were reluctant to reveal them to the site recorders, especially the more important sacred places. Further, the legislative protection of sites was weak and patchy across the different states. In South Australia, there was no legislative protection for sites outside of land reserved for the use and benefit of Aboriginal people (Vachon and Toyne 1983: 312–13). There was much unhappiness among anthropologists about this program and concern about how to improve it. In 1982, a French-owned exploring company, AFMECO, was granted a lease outside the eastern border of lands reserved for the Pitjantjatjara in northern South Australia, thus in an area where no site survey had been carried out. However, the company agreed to pay for a site survey to preserve good relations with the Pitjantjatjara Council, which represented the Aboriginal people with interests both inside the reserve area and outside it (Vachon and Toyne 1983: 313). It is not fully clear what the company's motivations for agreeing to this were, but perhaps it was hoping to smooth the way for later prospecting on the approximately one-hundred-thousand-square-kilometre reserve lands themselves. Having secured this agreement, the Pitjantjatjara Council extended the process to four other companies: Comalco, Layton Geophysics, Shell Oil, and Getty Oil. By agreeing to work in this way, Comalco secured agreement to explore on the reserve lands in a very rapid two months. This mode of working quickly evolved into the so-called "Pitjantjatjara model" of negotiation (Toyne and Vachon 1984: 112), which completely reversed the situation envisaged by the government. It was a highly strategic move in the control of knowledge. Under the government's model, it was not necessary to consult with Aboriginal people, just with the relevant authority that held the map of sacred sites in any state. Under the Pitjantjatjara model, the mining company would provide a map of the area that had been granted to them for exploration by the relevant state or territory authority, and then they would take it to the relevant Aboriginal council, which would then tell them where they could not go, without revealing the specific location of sites (Toyne and Vachon 1984: 112).

This approach is now known as the "work area clearance" process and remains vital to Aboriginal control of their land. It still goes along with the close control of maps and knowledge of site locations. However, this is now an obstacle for the creation of a "cultural future" as it relates to land.

It took a while for the land councils' lawyers organizing the land claims in the Northern Territory to pick up on the South Australian Pitjantjatjara model and apply it to the maps produced for the claims to unalienated land in the Territory; indeed it was not until after 1985 that the Aboriginal Land Commissioner who heard the claims stopped including the maps in his reports. From then on, the lawyers sought to have not only the maps but also all the material produced for the claims prepared by the land councils restricted. This carried over into the Native Title era, so that the mapping and all of the historical and related research for a native title claim is inaccessible to the claimants even after everything is finally resolved. The great irony in all this is that never again will so much money be spent on researching and consolidating cultural information about Aboriginal people and their relations to land in most parts of the continent, much of it information that is not part of Aboriginal common knowledge. Despite the fact that this information is recognized as of huge cultural significance for the Aboriginal people concerned, finding ways to make it accessible is complex. Keepers of secrets, especially lawyers, whose whole way of thinking is defined in terms of worst case scenarios, are enormously reluctant to endorse sharing this restricted information even in greatly changed times. Further, having got the courts to restrict access to the materials, the claimants find that organizing to have the restrictions removed is complex and expensive.[8]

For a Cultural Future

Since the development of the Pitjantjatjara model in the early 1980s, a great deal has changed in relation to land issues. The politics of knowledge control that was so enormously important in empowering Aboriginal people and in protecting their cultural landscapes is now less important. The principal reason for this is the *Mabo* judgment of 3 June 1992, recognizing the existence of native title, and the subsequent passing of the Native Title Act 1993 that laid down how the recognition was going to work. No development anywhere can now go ahead without first establishing whether a native title interest exists in the area concerned. This means that it is a legal necessity to establish whether and where such native title interests exist for any development project to proceed and for the proponents to enter into bona fide negotiations with the registered native title holders. So one of the major tactical concerns about releasing maps is that they may show some areas with few places, reducing the ability of the native title holders to oppose development should they wish to do so. However, development proponents would still have a legal obligation to negotiate in good faith (Burnside 2009).

There is no doubt that simply publishing the extremely professional and complex maps that have been compiled for land and native title claims in many areas exactly as they stand would not be a good idea, at this stage. They contain considerable information that almost inevitably would cause problems were it available. The most obvious of these problems has been present since the days of the sacred sites recording program. In particular, places to which Aboriginal people have always restricted access on the basis of gender and age, and which have always required that visitors, Aboriginal or non-Aboriginal, be accompanied by the correct people, would become easy to find independently by tourists and others. Many of the names of the important places are recorded in the published ethnographic literature, so, once their location was known, control over access would be lost, opening the way for unauthorized visits and potential for damage. Further places are frequently linked with other places conceptually, in what are known as dreaming tracks or song lines that are understood as the lines of travel of ancestral beings, and that are also shown on the maps prepared for the claim hearings. These dreaming tracks are major structuring features of the cultural landscape, and leaving them on the maps makes public the key to too much esoteric knowledge. Eliminating them from publicly available maps may pose a problem for remembering the tracks, but the details will be available in documentation held by the land councils.

There is a range of other issues that do not relate to outsiders but to internal relations of Warlpiri people with each other. Some places can be referred to by more than one name, so the choice of a name can possibly be interpreted in partisan fashion, in the place-based land tenure system, and adopting one particular name or spelling might inadvertently advantage one person or group over another. Further, having maps is seen as a way of assisting memory and transmission, so it may also come to devalue memorizing place names and locations, in a culture that has always placed a high value on memorizing songs, places, and myths.

Another complication is that by making all of the names and their locations available on a map, or even more via computer, the balance of everyday command of knowledge gets upset. That is, young people, especially those with computer skills, come to have control of the same body of place location knowledge as much older people, who up until that time have been the repositories of the knowledge and the people to be consulted about places and their location. It is not that this information is secret, but that only those with long years of moving across the country would have known it in the past, so making it easily available to all threatens to alter the relationship between young and old, and is an affront. Further, there is some evidence that knowledge of place names has become more restricted since people have left the bush, as old men have been limiting those to whom they will reveal some place names on the basis of age, gender, and race (e.g., to anthropologists; see Elias 2001: 196). There is also an enormous difference between knowledge of places, that is where they are and their general topographical features, and knowledge about places relating to their religious significance, which is often associated with esoteric knowledge available on the basis of age and gender and only revealed piecemeal over time, through ceremonies or formal visits to the location. My own view is that it is vital to remove the most important and restricted places from maps made available, as it is to remove the links between places, the dreaming tracks. However, there is no longer any case to restrict maps that show the majority of place names.

It is clear then, for all the reasons discussed above, that the maps compiled by anthropologists are not mediums for a cultural future in the terms set out by Eric Michaels. They cannot substitute for "traditional modes of cultural production" of knowledge about and the meaning of places. "For a cultural future" is a powerful slogan in a political project, just like the cry for "cultural maintenance." The danger is that powerful political rhetoric gets muddled with what makes sense anthropologically or even practically, to the detriment of people's understanding of the changes that are ongoing in their lives. There is no future for a cultural future that is simply an attempt to maintain the past, as that is impossible, nor indeed is there any indication that that is what people want. The maps do, however, have a very important place in a much more realistic understanding of what can be achieved in terms of a "cultural future." Apart from being the only way that much cultural information about the landscape inhabited by their forebears will be imparted across the generations, they are fundamental to demonstrating that what non-Aboriginal people call the bush, and see as wild and undifferentiated, is everywhere a culturally complex landscape with many named places, and a powerful and unavoidable reminder that Aboriginal people were here first.

Conclusion

This brief history of mapping is suggestive about the role of place in the ontology of at least some desert Aboriginal people today. The relationship of place to the sense of self and personal identity is not as central as other aspects of people's cultural world, like language and being embedded in a dense network of sociality. Most people are not living on their own land, and many younger people have only limited knowledge of it. The work with older people mapping the cultural landscape is a future-oriented activity in the production of cultural heritage materials. It is more about our culture of literacy and the production and conservation of objectified information than it is about the reproduction of ontological relationships to land among Aboriginal people. The fact that the political economy of knowledge in which these maps have been entangled for the last thirty years has meant that they have not been available to the relevant Aboriginal communities underlines this fact. The maps are, however, crucial to a cultural future but not to maintaining culture in dramatically changing times; rather they will have a central role in sustaining an ever-transforming cultural identity.

ACKNOWLEDGMENTS

I acknowledge many stimulating and insightful conversations with David Nash about things Warlpiri, and mapping in particular, and thank him for sending me a copy of his talk, "An Atlas of Indigenous Country in Central Australia?" presented at the 1st International Conference on Indigenous Place Names Sámi allaskuvla/Sámi University College, Guovdageaidnu, Norway, Tuesday, 7 September 2010. I would also like to thank Graeme Ward for information on the sites program, the editors for their comments, and Anna Kenny, Mary Laughren, Robert Graham, and Frances Claffey for sharing their knowledge about Warlpiri relations to land.

NOTES

1 Elodie Fache (in this volume) suggests that returning materials such as maps is best anthropological practice. However, as discussed below, return of materials is often a complex business with unexpected problems (e.g., see Batty 2005).
2 There are in fact two IPAs in the Tanami, a northern and a southern one, which together cover 141,600 square kilometres. This area has no precise relationship to the pre-contact area occupied by Warlpiri speakers, although it covers much of it. The pre-contact area occupied by the Warlpiri is hard to define precisely. Declaration of an IPA brings with it resources for the employment of a small number of Indigenous rangers to manage the area, thus making it possible for some people to get back to their own remote country from time to time (see Fache and Morphy in this volume for discussion of IPAs in Arnhem Land).
3 The situation described by Frances Morphy in this volume is uncommon to the extent that she is working with a community that is tightly knit, living on or close to the land of many in the community. More common is the situation described by Fache and Sachiko Kubota in this volume, where most people are a considerable distance from their own country, which they may not have visited for a "long time" (Fache, p. 102). This is not to say that their own patrilineal country is unimportant but that the nature of the identification with it is changing.
4 That is public lands held either by the state or Commonwealth of Australia. Aboriginal lands held under the Aboriginal Land Rights (Northern Territory) Act 1976 are inalienable, and can only be disposed of to the government for fair compensation. The same is true of native title land where there is exclusive possession.

5 The royalty regime is complex, involving statutory royalty equivalents as well as negotiated royalties. Statutory royalty equivalents are amounts any company pays to the government in respect of any productive resource project. Where the resource project is on Aboriginal land in the Northern Territory, the government pays the equivalent of double the statutory royalty amount to the relevant Aboriginal groups. Because in the Northern Territory Aboriginal people can veto prospecting on their land, they can negotiate with mining companies, so that if a mine goes ahead the traditional owners of the land on which the mine is located can receive an additional negotiated royalty.

6 Aboriginal people hold about 48 per cent in Aboriginal freehold under the Aboriginal Land Rights (Northern Territory) Act 1976 (Australia 1976), which gives much better rights than land claimed under the Native Title Act 1993 (Australia 1993). The old lands reserved for the use and benefit of Aboriginal people, which made up Schedule 1 lands and about 18 per cent of the Northern Territory, were transferred without a claims process on the passing of the Act. Native title claims are now being lodged principally over the cattle stations where Aboriginal rights can coexist with the pastoralists' rights. Over 50 per cent of the Territory is covered by cattle stations, a handful of which are owned by Aboriginal groups.

7 I have been involved in the preparation of claims to various areas of Warlpiri country jointly with Professor Françoise Dussart and others. Dr Anna Kenny and I recently prepared the native title claim to Mt Doreen Station, with particular assistance from Frances Claffey.

8 This has been an ongoing concern simmering along in the background of the statutory and native title claims, which is becoming more and more of an issue (see Koch 2008 for an early published account). The Federal Court of Australia, which holds all of the material generated in the hearings process for native title claims, is not only confronting a huge archiving task but is also concerned about how to deal with the increasing number of requests for access to these materials. Progress is slow in dealing with the access issues. For more information and links see http://www.aiatsis.gov.au/ntru/futureconnection.html.

REFERENCES

Anderson, Christopher, ed. 1995. *Politics of the Secret*. Oceania Monograph 45. Sydney: University of Sydney.

Austin-Broos, Diane. 2009. *Arrernte Present, Arrernte Past: Invasion, Violence, and Imagination in Indigenous Central Australia*. Chicago: University of Chicago Press.

Batty, Philip. 2005. "White Redemption Rituals: Repatriating Aboriginal Secret Sacred Objects." *Arena* 23: 29–36.

Berndt, Ronald. 1964. "The Gove Dispute: The Question of Australian Aboriginal Land and the Preservation of Sacred Sites." *Anthropological Forum* 1 (2): 258–95. http://dx.doi.org/10.1080/00664677.1964.9967198.

Berndt, Ronald. 1969. *The Sacred Site: The Western Arnhem Land Example.* Canberra: Australian Institute of Aboriginal Studies.

Burnside, Sarah. 2009. "Negotiation in Good Faith under the Native Title Act: A Critical Analysis." Canberra: Australian Institute of Aboriginal and Torres Strait Islander Studies, Native Title Research Unit Issue Paper 4(3).

Dussart, Françoise. 2000. *The Politics of Ritual in an Aboriginal Settlement: Kinship, Gender and the Currency of Knowledge.* Washington, DC: Smithsonian Institution Press.

Elias, Derek. 2001. "Golden Dreams: People, Place and Mining in the Tanami Desert." Unpublished PhD dissertation, Department of Archaeology and Anthropology, Australian National University.

Koch, Grace. 2008. "The Future of Connection Materials Held by the Native Title Representative Bodies: Final Report." Canberra: Australian Institute of Aboriginal and Torres Strait Islander Studies, Native Title Research Report 1.

Merlan, Francesca. 1989. "The Objectification of 'Culture': An Aspect of Current Political Process in Aboriginal Affairs." *Anthropological Forum* 6 (1): 105–16. http://dx.doi.org/10.1080/00664677.1989.9967398.

Michaels, Eric. 1989. *For a Cultural Future: Francis Jupurrurla Makes TV at Yuendumu,* vol. 3. Sydney: Art and Text Publications Monograph Series.

Munn, Nancy. 1970. "Transformation of Subjects in to Objects." In *Australian Aboriginal Anthropology,* ed. Ronald Berndt, 143–63. Perth: UWA Press.

Myers, Fred, and Betty Clarke. 1985. *Report on the First Contact Group of Pintupi at Kiwikurra.* Canberra: Australian Institute of Aboriginal and Torres Strait Island Studies.

Peterson, Nicolas. 1992. "Warlpiri." *In Encyclopaedia of World Cultures Volume 2: Oceania,* ed. Terrence Hays, 373–6. Boston: G.K. Hall.

Peterson, Nicolas. 2015. "Place, Personhood and Marginalization: Ontology and Community in Remote Desert Australia." *Anthropologica* 57: 491–500.

Toyne, Philip, and Daniel Vachon. 1984. *Growing Up the Country: The Pitjantjatjara Struggle for Their Land.* Melbourne: McPhee Gribble.

Vachon, Daniel, and Philip Toyne. 1983. "Mining and the Challenge of Land Rights." In *Aborigines, Land and Land Rights,* ed. Nicolas Peterson and Marcia Langton, 307–26. Canberra: Australian Institute of Aboriginal Studies.

Ward, Graeme. 2013. "Australian Institute of Aboriginal and Torres Strait Islander Studies (AIATSIS): Its Role in Australian Archaeology." In *The Encyclopaedia of Global Archaeology*, ed. Carol Smith, 665–76. New York: Springer.

Afterword

MICHAEL ASCH

The contributions in this book offer significant insights into at least three themes of great import to our discipline. The first, which has long been prominent in the field, concerns how to represent the impact on Indigenous peoples of their encounter with Modernity; the second, which has moved to prominence in recent years among those of us who work with those often referred to as "hunter-gatherers," is the extent to which there are fundamental differences between the understandings that orient the worlds of Indigenous peoples and those that orient those connected to Western ways; and a third, which does not feature greatly in our discourse at present but soon will, that addresses the ways in which Indigenous intellectuals are dealing with the disappointment resulting from the presumption (beginning perhaps in the 1970s) that recognition by settler states (such as Canada and Australia) of the life-ways of Indigenous peoples as well as their historic and (from a Western perspective at least) legal connection with the territories on which these states were established has had on reforming the actions of those governments. And in Nicolas Peterson's soul-searching contribution, I catch a glimpse of a fourth theme of great significance to our community: what is the proper role of establishing the existence of cultural difference in general, and of the fidelity of the transmission of cultural difference across generations in particular, to the validation of Indigenous rights to the ownership of property and to self-determination with respect to the settler states within which they have been incorporated?

The Impact of Modernity on Indigenous Life-Ways

With regard to the first theme, most anthropologists who do not work with Indigenous peoples (and hunter-gatherers in particular) take one of two positions. In recent decades, by far the most prominent line has been that modernity overwhelms Indigenous ways. Using Dene as an example, there is the work of Elman Service, who suggested that this came quickly. As he put it in his influential book, *Primitive Social Organization*, first published in 1962: "Athapaskans who survived the early disasters became employees (or, more accurately, debt-peons) of European fur-trading companies almost 200 years ago" (1971: 77). Or, as Robert Murphy and Julian Steward suggested in their seminal 1956 article, "Tappers and Trappers: Parallel Processes in Accultura-tion," it was a process that went through stages and took some time. In either case it was inevitable either because – as Murphy and Steward argued – Indigenous peoples, when faced with the obvious advantages of modernity, eventually voluntarily abandoned their ways of life, or because, in Eric Wolf's version, which now takes precedence, as dis-cussed in his 1982 book, *Europe and the People without History* (1982; see also Hancock 2011), the power of the world system forced them into submission. A second line, the only prominent adherent of which I can name is Marshall Sahlins, but which is sometimes echoed by others and is represented most prominently in Sahlins's 1999 article "What Is Anthropological Enlightenment? Some Lessons of the Twentieth Cen-tury," takes the view that Indigenous peoples have been able to absorb the ways of capitalism – the central feature of Modernity he addresses – and reshape them to their own ends.

In contrast, most of us who work with Indigenous peoples over-whelmingly take the position that, while Modernity impacts Indige-nous ways, it does not necessarily overwhelm them. It is to this view that the authors in this book – including myself – subscribe. Often, at least historically, described as a process of "continuity and change," this approach looks more closely at what is transpiring at a fine-grained level and seeks a more nuanced explanation of the processes and the consequences. At one time called "the study of acculturation" (used in a different sense than in the Murphy and Steward article, in which it is a synonym for assimilation), it has been through a number of ter-minological and substantive iterations. "Hybridity," described aptly by Sylvie Poirier in this volume as a perspective that "tends somehow to underestimate, and even negate, differences" (p. 216) and which I see as a misplaced vision of an inevitable fusion of a way of life shaped prin-cipally by Modernity, is of recent vintage. This perspective is, however, negated by the fact of "life projects" (Blaser 2004; Feit 2004) that remain remarkably faithful to long-standing understandings and practices that lie significantly outside the parameters that Modernity seeks to shape.

To the scholars in this book, "entanglement" is the term of art used to describe what is taking place. This concept, in its original formulation, appears to me to be a product of the period in which anthropologists were particularly concerned with establishing that cultures are less (to use Wolf's words) billiard balls that protect members from what is outside than membranes that permit flows in and out. Or to put it another way: there is no such thing as purity. Ways are always entangled, and as Nicholas Thomas argued in his 1991 book *Entangled Objects* (on which Dussart and Poirier, in their chapter in this volume, principally rely), this understanding is pertinent particularly in the context of colonization. Used in this sense, the term in my estimation is nothing more than yet another concept formulated to chastise founding figures in our field, and particularly Franz Boas, for failing to take into account in their work the profound ways in which the cultures of the peoples with whom they worked had been impacted by colonialism. It is, in my estimation, a rather myopic lens that really deserves no more exposure (Asch 2007–8; Asch 2015).

Fortunately, as described lucidly in chapter 1 in this volume, Dussart and Poirier here take their meaning of entanglement from another place in Thomas's text, and that is the passage in which he argues: "The notion of entanglement aims to capture the dialectic of international inequalities and local appropriations; it energizes a perspective situated beyond the argument between proponents of the view that the world system is essentially determinate of local social systems and those asserting the relative autonomy of individual groups and cultures" (1991: 207). Looked at in this way, the concept of "entanglement" offers an important perspective on the encounter between Indigenous people and – as I will now put it – colonialism and capitalism, for it focuses on the nexus of the encounter without prejudicing the direction it will take. And we hope that the fine-grained analyses of the modalities of entanglement presented in this volume will assist not only specialists in the area but also the anthropological community at large to better understand the complexities of the encounter between Indigenous peoples and the processes of capitalism and colonialism.

On Ontology

The second theme is the extent to which different ways of life are incommensurate. It is one of the most important questions facing the cultural anthropologist. How it is answered not only has profound implications for ethnographic work and theory building but also, at least for those like myself, provides the conceptual frame on which we begin to understand how it might be possible, notwithstanding our colonial roots, to find a way to care for each other and justly share the lands on which our communities now dwell.

On this matter all the authors – including myself – are in agreement. The Western way of life, and particularly in the form taken by Modernity, has a very different ontology (operates on a very different set of principles and understandings) from Indigenous ways, up to and including the present day. As discussed by Dussart and Poirier, the distinction represented in this volume is drawn between what is labelled "a naturalist ontology" and which, as they describe it following Sahlins, "supposes a world from which spirit and subjectivity were long ago evacuated" (Sahlins 1995: 163) and a relational ontology, which is premised on understanding (to quote Dussart and Poirier) "the volition and agency of non-human others to be facts of life, and that sociality and historicity are indisputably inclusive of non-human others" (p. 215). That is, there is a distinction between an ontology that insists on a category boundary between human and other than human and one that refuses such a division. It is a distinction that, as Dussart and Poirier show clearly, has profound implications for how one lives in this world.

It is fair to say that most (if not almost all) of us who work with Indigenous peoples and many, many others (including a large number of Indigenous peoples) do clearly see such a distinction between the two orientations (and most frequently express it in terms compatible with that drawn between naturalist and relational forms offered in this text – however, as I will mention below, I would frame it in a different way). That is, there is near universal agreement that these two orientations are radically different. The crucial question is whether this difference represents "a gulf that cannot be bridged." It is a turn of phrase I use deliberately, as it is the one deployed by the Law Lords of the Privy Council of Great Britain in their 1919 judgment *In Re Southern Rhodesia*. As they put it:

> The estimation of the rights of aboriginal tribes is always inherently difficult. Some tribes are so low in the scale of social organization that their usages and conceptions of rights and duties are not to be reconciled with the institutions or legal ideas of civilized society. Such a gulf cannot be bridged. It would be idle to impute to such people some shadow of the

rights known to our law and then to transmute it into the substance of transferable rights of property as we know them. (*In Re Southern Rhodesia* 1919, A.C., 234)

That is (to use the evolutionary, racist logic of those times and these), Indigenous peoples were too primitive to have laws reconcilable with those of the civilized. Consequently, the Law Lords concluded that the practices of these peoples could not be translated into rights recognized in English law.

The response of British social anthropology at that time, I should add, was to reject this premise in the strongest possible terms (Asch 2011). Thus, Malinowski asserted forcefully in a 1930 piece:

The Judicial Committee plainly regard the question of native land tenure as both beyond the scope of practicable inquiry and below the dignity of legal recognition. On the contrary, I maintain that there is no people "so low in the scale of social organization" but have a perfectly well-defined system of land tenure. It is absurd to say that such a system "cannot be reconciled with the institutions or legal ideas of civilized society." (Malinowski 1930: 414–15)

And, may I add, it is a position with which I have much sympathy, notwithstanding my views on ontological difference.

At the same time, it is very interesting that there are those today (but they will not be mentioned here) who appear to argue that, while the racist, evolutionary argument in that judgment is entirely false, its conclusion was substantively correct in this respect: there is, indeed, no way to bridge the gulf between the two ontologies. It is a finding that leaves people like me, who are seeking ways to live together in a place like Canada, no purchase on which to build such ways.

What is most helpful is that the scholars in this volume take a nuanced approach to this matter. That is, on the one hand, their contributions affirm the existence of a clear "gulf" between the two ontologies, which they exemplify largely in the contrast between one that finds no divide between humans and animals – in that both have agency and are spiritual beings – and one that distinguishes between animals and humans on just those grounds. On the other hand, the chapters show clearly that, if the two sides are not necessarily (fully) reconcilable, people are still able to engage in meaningful communication across the divide. People, as is so well illustrated in Harvey Feit's chapter, are not, as I would put it, "uni-ontological" – that is, limited to the use of a single ontology – and in that sense at least the possibility of building a bridge across the gulf always is present. In particular, the contributions demonstrate over and over again that Indigenous peoples – and generally the contributors to this volume limit their focus to the Indigenous side – are able to communicate effectively and negotiate expertly with governments and settlers who live in a world constructed through a naturalist ontology, notwithstanding that they themselves live and are determined to continue to live within a relational one. And in this regard, the contributions provide much evidence to demonstrate the skill with which Indigenous peoples search for and find concepts and language from a naturalist point of view with which to communicate principles and practices dear to them to those who believe that the naturalist ordering of things is the only right one.

As such, the book begs the question of whether those of us schooled within the naturalist ordering have the same conceptual dexterity, and if so whether our refusal to engage in the process results from our power to impose rather than from an inability that lies at the core of the ontology within which we live. In that regard, I go to some length in my recent book to offer the possibility that the fault lies in our power to ignore other ways of understanding rather than in an inability to learn (Asch 2014: 117–51). This exploration led me to search for abstract principles that can generate the distinction drawn in this volume between those for whom animals and humans belong together in the dimensions mentioned above and those who see them as separate. And I hope it is not too much of a diversion to offer a few words on that matter here.

To my mind, central to the distinction is the manner in which categories are conceptualized. To the Western mind – and here I am following R.B.J. Walker (1991) – we operate on the principle that all things that are alike belong in the same fixed container, and all things different – but the same with respect to each other – in a separate one; and then we ask what is the relationship between them. Thus, for example, we imagine that all humans with the identity of "Cree" first belong in a container we call "Cree" that contains them all, and (e.g.) another in which all humans with the identity "Anishinaabe" first belong in a container called "Anishinaabe" (etc.), and only then do we ask what is the relationship between them. Thus, to use the example cited above, at least in the formulation I described, we are asking whether they belong in container one (the relational ontology) or two (the naturalist ontology). But in either case it is the notion of the container that comes first.

Here is where I see the distinction with the relational approach. Rather than beginning by putting identities (such as Cree and Anishinaabe) into separate containers and then asking what is the relationship between them, we begin with how people's identities (such as Cree and Anishinaabe) are linked to one another by interest and obligation on the understanding that they seek through this process to build a container that fits them well – and by extension all creation, if you conceptualize this generatively.

My thinking is animated through the words of Kiotseaeton, Mohawk Chief of the Six Nations – which I found by searching for the origin of the phrase "linking arms together," used by Robert A. Williams, Jr, as the title of one of his books (1997) – which Kiotseaeton uttered at the conclusion of a 1645 treaty of peace between the French, the Iroquois, and other nations. In his speech, he uses the concept of "linking together" to describe the relationship that ensues from the agreement just reached in these graphic words:

> [Kiotseaeton] took hold of a Frenchman, placed his arm within his, and with his other arm he clasped that of an Algonquin. Having thus joined himself to them:
>
> "Here," he said, "is the knot that binds us inseparably; nothing can part us … Even if the lightning were to fall upon us, it could not separate us; for, if it cuts off the arm that holds you to us, we will at once seize each other by the other arm."
>
> And thereupon he turned around, and caught the Frenchman and the Algonquin by their two other arms, – holding them so closely that he seemed unwilling ever to leave them. (Quoted in Asch 2014: 118)

To reiterate: What I take from this is that in the relational way of doing things one does not begin with fixed containers, but with the principle of linking together so tightly that whatever is the substance of each is fused with (but not assimilated into) the other and cannot come apart. Hence, in this way of thinking, the container is formed from the relationship, rather than, as in the naturalist ontology, the relationship only coming into being once separate containers have been formed. Thus, the shape of the container in the relational approach is not fixed, for it changes shape as other links of mutual reciprocity are forged.

Let me illustrate by way of this example. To our way of thinking, Cree and Anishinaabe belong in separate containers. And it is only natural that we imagine that (without the state to impose another form of unifying identity) people from each community would prefer to live among their own kind. However, in point of fact, while it is true that people may live in separate communities based on identity as Cree or Anishinaabe – as we would imagine is normative – that is not the only form of community building among Indigenous communities (including Cree and Anishinaabe), for equally there are communities that include both Cree and Anishinaabe, and, as Rob Innes points out in his 2014 book, *Elder Brother and the Law of the People*, this principle is extended even more broadly indeed (Innes 2014). Thus, there is clear evidence that, among the groups that negotiated Treaty 4 with the Crown in 1874, there was one, and this is just one example, "comprising five major groups – the Plains Cree, Saulteaux, Assiniboine, Métis, and English half-breeds, although individuals from other cultural groups were also part of the band" (quoted in Asch 2014: 138).

Thus, by establishing a relationship with animals, treaties if you will, we join together to forge a container that in our imaginary includes both as separate connected entities and at the same time will continue to expand through treaties with others – human or not. Therefore there can be no fixed borders – everything is porous, not because the membrane is porous, but because we only establish membranes through the process of forming relationships with what is outside of the (individual or collective) self. It is a world view that is rarely described in Western thought. One example, as discussed in my book (2014), is found in Lévi-Strauss's notion of dual organizations. Another is in Martin Buber's description in *I and Thou* of an understanding in which the I cannot stand alone, but only exists as linked to that which stands outside of the I. Thus as he writes, "When one says You, the I of the word pair I-You is said, too. When one says It, the I of the word pair I-It is said too" (Buber 1970: 54).

The point then is that, if this is so, then there are ways to bridge or at least to begin to bridge "difference" by reordering how we think about categorization, by joining together what we would describe as "different," and thus begin to work our way into imagining how to live within a relational ontology. But what is required, at least at the outset, is a willingness to do so, and that means an openness to what we do not know. And that I think is where we fail, partly because we are embedded in an ontology of certainty, but also because we are the powerful who live within an ontology in which the ability to dominate plays a key organizational role.

And that, I would suggest, is the principal failure of the colonial mind revealed in this book. What the articles show clearly, at least by implication, is that we are not prepared to accept the validity of ways that are not our own, or to put it another way, we are determined to be "uni-ontological." For example, I found it helpful to understand – as per Petronella Vaarzon-Morel – how it came to be that Indigenous peoples in Australia incorporated what was initially strange to them into their world view. At the same time, I asked myself how the colonists did the same thing, for after all there were people and animals living there that they had not encountered before. And the answer, of course, was that they immediately placed those peoples in a category of inferiority based on a very superficial understanding and a set of racist principles. What a difference it might have made had they paused to wonder and reflect on such a rich difference – but that is the impact of a colonial mind steeped in a naturalist way. Indeed what is most glaring in these chapters is the arrogant certainty the Western mind has of the superiority of our own ways. And moreover, as seen in Colin Scott's chapter, our willingness to ignore or, perhaps better, to violate the boundaries of the containers we set for ourselves – in this case legal agreements with Cree – when it comes to relations with those who we imagine stand outside of and in an inferior position to ourselves.

On Recognition

On this point, many of the authors in this volume discuss the state recognition of Indigenous rights as an important milestone in relations with Indigenous peoples, and as someone who began his career before this took place in Canada, I know firsthand how important it is. But the truth is that recognition has not done the work it was intended to do. Many of the chapters, such as the one by Colin Scott cited above, speak to that. What I know well, now that I have been at the University of Victoria for more than fifteen years, is that Indigenous intellectuals are keenly aware of this issue. For many, this has led to a full-blown critique of recognition, some arguing, as does Glen Coulthard in his 2014 book, *Red Skin White Masks*, that it is a form of appropriation and forced transformation. This view is exemplified in the Australian self-determination movement discussed by Frances Morphy and Sachiko Kubota in this volume and can also be seen in the work of scholars such as Nadasdy (2002) and Povinelli (2002). As I see it, this critique has spawned a number of different movements. There are those who place emphasis on what is termed "Indigenous resurgence," in which the goal is to disengage as much as possible with the State and with settlers and to live using their own principles – life projects as it were (Alfred 2005; Alfred and Corntassel 2005).

Another movement is carried by those who are looking deeply into the manner in which the understanding I am calling "linking" integrates Indigenous life-ways today. Among these is the author Robert Innes, mentioned before, whose work on the complex entanglements within the socio-political organization of the Cowessess community ought to be a must-read for anthropologists. Furthermore, the notion of linking together through relationality also provides an opening for settlers to begin to imagine building a just and enduring relationship with Indigenous peoples based on responsibilities and possibilities entailed in the links we forged through treaties (such as Treaty 4) as they were negotiated, notwithstanding that today we now live in a world in which such a possibility appears to be a fantasy. But, as Michel Foucault rightly argued in "Society Must Be Defended" (2003), to move beyond a world determined by the existence of power relations dictated by capital and the state as it is now organized and our need to resist them, it is necessary to also think of what can exist "outside of that box."

Conclusion: On the Contribution of Ethnographic Knowledge to Cultural Reproduction

Nicolas Peterson's chapter provides an insight into the complexities of understanding the processes of cultural reproduction in a world in which knowledge held by Indigenous peoples collides with the imperatives of living in a world dominated by values, practices, and technologies spawned by Modernity as it exists today. To take but one of many examples he provides, how does one imagine the impact on cultural transmission when the highly valued ability to memorize songs about and names of places collides with the existence of accurate maps produced by community members that enable anyone to glean this knowledge? It is a question to which, rightly in my view, he responds by saying that maps and other tools of Modernity are better understood not as means by which the culture – and therefore the right of land ownership – of the Indigenous becomes diluted to the point of disintegration, but rather as new tools that enable the people to sustain "an ever-transforming cultural identity" as the original owners of the land (Peterson in this volume, p. 248).

And behind this, in my view, lies the whole question of whether cultural identity and therefore culture difference itself are appropriate tools by which to measure the validity of a claim to an Indigenous right to own land or to aspire to political self-determination. And in my view, they are not, for I would judge that the right of Indigenous peoples to self-determination and to their ownership of land would not go away if it was demonstrated that they have now become completely assimilated culturally or even if they shared the same culture as those who colonized them at the time of colonization. To put it as did Indigenous leader Bill Wilson, at a constitutional conference in Canada in the 1980s,

> When the German forces occupied France, did the French people believe they didn't own the country? I sincerely doubt that there was one French person in France during the war that ever had the belief that France belonged to Germany, which is why, of course, they struggled with our assistance to liberate their country and once again take it back for themselves. (Quoted in Asch 1984: 29)

In other words, the fact that Germans and French share, in a basic way, a similar culture did not matter. France had every right to free itself from German rule. And that holds for Indigenous peoples too. That is, as Lord Dufferin, one of Canada's early post-Confederation governors-general, put it, when it comes to ownership of the land, we must "acknowledge that the original title to the land existed in the Indian Tribes," so that "before we touch an acre we make a treaty with the chiefs representing the bands ... but not until then do we consider that we are entitled to deal with a single acre" (quoted in Asch 2014: 8). In short, as I see it, an appeal to cultural distinctiveness has become the normative space for legitimating Indigenous rights primarily because we have built our societies by violating a value fundamental to the naturalist ontology as it is practised today: you do not go on lands that belong to other people without their permission.

REFERENCES

Alfred, Taiaiake. 2005. *Wasáse: Indigenous Pathways of Action and Freedom.* Toronto: University of Toronto Press.

Alfred, Taiaiake, and Jeff Corntassel. 2005. "Being Indigenous: Resurgences against Contemporary Colonialism." *Government and Opposition* 40 (4): 597–614. http://dx.doi.org/10.1111/j.1477-7053.2005.00166.x.

Asch, Michael. 1984. *Home and Native Land: Aboriginal Rights and the Canadian Constitution*. Toronto: Methuen.

Asch, Michael. 2007–8. "Folkways Records and the Ethics of Collecting: Some Personal Reflections." *MUSICultures* 34–5: 111–27.

Asch, Michael. 2011. "Radcliffe-Brown on Colonialism in Australia." *Histories of Anthropology* annual volume 5: 152–65.

Asch, Michael. 2014. *On Being Here to Stay: Treaties and Aboriginal Rights in Canada*. Toronto: University of Toronto Press.

Asch, Michael. 2015. "Colonialism and the Reflexive Turn: Finding a Place to Stand." *Anthropologica* 57 (2): 481–9.

Blaser, Mario. 2004. "Life Projects: Indigenous Peoples' Agency and Development." In *In the Way of Development: Indigenous Peoples, Life Projects, and Globalization*, ed. Mario Blaser, Harvey A. Feit, and Glenn McRae, 26–44. London and New York: Zed Books and Ottawa: Canadian International Development Research Centre.

Buber, Martin. 1970. *I and Thou*. Trans. Walter Kaufmann. New York: Scribner.

Coulthard, Glen S. 2014. *Red Skin White Masks: Rejecting the Colonial Projects of Recognition*. Minneapolis: University of Minnesota Press. http://dx.doi.org/10.5749/minnesota/9780816679645.001.0001.

Feit, Harvey A. 2004. "James Bay Crees' Life Projects and Politics: Histories of Place, Animal Partners, and Enduring Relationships." In *In the Way of Development: Indigenous Peoples, Life Projects, and Globalization*, ed. Mario Blaser, Harvey A. Feit, and Glenn McRae, 92–110. London and New York: Zed Books and Ottawa: Canadian International Development Research Centre.

Foucault, Michel. 2003. *"Society Must Be Defended": Lectures at the Collège de France, 1975–1976*. Ed. Mauro Bertani and Alessandro Fontana; trans. David Macey. New York: Picador.

Hancock, Robert L.A. 2011. "Eric Wolf and the Structural Power of Theory." *Histories of Anthropology Annual* 7 (1): 191–215. http://dx.doi.org/10.1353/haa.2011.0005.

In Re Southern Rhodesia. 1919. A.C. 211–49.

Innes, Robert Alexander. 2014. *Elder Brother and the Law of the People: Contemporary Kinship and Cowessess First Nation*. Winnipeg: University of Manitoba Press.

Malinowski, Bronislaw. 1930. "The Rationalization of Anthropology and Administration." *Africa: Journal of the International Africa Institute* 3 (4): 405–30. http://dx.doi.org/10.2307/1155193.

Murphy, Robert F., and Julian H. Steward. 1956. "Tappers and Trappers: Parallel Processes in Acculturation." *Economic Development and Social Change* 4 (4): 335–408. http://dx.doi.org/10.1086/449720.

Nadasdy, Paul. 2002. "'Property' and Aboriginal Land Claims in the Canadian Subarctic: Some Theoretical Considerations." *American Anthropologist* 104 (1): 247–61. http://dx.doi.org/10.1525/aa.2002.104.1.247.

Povinelli, Elizabeth A. 2002. *The Cunning of Recognition: Indigenous Alterities and the Making of Australian Multiculturalism.* Durham, NC: Duke University Press. http://dx.doi.org/10.1215/9780822383673.

Sahlins, Marshall. 1995. *How "Natives" Think: About Captain Cook, for Example.* Chicago: University of Chicago Press. http://dx.doi.org/10.7208/chicago/9780226733715.001.0001.

Sahlins, Marshall. 1999. "What Is Anthropological Enlightenment? Some Lessons of the Twentieth Century." *Annual Review of Anthropology* 28 (1): i–xxiii. http://dx.doi.org/10.1146/annurev.anthro.28.1.0.

Thomas, Nicholas. 1991. *Entangled Objects: Exchange, Material Culture, and Colonialism in the Pacific.* Cambridge, MA: Harvard University Press.

Walker, R.B.J. 1991. "State Sovereignty and the Articulation of Political Space/Time." *Millennium* 20 (3): 445–61. http://dx.doi.org/10.1177/03058298910200030201.

Williams, Robert A., Jr. 1997. *Linking Arms Together: American Indian Treaty Visions of Law and Peace.* New York: Oxford University Press.

Wolf, Eric R. 1982. *Europe and the People without History.* Berkeley and Los Angeles: University of California Press.

Contributors

Michael Asch is Professor (Limited Term) in the Department of Anthropology and Adjunct Professor in Political Science at the University of Victoria, and Professor Emeritus of Anthropology at the University of Alberta. His publications include *Home and Native Land: Aboriginal Rights and the Constitution* (1984), *Aboriginal and Treaty Rights in Canada: Essays on Law, Equality and Respect for Difference* (1997), and *On Being Here to Stay: Treaties and Aboriginal Rights in Canada* (2014). Dr Asch has served as an expert witness in court and at public hearings, including the Mackenzie Valley Pipeline Inquiry. He served as Senior Research Associate for Anthropology with the Royal Commission on Aboriginal Peoples, and as Research Director of the Dene/Métis Mapping Project for the Dene Nation. He maintains a keen interest in finding ways to justly resolve political relations between Indigenous Peoples and Canada.

John Borrows is the Canada Research Chair in Indigenous Law at the University of Victoria Law School. His books include *Recovering Canada: The Resurgence of Indigenous Law* (2002), *Canada's Indigenous Constitution* (2010), *Drawing Out Law: A Spirit's Guide* (2010), and *Freedom and Indigenous Constitutionalism* (2016). He is a Fellow of the Pierre Elliot Trudeau Foundation, the Canadian Academy of Social Science (FRSC), and a member of the Chippewas of the Nawash First Nation.

Françoise Dussart is Professor of Anthropology at the University of Connecticut. She is the author of *La Peinture des Aborigènes d'Australie* (1993*)*, *The Politics of Ritual in an Aboriginal Settlement: Kinship, Gender and the Currency of Knowledge* (2000), and two edited volumes, *Media*

Matters: Representations of the Social in Aboriginal Australia (2006), and *Engaging Christianity in Aboriginal Australia* (2010) (with C. Schwarz). She just curated the very first major exhibition in Canada (*Lifelines: Contemporary Indigenous Art from Australia*) of Indigenous Art from Australia. Her most recent project investigates Indigenous ill-health in Australia.

Elodie Fache (PhD, 2013, Anthropology, Aix-Marseille Université/ CREDO) is conducting research on environmental conservation, sustainable development, and local empowerment in Oceania. Her PhD thesis presents a critical analysis of formalized land and sea management programs implemented by Indigenous rangers in Northern Australia. Her postdoctoral research is focusing on "community-based" management of coral reefs in Fiji.

Harvey A. Feit is Professor Emeritus at McMaster University. He has done long-term research with and for Eeyouch (James Bay Crees). His main research interests are co-governance, political ontologies, knowing as a practice of everyday life, and local conservation. His publications include *In the Way of Development: Indigenous Peoples, Life Projects and Globalization*, edited with Mario Blaser and Glenn McRae (2004); "Myths of the Ecological Whitemen," in *Native Americans and the Environment*, edited by Michael Harkin and David Rich Lewis (2007); and "Governmental Rationalities and Indigenous Co-Governance," in *Unsettled Legitimacy*, edited by Steven Bernstein and William D. Coleman (2009).

Sachiko Kubota is Professor of Anthropology at Kobe University, Japan. Her main domains of research include the gender anthropology, anthropology of art, and contemporary hunters and gatherers in northeastern Arnhem Land in Australia. Her research also includes comparative study on Indigenous political claims in Australia and Japan. She is the author of a number of articles and monographs, including "Gender Anthropology on Aboriginal Soceity – Indigenous People, Women and Social Change" (2005) and "Who Are 'Indigenous People'?" (2009).

Frances Morphy is currently a Research Associate at the Center for Advanced Study in the Behavioral Sciences, Stanford University, and an Honorary Associate Professor at the Centre for Aboriginal Economic

Policy Research, The Australian National University. Her recent research has addressed, broadly, problems of "translation" across difference, focusing on Indigenous Australian organizations as sites of articulation with the state and on a critique of the national census that highlights the silences and distortions imposed on remote Indigenous populations by conventional demographic categorizations of concepts such as "residence," "family," and "household." She is coeditor (with Bill Arthur) of the *Macquarie Atlas of Indigenous Australia: Culture and Society through Space and Time* (2005).

Nicolas Peterson is Professor of Anthropology at the Australian National University. He has a long-standing interest in Australian Aboriginal anthropology, land and sea tenure, economic and development issues, fourth world people and the state, and the photography of anthropological subjects. His most recent book, coedited with Fred Myers, is *Experiments in Self-Determination: Histories of the Outstation Movement in Australia* (2016).

Sylvie Poirier is Professor in the Department of Anthropology, Université Laval (Quebec). She has been conducting research with Aboriginal people in the Australian Western Desert since 1980 and with the Atikamekw, a First Nation in north-central Quebec, since 1990. She is the author of *A World of Relationships: Itineraries, Dreams and Events in the Australian Western Desert* (2005) and coeditor (with John Clammer and Eric Schwimmer) of *Figured Worlds: Ontological Obstacles in Intercultural Relations* (2004). In collaboration with the Council of the Atikamekw Nation, her current project focuses on the documentation, valorization, and transmission of Atikamekw knowledge of the forestlands.

Colin H. Scott is an Associate Professor in the Department of Anthropology at McGill University in Montreal. His research focuses on Indigenous ecological knowledge, land and sea tenure, conservation governance, and the political and legal process of Indigenous rights among hunting and fishing peoples in northern Canada and northern Australia. He directs the INSTEAD (Indigenous Stewardship of Environment and Alternative Development) research team and CICADA (the Centre for Indigenous Conservation and Development Alternatives), transnational partnerships with Indigenous communities and organizations that seek improved conditions for the integrity of Indigenous land- and sea-based livelihoods and ecologies.

Brian Thom is Associate Professor at the University of Victoria. He has worked as a researcher, advisor, and negotiator for Coast Salish peoples since the mid-1990s. His research focuses on Indigenous land rights and self-determination, and examines the political and ontological challenges encountered as Indigenous peoples engage state institutions. He is author of numerous articles, including "Reframing Indigenous Territories" (2014) and "The Paradox of Boundaries" (2009).

Petronella Vaarzon-Morel is a Research Associate at PARADISEC, Sydney Conservatorium of Music, the University of Sydney, and Sessional Lecturer in Anthropology NYU Sydney. Her interests include Australian Indigenous relations to the land, personhood, identity, human-animal relations, visual culture, and history. Over many years she has conducted extensive research with Aboriginal people in central Australia for their land and native title claims. Currently, she is working on the Central Land Council Cultural Media Project. Recent publications include "Pointing the Phone: Transforming Technologies and Social Relations among Warlpiri" (2014).

Clinton N. Westman is Associate Professor in the Department of Anthropology at the University of Victoria. He has published numerous articles, book chapters, and technical reports examining the ecologies and ontologies inhabited by Cree and Métis people in northern Alberta, on Aboriginal and environmental politics and research in Canada, on the Cree language, and on ritual studies. His work is based on long-term ethnographic, archival, and policy studies in partnership with First Nations and Aboriginal organizations.

www.ingramcontent.com/pod-product-compliance
Lightning Source LLC
Chambersburg PA
CBHW021855020426
42334CB00013B/340